The Resume Kit

THE RESUME KIT

THIRD EDITION

RICHARD H. BEATTY

JOHN WILEY & SONS, INC.

New York • Chichester • Brisbane • Toronto • Singapore

Library of Congress Cataloging in Publication Data:

Beatty, Richard H., 1939–
    The resume kit / Richard H. Beatty. — 3rd ed.
       p.   cm.
    Includes index.
    ISBN 0-471-12403-6 (pbk. : alk. paper)
    1. Résumés (Employment)   I. Title.
HF5383.B33   1995
650.14—dc20   95-16942

Printed in the United States of America
10 9 8 7 6 5 4 3 2 1

To my wife Carolyn
and my sons, Chris and Scott,
who have added considerable joy and
fullness to my life

PREFACE

You are about to embark on the single most important aspect of your job-hunting campaign—preparation of your resume. At first blush this may sound like a dramatic overstatement, but if you bear with me for a few paragraphs, I am sure I can convince you.

Managers of most companies are extremely busy people who cannot afford to waste time. They will almost always insist on reviewing a complete employment resume before agreeing to grant an employment interview. Most simply refuse to waste time interviewing candidates whose backgrounds are totally unrelated to their employment needs, or who are so poorly qualified that it is obvious in advance that no employment offer will result. In fact, authorities in the employment field estimate that approximately 95 percent of all employment interviews are granted only *after* the company has received and read the candidate's resume.

Your employment resume is therefore critical to your job-hunting campaign. It must do a sufficiently good job of both representing and selling your qualifications to warrant an employment interview. Without an employment interview one can hardly expect to land a job.

The employment process itself is designed to be a "negative" screening process. The employer establishes certain candidate selection criteria or specifications against which the candidate's qualifications are to be measured. A candidate who is poorly qualified or lacks some of the basic qualifications to fill the position is "screened out" of the process. If you have a poorly prepared resume, you will be screened out before you have a chance to get started.

In addition to the critical role of helping you secure an employment interview, the resume also plays an additional important role—it serves as the basic reference guide used by the employer as a sort of "road map" in conducting the employment interview. As with a poor road map, the poorly written resume will lead the interviewer down side streets, back roads, and dead-end streets. Key pieces of information are missing, and the interviewer has difficulty identifying and focusing in on key qualifications and accomplishments. A lot of valuable interview time can be wasted, with the interviewer coming away from the interview with little or no understanding of your qualifications for the position. The likely outcome is a "no interest" letter in your mailbox a week or two following your interview date.

By contrast, the well-prepared resume serves as a road map that expertly leads where you want the interviewer to go. It efficiently guides the interviewer through your background in a logical, concise manner with clearly marked road signs that highlight your major accomplishments and key qualifications. It leaves a favorable and lasting impression which, in many cases, will result in serious consideration and enhance the possibility of an employment offer being made.

Another important point to consider when preparing your resume is that it continues to serve as a permanent, lasting record for review by the employer after the interview has been conducted. It is often used by the employer in recalling the specifics of your qualifications and as a base of reference in comparing your qualifications with the qualifications of other candidates under consideration by the employer. If your resume is well prepared and does a good job highlighting your strengths and major contributions, you will have a distinct advantage over your competition.

I am hopeful that by now I have been successful in convincing you that a good resume is critical in your job-hunting game plan. I also hope that this has served to motivate you to invest the necessary time, effort, and patience to assure the preparation of a thorough and efficient resume. The rewards of landing an outstanding job and assuring a bright future should be well worth this effort.

As author of this book, I think it is important to present my credentials as an employment professional so that you know you are receiving the advice of someone who has more than just a casual acquaintance with the employment field. I am an employment professional with over 30 years of experience in the field of human resources. I am currently president of the Brandywine Consulting Group, a broad-based consulting firm offering a wide range of human resource consulting services, including executive search and outplacement consulting. I was previously a vice president with MSL International Ltd., a major U.S. executive search firm with offices throughout the world.

Earlier in my career, I spent nearly 17 years as a human resources executive with Scott Paper Company. This included nearly three years as manager of corporate staff human resources, seven years as corporate manager of technical employment, and an additional two years in a division level assignment as manager of recruiting and personnel services.

Over the years, I have read an estimated 100,000 to 150,000 resumes, conducted approximately 2,000 employment interviews, and hired several hundred professionals and managers. Recruiting assignments for which I have been responsible have run the gamut from entry level college graduate through company president.

I have seen almost every type, style, and format of employment resume imaginable. As both a corporate employment manager and a human resource consultant, I have gained an excellent "insider" understanding of what employers look for in a good resume. You are thus benefiting from this unique perspective and should end up with an excellent resume if you follow the instructions in this resume preparation kit.

I will not guarantee that this will be a totally painless process; however, this kit will substantially simplify an otherwise difficult task by providing you with a logical, easy-to-follow, step-by-step approach.

This Third Edition of *The Resume Kit* has been completely updated to include the latest thinking and concepts in modern resume writing. This includes two new chapters that describe the linear resume, a new resume format that has gained enormous popularity and usage in the last few years. In addition to the step-by-step instructions for preparing a liner resume (see Chapter 7), Chapter 8 provides you with 20 examples of this popular resume format.

An entirely new chapter (Chapter 12) has been added on the "electronic resume." Whether you are surfing the Internet looking for a job, or having your resume scanned into an employer's or search firm's resume database, it is important that your resume be in proper form—electronically speaking. This new chapter provides you with answers you will need for your resume to be effective in this new electronic age.

Armed with the careful instructions contained in this book, you should have everything you will need to prepare an excellent resume. My best wishes to you for a successful job search and a rewarding career!

RICHARD H. BEATTY

West Chester, Pennsylvania

CONTENTS

1

THROUGH THE EYES OF THE EMPLOYMENT MANAGER

The employment resume—its style, organization, and content—has long been a topic of considerable discussion and debate. Like religion and politics, this is a subject fraught with controversy. It is one of those topics where there are many "experts" who will provide you with considerable "professional" advice and counsel as long as you are willing to listen.

Should you wish to put this statement to the test, let me suggest that the next time you are at lunch or dinner with a group of friends or business colleagues, introduce the subject of "resume preparation" and ask a few of the following questions:

1. How long should a resume be?
2. What is the best resume format? How should it be organized?
3. Should there be a statement of job objective? If so, how should it be worded?

4. Should the resume contain personal data—age, height, weight, marital status, number of children?

5. Should hobbies and extracurricular activities be included?

6. How important is salary history? Should it be shown at all?

7. Where should education be described—near the end or the beginning of the resume?

8. What writing style is the most effective?

9. What is the best format for computer scanning and resume database search?

These, and similar questions, are guaranteed to spark a lively discussion punctuated with considerable difference of opinion. There will be those who claim that "Everyone knows that a resume should never be longer than a single page." Others will assert that "Two pages are quite acceptable." Still others will be adamant that "Two pages can never begin to do justice to 10 years of professional experience and accomplishment." All may use logical and persuasive arguments, with each sounding more convincing than the last. Who is right? Which argument should you believe? What works best?

As a consultant and executive with considerable employment experience, I can tell you that there are good answers to these questions. There is a right and a wrong way to prepare an employment resume. There are items that should definitely be included in the resume, and there are those that are best left out. There are resume formats that have consistently proven more effective than others, and there are those that should be avoided.

There are appropriate answers to these and many other questions associated with the subject of effective resume preparation. But you cannot expect to get expert advice on resume preparation over casual dinner conversation with a few friends whose expertise consists mainly of preparation of their first resume and a few articles read somewhere in a trade journal. This is hardly the type of advice that you need to prepare a resume that will be successful in launching you on a new and prosperous career track.

What I am about to share with you are the observations and advice of a human resources consultant and former personnel executive who has had considerable experience in the corporate employment function of a major Fortune 200 company. This is knowledge gleaned from years of employment experience—knowledge gained from the reading of thousands of employment resumes and the hiring of hundreds of employees at the professional, managerial, and executive level. This advice is based on firsthand observation of those resumes that resulted in job interviews and those that did not. This is advice based on "inside" knowledge of what makes professional employment managers tick—what motivates them to respond favorably to one resume and "turns them off" on the next. It will guide you in preparing a resume that will best display your qualifications and maximize your potential for landing interviews.

This chapter will provide you with an understanding of what happens in a typical company employment department. Where does your resume go? Who reads it? What is the basis for determining interest or lack of interest? What does the employment manager look for in a resume? How is the resume read? Who makes the final decision on your resume? Answers to these and similar questions should provide you with valuable insight that will enable you to design your resume to successfully compete for an employment interview. They will also serve as the basis for better understanding the recommendations made later in this book on such topics as resume format, content, style, appearance, and so on.

COMPETITION

In larger companies, it is not uncommon for the corporate employment department to receive as many as 40,000 to 50,000 resumes during the course of an average business year. Some receive considerably more. The annual employment volume of such firms typically runs in the range of 200 to 300 hires per year. Assuming an average of two to three interviews per hire, these firms will interview 400 to 900 employment candidates in meeting their employment requirements. This means that only 400 to 900 of the total 40,000 to 50,000 resumes received will result in an employment interview. In other words, only one or two out of every 100 resumes will result in an employment interview. Those are not very encouraging odds!

You are thus beginning your employment search at a decided statistical disadvantage. For every 100 resumes mailed to prospective employers, on the average you can expect only one or two interviews to result. These statistics alone should persuade you of the importance of a well-prepared and effective resume.

It is estimated that the average employment manager of a major corporation will read more than 20,000 resumes a year. Assuming no vacation time and 260 workdays in a year, this is equivalent to a weeknight workload of more than 75 resumes. Since employment managers must frequently travel, however, and most do take time off for holidays and vacations, it is estimated that this number is actually closer to 100. Since each resume averages 1½ pages in length, the employment manager has an average of 150 pages of reading to do each evening—a sizable chore!

Since the employment manager frequently spends the entire workday interviewing employment candidates, most resumes are normally read during the evening hours. Additionally, since evenings are often used by the manager to plan employment strategies, write recruitment advertising, and do other planning work necessary to the employment process, the amount of evening time left to read resumes may be only an hour or two.

In many cases, the employment manager is unable to read resumes until later in the evening. The early evening hours must often be used by the manager to make telephone calls to make job offers, follow up with candidates on outstanding offers, prescreen prospective candidates, and so on. These calls can usually be made only during the early part of the evening, leaving resume reading until later.

As you can well imagine, by 10 or 11 P.M. (following a full day of interviewing and several early evening phone calls) the typical employment manager is probably tired. He or she must now read an estimated 150 pages of resumes before retiring for the evening. You can well imagine how thoroughly these resumes will be read.

The technique used by most employment managers in reviewing resumes is not an in-depth, step-by-step reading process. Instead, it is a process of rapidly skimming the resume in a systematic way to determine whether or not the individual has qualifications and career interests consistent with the company's current employment requirements.

Considering all of these factors, resumes that are poorly prepared, sloppy, or in any other way difficult to read will receive very little consideration. Resumes are thought to be indicative of the overall personal style of the writer. Thus the inference that is frequently drawn from such poorly written resumes is that the applicant is likewise a sloppy, uncaring, or disorganized individual. Why then should the employment manager risk bringing this individual in for interviews? In such cases, the resume will more likely than not be stamped "no interest," and the employment manager will quickly move on to the next resume.

By now I hope that you are convinced that the general appearance of the resume is critical to its impact and effectiveness. It should be obvious that readability is likewise a major criterion for resume success. Resume organization and format are therefore extremely important factors to consider if your resume is to be successful in this difficult and competitive arena.

We now move on to a general discussion of the organization and operation of the typical company employment department. We carefully trace the steps through which your resume will likely pass, from the point of receipt by the department to final determination of application status.

RESUME PROCESSING

In the case of a company with a large employment department, the department is normally subdivided into functional specialties with each employment manager having accountability for a given area. For example, there may be an Administrative Employment Manager who has accountability for all administrative hiring: Accounting, Finance, Law, Data Processing, Human Resources, and so on. A Technical Employment Manager may also exist with accountability for all technical hiring: Research and Development, Central Engineering, Technical Services, Quality Control, and so on. Likewise, there may be an Operations Employment Manager with responsibility for all hiring related to manufacturing or plant operations. Marketing and Sales may also be represented by a separate employment manager.

As resumes are received by the employment department, there is usually one person who is designated to open and sort the mail into the appropriate categories for distribution to the individual employment managers. Once received by the employment manager's administrative assistant, the screening process will begin with the assistant "screening out" those resumes that are clearly not of interest to the employment manager. Thus if the employer is a steel company, the resumes of botanists, foresters, artists, and so forth are likely to be "screened out" at this point. Likewise, the administrative assistant may eliminate illegible, sloppy, or otherwise undesirable resumes.

The next step is for the employment manager to read the resume to determine whether there is an opening that is an appropriate match for the applicant's credentials. If not, the resume is usually marked "no interest," coded, and sent to Word Processing where an appropriate "no interest letter" is prepared and sent to the applicant. A copy of this letter along with the original resume is then returned to the employment department for filing and future reference.

At this point, "no interest" resumes are normally divided into two categories: (1) those in which the employer will probably have no future interest and (2) those having a high likelihood of interest at some future time ("future possibles"). Those in which the company is likely to have future interest are normally placed in an active file for future reference and review. In some cases, these "future interest" resumes are electronically scanned and stored on a computer resume data base. The remaining resumes are placed in a dead file with no possibility of future review.

When the employment manager determines that there is a reasonable match between the candidate's qualifications and the employment needs of a given department, the next step is a review of the resume by the hiring manager (the manager having the employment opening). Having reviewed the resume and determined that there is a probable match between the candidate's qualifications and interests and the requirements of the position, the hiring manager then notifies the employment manager of this interest and requests that the employment manager schedule the candidate for an interview. If, on the other hand, there is no interest, the hiring manager indicates this to the employment manager, and the resume is processed as described above.

In the case of the more sophisticated employers, there is usually one additional step in the process prior to extending an invitation for an interview. This step is referred to as the "telephone screen." This means that either the hiring manager or the employment manager will phone the candidate for the purpose of conducting a mini-interview. This telephone interview is intended to determine whether the candidate has sufficient qualifications and interest to warrant the time and expense of an on-site interview. Additionally, employers frequently use this preliminary interview to determine the validity of the information provided on the resume—a good reason to be factual in describing your qualifications and accomplishments!

There are three critical points in the resume-processing procedure at which your resume may be screened out and marked "no interest":

1. Administrative Assistant—screened for obvious incompatibility, incompleteness, sloppiness, or illegibility.
2. Employment Manager—screened for incompatibility with current openings and required candidate specifications.
3. Hiring Manager—screened for insufficient or inappropriate qualifications when compared with job requirements.

The highly competitive nature of the employment market, coupled with the thorough screening provided by the prospective employer, makes the preparation of a professional and effective resume an absolute must if one expects to be successful in the employment or job-hunting process! The resume cannot be left to chance. It must be carefully and deliberately designed if it is to successfully survive the rigors of the company's screening process.

Let's now take a closer look at the process used by the employment manager to screen resumes. How does he or she read a resume? What is the employment manager looking for? What will determine which resumes are screened out?

CANDIDATE SPECIFICATION

The very first step in the typical employment process is the preparation of an "employment requisition" by the hiring manager. This document is normally signed by the hiring manager's function head and human resources manager and is then forwarded to the appropriate employment manager. The purpose of the employment requisition is normally threefold:

1. Provides management authorization to hire.
2. Communicates basic data about the opening—title, level, salary range, reporting relationship, maximum starting salary, key job responsibilities, and so on.
3. Communicates basic or fundamental candidate specifications—type and level of education required, type and level of experience sought, technical and administrative skills required, and so forth.

Any good professional employment manager knows that the employment requisition seldom provides sufficient information to do a professional job of identifying and recruiting a well-qualified candidate. Considerably more information will usually be needed, and the employment manager is quick to arrange a meeting with the hiring manager to develop a more thorough and comprehensive candidate specification. The following are examples of typical "candidate specs."

Both of these candidate specs are highly detailed and very particular about the kind of qualifications that will satisfy the employment requirement. Very little has been left to chance. There is a clear understanding of both the educational and experience requirements for candidates who would receive serious consideration for employment.

Job Title: Chief Project Engineer

Job Level: 600 Points

Department: Central Engineering

Group: Mechanical

Education:

  Preferred: M.S. Mechanical Engineering

  Acceptable: B.S. Mechanical Engineering

Experience:

  Eight plus years experience in the design, development, installation, start-up, and debugging of Herrington Winders and auxiliary equipment. Demonstrated project leadership of projects in the eight to ten million range. Must have managed groups of five or more professionals.

  Maximum Starting Salary: $85,000

Now let's look at another example.

Job Title: Director—Human Resources

Job Level: 1,200 Points

Department: Human Resources

Reporting Relationship: Sr. Vice President—Administration

Maximum Starting Salary: $100,000

Estimated Bonus: 20% to 30%

Education: <u>Masters in Human Resources Management</u>

Experience:

<u>Requires a minimum 15 years experience in Human Resources in a corporation of 20,000 plus employees. Experience must include a broad range of Human Resources experience to include: Employment, Compensation & Benefits, Training & Development, and Employee Relations. Must be up-to-date with modern concepts in such areas as Human Resources Planning, Organization Effectiveness, and Executive Assessment. Experience must include demonstrated management leadership in the direction and guidance of decentralized, autonomous division Personnel functions in a multidivision and highly diversified company. Must have played key role in the development and execution of corporate-wide labor relations strategy in a multiunion setting. Must have managed a staff of at least 20 mid-management and professional level Human Resource professionals.</u>

HOW RESUMES ARE READ

The candidate specification, as shown in the examples, is the basic tool of the employment manager when it comes to reading an employment resume. Actually the term "reading" is misleading when describing the process by which most employment managers review employment resumes. More precisely, the experienced employment manager rapidly scans for basic qualification highlights. The question that is constantly being asked by the employment manager is "Does this individual meet all of the critical qualifications of the candidate spec?"

The typical employment manager does not bother to read a resume in any degree of detail unless the preliminary scan indicates that the applicant has some of the essential skills and experience sought. In such cases, as key phrases and headings begin to match the candidate spec, the manager slows down and begins to read with a more critical eye. If several key criteria appear to be met, the employment professional will usually return to the beginning of the resume and begin a more thorough, detailed reading. To the contrary, if quick scanning of the resume indicates that few, if any, of the candidate's qualifications appear to match the current requirements, no time is lost in moving on to the next resume.

QUICK "KNOCKOUT" FACTORS

In scanning the employment resume, the employment manager is looking for key "knockout" factors—factors that clearly spell no interest and signal the employment manager to stop reading and move on to the next resume. Some of these quick knockout factors are:

1. Job objective incompatible with current openings
2. Inappropriate or insufficient educational credentials
3. Incompatible salary requirements
4. Geographic restrictions incompatible with current openings
5. Lack of U.S. citizenship or permanent resident status
6. Resume poorly organized, sloppy, or hard to read
7. Too many employers in too short a period of time
8. Too many pages—a book instead of a resume

Any of these factors quickly signals the employment manager that it would be a waste of time to read any further. These are generally sure knockout factors and warrant use of the no interest stamp. These same factors should be consciously avoided when preparing your employment resume.

CRITICAL READING

Having successfully passed the quick knockout factors test and avoided the no interest stamp, your resume must now undergo a more thorough and critical scanning. Concentration is now centered on the Work Experience section of the resume as the following questions are considered:

1. Are there sufficient years and level of experience?
2. Is experience in the appropriate areas?
3. Is the candidate missing any critical experience?
4. Does the candidate have sufficient breadth and depth of technical knowledge?
5. Does the applicant have sufficient management or leadership skills?
6. Are any technical or managerial skills missing?
7. Is there a solid record of accomplishment?
8. How does this candidate compare with others currently under consideration?
9. Based on overall qualifications, what are the probabilities that an offer would be made—50%, 75%, 90% (as measured against past candidates with similar credentials)?

There is little advice that can be given to the resume writer in this area. You are what you are, and the facts cannot be changed. You either have the qualifications and experience sought, or you don't. At best, you can hope that through diligent application of professional resume preparation techniques, you have done an excellent job of clearly presenting your overall skills, knowledge, accomplishments, and other pertinent professional qualifications. This book is intended to provide you with the expert guidance and advice to do just that!

There is nothing mysterious or mystical about the resume-reading process. It is essentially logical and straightforward. It is a process whereby the employment manager or hiring manager simply compares the candidate's qualifications and interests with the candidate's hiring spec in an effort to determine the candidate's degree of qualifications and the desirability of moving to the interview (or phone screen) step. Neatness, clarity, organization, style, and format are the key ingredients; they are critical to the impact and effectiveness of the employment resume. These topics are covered in subsequent chapters of this book.

2

TWELVE COMMON RESUME MYTHS

The field of resume writing abounds with myths. Many of these myths are carryovers from previous decades, when the employment market was less sophisticated than it is today. Others simply exist and have been around since "time immemorial." Unfortunately, these myths are frequently supported by otherwise respected and knowledgeable people who are well intentioned and who feel strongly that what they espouse is the truth. This solid conviction is bound to manifest itself in strongly stated opinions during informal discussions of the resume preparation process. Heard frequently enough, these myths can be misinterpreted as "facts" by the inexperienced, unenlightened professional.

In this chapter, we examine 12 of the most commonly held resume myths and dispel the underlying logic that has caused these myths to survive and flourish in the annals of resume folklore. You may still find yourself stubbornly clinging to some of these long-cherished fables, but let me strongly encourage you to abandon them. These myths aren't worth believing if your resume is to succeed in this highly competitive labor market!

Myth 1. Resumes should never exceed one page in length.

Advocates of this myth argue that no matter how many years of experience or how extensive the skills and qualifications of the candidate, all pertinent information necessary for a trained human resources professional to make an informed employment judgment can be condensed to a single page. Proponents of this viewpoint frequently argue that the inability to write a one-page resume is reflective of a candidate who is overly verbose or poorly organized.

This myth is based on the premise that most employment managers will simply not take the time to read a resume that is greater than one page in length. Thus, the argument continues, two-page (or longer) resumes will only be given a cursory scan and will quickly receive the no interest stamp.

Although there is much to be said in favor of brevity, there is little basis for this myth. Since the key motivation of the employment manager is to find well-qualified candidates to fill the company's employment needs, conscientious employment managers read most resumes with equal intensity and interest if the resumes are kept to a reasonable length. Resumes of two and three pages are, in fact, a fairly common phenomenon and are treated with the same degree of interest as the single-page format.

It is my belief that individuals having 10 or more years of experience will find it difficult to adequately describe their extensive experience and professional qualifications on one page. By forcing this information on to a single page, major accomplishments and significant contributions may have to be omitted. So, if you are an individual who fits the 10-year-plus experience category, by all means use a two-page format!

Myth 2.   Longer resumes better describe qualifications and are more effective.

Proponents of longer resumes (three pages or more) will tell you that it is virtually impossible to condense 15 or 20 years of professional experience to a few short pages. They will argue that you are unnecessarily depriving yourself of the opportunity to present your full and complete credentials to the prospective employer.

Although it is probably true that longer resumes do a more thorough job of describing employment qualifications, the important counterpoint to this argument is that such resumes are rarely read as carefully or fully as their shorter (one- or two-page) counterparts. In fact, the truth of the matter is that lengthy resumes frequently elicit a good deal of disdain from employment managers, and for good reason. Such resumes are far less concise. They make it difficult, if not impossible, for the reader to determine which of the candidate's qualifications and accomplishments are most significant. They encourage a feeling of ambivalence on the part of employment managers—an unwillingness to invest much time or energy in ferreting out key qualifications. Resumes of unreasonable length, in fact, frequently cause employment managers considerable frustration and have been known to incur the ultimate penalty in the form of the manager's no interest stamp.

Although I do not feel it necessary to cram all information on to a one-page format, I do feel that an employment resume should not resemble a book! I can remember more than one evening when, at 11 P.M. or so, I encountered a resume of 15 or 20 pages. Such resumes would incur my ire, and my no interest stamp would be applied with a vengeance!

When deciding on an appropriate resume length, use the following rules of thumb. If you have less than 10 years' experience and have had two or fewer employers, use a single-page format. Candidates with more than 10 years' experience, or who have had more than three employers, should feel comfortable moving to a two-page format. In extremely rare cases, extensive experience may force the resume on to a third page, but this is strongly discouraged. The *absolute limit* should be 2½ to 2¾ pages.

Myth 3.   Unique or unusual resumes attract attention and are better read.

Although unique or unusual resumes will unquestionably attract attention, they are usually viewed with a high degree of suspicion by employment professionals. Disciples of this myth would have you believe that the unusual resume will foster the image of a creative, innovative, and desirable candidate. They believe that such formats suggest candidates of high intelligence.

There are times that I am sure that I have seen every conceivable kind of resume! One resume, for example, was neatly folded into a wad and was inserted in a plastic pill box, which the applicant had designed. The only problem was that the resume was so wrinkled that it was barely legible. I gave up trying to read it.

Other unusual examples include resumes written on the backs of envelopes, some on vacation postcards, one typed on toilet tissue, one on pink construction paper, several bound in book form, some uniquely folded with pop-out parts, one with a photograph of the applicant wearing a skimpy bikini, one including a dime and suggesting I read his resume over a cup of coffee (coffee at that time cost 25¢ at our company cafeteria), and others too ridiculous to mention.

I can assure you that none of the above compelled me to extend an invitation for an interview with my employer! To the contrary, most unusual resumes, rather than conveying an image of originality, creativity, or intellect, raise some "red flags" for the employment professional. Unusual formats frequently raise the specter of a nonconformist, loner, oddball, or some other highly undesirable label.

Myth 4.   Resume content is more important than style or format.

The arguments set forth by supporters of this myth are very similar to those advocated by proponents of Myth 2 (longer resumes are better). They believe that as long as an individual has outstanding credentials, resume style or format is completely irrelevant! The underlying belief is that employment managers are willing to weed through miles and miles of disorganized, difficult-to-read presentations to get to an applicant's outstanding credentials. Most employment professionals will do no such thing!

Few things turn an experienced employment manager off more quickly than a poorly written or disorganized resume. Such resumes require an inordinate amount of time to sift through and severely test the patience of a busy manager. They suggest a candidate who is insensitive, inconsiderate, sloppy, disorganized, confused, uninformed, undisciplined, or worse. Seldom will seasoned employment managers invest the time necessary to read poorly prepared resumes. Instead, they will simply mark the resume no interest and move on.

Myth 5. Exaggerate accomplishments— nobody ever checks.

Although it is probably true that exaggerated accomplishments will create increased interest in your qualifications and therefore increase the number of interviews proportionately—beware of this practice! Skillful interviewers will sooner or later discover your exaggeration and that will prove embarrassing.

Proponents of this myth have probably never encountered the well-trained employment interviewer. They believe that most interviewers are willing to accept superficial answers. For this reason, they believe that they have a high probability of surviving the interview and landing the job offer. Although the odds may be somewhat in their favor, the longer range prospects of being hired and unable to perform can be destructive or even fatal to a career.

You should also be aware that not all interviewers are unskilled and inept. To the contrary, some have been intensely trained and are unusually skilled at distinguishing truth from fantasy. Some employ a patterned interview technique, in which they intentionally ask the same questions more than once during the interview. These individuals can be quite adept at disguising such questions and spacing them throughout the interview so that they are not easily detected. The purpose of this "patterning" technique is to uncover specific inconsistencies that suggest puffery, exaggeration, or outright dishonesty. I have mastered this technique and have seen more than one employment candidate squirm with discomfort or turn red with embarrassment when confronted with such inconsistencies. Nothing can destroy an interview faster than exaggeration or outright dishonesty!

Additionally, although some companies do not check business references, many still do! And for higher level positions, they are checked very thoroughly. This includes detailed discussions with past superiors and peers to verify specific accomplishments. In some cases where credentials were exaggerated or otherwise misrepresented, offers of employment were even withdrawn. In more than one such case, the candidate had already tendered his or her resignation to the current employer.

The best advice is—don't exaggerate or misrepresent your qualifications to a prospective employer. It's not worth the risk.

Myth 6.   Listing references is important and conveys "solid" character.

The idea of listing references on the resume because this conveys a sense of honesty, integrity, and solid character is a badly outdated notion. Yet proponents of this myth persist.

The modern approach to resume organization excludes personal and business references from the format. The purpose of the employment resume is to elicit sufficient interest in your credentials to warrant an interview, and references do little to effect that outcome. Resume checking comes later, when the decision has been made by the employer to extend an offer. Up to that time, little if any attention is paid to references. The only thing references do is take up valuable space that could be more effectively used in describing your qualifications. Qualifications are of considerably more interest to the prospective employer than references at this point.

The listing of references can, in some cases, prove detrimental to your employment candidacy. Since this is no longer an encouraged resume practice, it could signal an alert and image-conscious employer that you are not up-to-date in your thinking—that you are not in tune with modern-day concepts.

If currently employed, you had better think twice about listing references on your resume (particularly if your employer is unaware that you are looking). More than once I have heard some pretty bad "war stories" from other employment professionals where an insensitive and unthinking potential employer has prematurely checked a candidate's references (before receiving permission to do so). The results can be disastrous!

Additionally, some companies check references on a routine basis as part of their prescreening process. That is, they call the candidate's references as part of the process for determining whether the candidate should be brought in for interviews. A less than glowing reference can do a lot to squelch any possibility of an on-site interview. Why take the chance? At least give yourself the benefit of a solid interview before your references are inspected.

Myth 7.   Listing hobbies and extracurricular activities is important and conveys the image of a diversified, well-rounded person.

As with references, modern resume concepts normally exclude hobbies and extracurricular activities from the format. Unlike references, however, there are some bona fide exceptions.

Proponents of this myth insist that the inclusion of hobbies or extracurricular activities adds a dimension to the resume that suggests a candidate who is diversified, well-rounded, resourceful, complex (meant to be complimentary in the intellectual sense), efficient, sociable, energetic, interesting, and so on. What valid conclusion can be drawn from a huge list of hobbies and outside activities? Perhaps such listings connote an individual who hates a job and thus finds an outlet for frustration. Perhaps it reflects a person whose marriage is unhappy and who wishes to get away from their spouse. Anyway, how can a person who is truly committed to a job be spending so many of his or her evenings immersed in so many other endeavors?

I have heard the story of the jogger who listed this fact on his resume in hopes that it would convey a sense of health, well-being, energy, and so forth. Upon arriving at the interview he was greeted by his prospective boss—a 300-pound, cigar-smoking vice-president. The interview started, "I see that you're a jogger. I never could get interested in jogging— a waste of time, don't you think?" This interview was not off to the best of starts.

As with references, hobbies and extracurricular activities take up valuable space on the resume that could be used more effectively to describe qualifications or work-related accomplishments—information of considerably more interest to the employer at this time. Most employers are not going to hire you simply because you play golf, are president of the Lions Club, or have chaired the annual flower show. They are going to hire you because you are going to help them solve problems and add profits to their company.

There are only two situations that warrant the inclusion of these items on the resume. First, if they are directly job related, they may enhance your value and marketability to the prospective employer. Second, you may wish to list them if you are applying to a firm that is known to place a high value on such activities. With the exception of these two specific cases, however, I recommend exclusion of all hobbies and extracurricular activities from your resume.

Myth 8.   *Indicating one's status as married conveys a mature or stable image.*

Modern resume formats specifically exclude such personal data as age, height, weight, health, and marital status. Such information is not considered to be job-relevant.

Showing marital status is particularly disadvantageous for female applicants. If you're young and married, some employers will consider your pregnancy an imminent probability. Fair or not, these are the harsh realities of the employment market. Even civil rights legislation, although substantially improving the environment, has not totally eradicated attitudes of this kind.

The best rule to follow is to simply exclude all personal information from the resume. In this way, you will not invite discrimination.

Myth 9.   Personal photos improve resume appearance and enhance marketability.

The use of personal photographs as part of the resume was a customary practice until the early 1960s. The year 1964, however, saw the passage of the strongest civil rights act in the history of the United States. This law made it illegal for employers to discriminate against an individual on the basis of race, color, religion, or national origin. Further, it provided for the establishment of the Equal Employment Opportunity Commission for the purpose of enforcing fair employment practices. With the advent of this legislation, the practice of including a personal photograph with one's resume became obsolete!

Today, most employers are intolerant of candidates who insist on including a photograph. Employment managers simply don't want to see them! Such photographs render the employer vulnerable to possible charges of racial discrimination in their employment practices. Resultant suits can be costly and can cause considerable damage to the firm's public image. As a result, some companies have adopted a standing policy of not interviewing anybody who submits a personal photograph along with employment credentials.

Personal photographs included with the resume strongly suggest an applicant who is totally out of touch with current practices—an individual who is considerably behind the times. Such candidates may be quickly dismissed as uninformed, insensitive, or both.

Myth 10.   Use of salary history on a resume can enhance the image of a high potential, fast-track candidate.

Proponents of this myth feel that in the case of an individual who has had extremely favorable salary treatment and rapid salary progression, salary history should definitely be shown on the resume. Proponents argue that this is clear and tangible evidence of your value to your current employer. It shows that your contributions are recognized and rewarded.

Although this may sound right and logical to you, unfortunately from a professional resume standpoint it's incorrect. Modern resume concepts strongly recommend omitting salary or salary history from the resume. There are several good reasons for this:

1. Showing salary information on the resume is considered to be in poor taste. It can create an impression that the candidate is ostentatious, showy—a braggart. Such practice lacks a certain touch of subtlety, diplomacy, and class.

2. Employers are interested in your accomplishments and contributions, not your cost. By including salary information on the resume, you draw attention to your cost instead of to your potential value. You may thus never reach the interview stage and therefore forfeit the opportunity to personally convince the prospective employer that you're really worth it.

3. Inclusion of salary history may give the impression that you are "money hungry." This may suggest to some potential employers that you have a rather shallow value system—that you lack real depth and character. It may lead them to believe that you are one of those individuals who is always asking for more money—a malcontent who is never satisfied.

4. Most importantly, premature disclosure of salary or salary requirements may automatically screen you from consideration for a position in which you might have considerable interest. Many people have taken lateral moves or slight salary decreases to accept positions offering considerable long-term advancement opportunity.

The rule of thumb recommended by most experts in the employment field is "Don't show either salary history or current salary on the resume. Only volunteer current salary or salary history in a cover letter if specifically asked by the employer to furnish this information." Even in those cases where you have been asked to furnish salary requirements in your cover letter, try to avoid being specific. In handling these requests, you should state a range—mid-$70K range, low-$80K range, and so on. In doing so, you are not automatically screening yourself out, yet you are still preserving some flexibility for future salary negotiations.

Myth 11.   Cover letters are better read than resumes.

There are some who argue that the cover letter that accompanies the resume is more important than the resume itself. They contend, therefore, that an individual should devote considerably more time and effort to the development of an outstanding cover letter than to the actual resume. It is believed that the cover letter captures the attention of the employment manager and compels him or her to read the accompanying resume with more interest and intensity.

Although I agree that it is important to have a good cover letter, I would take strong issue with the contention that this letter plays a more important role than the resume itself. In fact, as a seasoned employment professional who has read resumes and cover letters numbering in the hundreds of thousands, I can assure you that the resume is considerably more important. Cover letters are frequently poorly written and usually provide little or no additional information beyond what is already covered in the resume. This has conditioned many employment professionals to pay little attention to the cover letter and to move right on to the actual resume.

In addition to providing little meaningful supplementary information, many cover letters tend to be rather boastful, with paragraph after paragraph extolling the applicant's virtues. They can speak in absolutely glowing terms about their many accomplishments and achievements as well as their many outstanding strengths. Instead of adding to the value of the applicant's credentials and increasing interest in his or her employment candidacy, many cover letters do just the opposite—leaving an impression of an individual who is overly self-impressed. Again, having been conditioned by such a high proportion of poorly written cover letters, most employment professionals read them skeptically (if they read them at all). Most are only being read to see if there is any personal contact with the company that would suggest the need for something other than the normal form letter response.

If you put extra emphasis anywhere at all, focus concentration on the resume itself. Resumes are much better read than the cover letters that accompany them. It is the resume that sets forth the candidate's overall qualifications and is the primary document from which decisions to interview are made. Don't rely on the cover letter to accomplish this objective for you.

Myth 12.   The functional resume is the most effective format.

The functional resume (see description in Chapter 9) is considered by many to be the most effective resume format. Proponents of this view base their arguments on firm marketing strategy. They believe that in order to increase the employment professional's interest in your credentials, you must get his or her attention right from the start. This is done by summarizing your major accomplishments and achievements at the very beginning of the resume.

Although I like the logic behind the functional resume, I am less impressed with the end result. The marketing strategy is sound, yet this particular format has some shortcomings of which you should be aware. First, and foremost, this is a format often used by those who have something to hide, for example, a considerable number of past employers, long periods of unemployment, limited direct work experience in the area for which they are applying, and so on. Employment managers are so conditioned to this fact that red flags go up immediately when this format is used by the applicant. This often sets into motion a very negative process, a kind of "witch hunt" to find the major flaw in the applicant's credentials. What is it that the applicant is attempting to hide? In choosing this particular format, therefore, you should do so with full knowledge that many employment professionals will be reviewing your resume with some suspicion.

A second major shortcoming of the functional resume format is that it is considerably more difficult to read and comprehend than the chronological format. Since functional accomplishments are not shown at the same place in the resume as employers, it may leave the employment manager in a quandary as to which accomplishment was with which employer. This can cause considerable frustration since, in order to properly evaluate the candidate's qualifications, it is often necessary to have this information. In order to get this information, the manager must call the applicant, which many employment managers are loath to do. Unless there is a scarcity of applicants, and the current opening will be a very difficult one to fill, the employment manager is likely to stamp the resume no interest and move on to the next.

This is not to say that the functional resume does not have a role in the employment process—it does. In most cases, it is simply not the most effective resume format to use to increase your chances of landing a job interview. Chapter 9 will help you determine whether this format should be used in your particular case.

Having read this chapter, you must realize that the subject of resume writing abounds with well-intentioned but nonetheless erroneous myths. Many of these sound very logical and quite innocent on the surface; however, they can prove to be detrimental to the effectiveness and impact of your employment resume. Don't let yourself fall into any of these resume traps. And, if you need help, seek the advice of an experienced employment professional. It can be well worth your time.

3

PREPARING
TO WRITE

If you are feeling a little apprehensive by the challenge of writing an effective resume, relax—you have a lot of company. Resume writing is not a process that comes easily to most. On the contrary, the great majority of people find this exercise a difficult one. I have seen very bright, talented, and highly successful people rendered almost helpless when it came to reducing their outstanding credentials to a concise, forceful, and effective employment resume document. Additionally, I have read the resumes of thousands of highly qualified individuals in which it was painfully clear that the author had experienced considerable difficulty in developing this all-important summary.

This chapter will help you overcome this initial anxiety and to provide you with the structure and techniques needed to approach this task with confidence. If you carefully follow the advice and instructions contained in this chapter, you should be fully prepared to construct an effective resume that does full justice to your background and professional qualifications.

RESUME ANXIETY

When dealing with the feelings of apprehension or un-easiness associated with resume writing, a little careful analysis can go a long way. Generally speaking, fear or un-easiness is normally associated with the unknown or unexpected. People feel least uncomfortable with those things with which they are most familiar. In fact, where the individual has firsthand, intimate knowledge of the subject, there is a strong sense of security and self-confidence. To the contrary, when the individual has little or no experience, there is a lack of security and confidence. Applying this logic to the subject of resume writing, it is easy to see why so many people have a feeling of uneasiness. Few have had much experience in this important undertaking.

Generally, anxiety over resume preparation falls into one or more of the following three categories:

1. Content (What do I say/not say?)
2. Format (How should it be organized?)
3. Style (How should I say it?)

If you know what to say, how to organize it, and how to say it, there should be little reason to feel uncomfortable about this process. In addition, the more you have prepared, organized, and rehearsed, the more comfortable and confident you will feel in your skill and ability to write an effective employment resume. This chapter is designed to help you develop these resume-preparation skills and the confidence necessary to move on to the actual writing process.

More specifically, this chapter is intended to assist you in two areas. The first is the area of advance preparation. Basic guidelines for collecting and organizing all of the advance data that you will need for resume preparation are provided. Second, assistance in developing the writing skills and style necessary for an effective and forceful resume is offered. Our focus will thus be on content and style. The subject of resume format or structure is dealt with in depth in Chapters 5, 7, and 9 and is not covered here.

ADVANCE PREPARATION

With most difficult tasks, the need for organization and advance preparation is paramount. Resume writing is no exception! Before you can proceed with the actual writing, you will need to have a number of facts and details at your fingertips. Further, these facts will have to be organized in such a way that they may be found when you need them. This advance-preparation step then is essential to an efficient and orderly process. It will save you considerable time and frustration as you proceed with the writing process.

The following forms are designed to organize these data in an orderly manner that will allow you to locate information quickly and efficiently.

Education

In the spaces provided, fill in all the information requested, starting with most recent degree first.

Degree: _____

School: _____   Date Graduated: _____

Major: _____   Grade Point Average: _____

Honoraries: _____

_____

Scholarships: _____

_____

Offices Held: _____

_____

Degree: _____

School: _____   Date Graduated: _____

Major: _____   Grade Point Average: _____

Honoraries: _____

_____

Scholarships: _____

_____

Offices Held: _____

_____

Degree: _____

School: _____   Date Graduated: _____

Major: _____   Grade Point Average: _____

Honoraries: _____

_____

Scholarships: _____

_____

Offices Held: _____

_____

Professional Designation: _____

Date Certified: _____

Certifying Organization: _____

Professional Designation:

Date Certified: _____

Certifying Organization: _____

Work Experience

Starting with your most recent employer first, list all employers for whom you have worked, including dates of employment, title of position held, and key job accountabilities.
In those cases where you have held more than one position
with a given employer, indicate this by writing "Same" in the
space provided for the employer's name. List such positions
in reverse chronological order (starting with the most recent
position first), again showing dates that positions were held
and key job responsibilities.

1. Dates Employed: From: _____ To: _____

   Employer: _____

   Division: _____

   Position Title: _____

   Key Responsibilities: _____

   _____

   _____

----

2. Dates Employed: From: _____ To: _____

Employer: _____

Division: _____

Position Title: _____

Key Responsibilities: _____

_____

_____

_____

_____

----

3. Dates Employed: From: _____ To: _____

Employer: _____

Division: _____

Position Title: _____

Key Responsibilities: _____

_____

_____

_____

_____

_____

----

4. Dates Employed: From: _____ To: _____

Employer: _____

Division: _____

Position Title: _____

Key Responsibilities: _____

_____

_____

_____

_____

----

5. Dates Employed: From: _____ To: _____

Employer: _____

Division: _____

Position Title: _____

Key Responsibilities: _____

_____

_____

_____

_____

----

6. Dates Employed: From: _____ To: _____

Employer: _____

Division: _____

Position Title: _____

Key Responsibilities: _____

_____

_____

_____

_____

If you have worked for more than six employers or held more than six positions with a number of different employers, continue this exercise on a separate piece of paper. Continue to list the information in the same format until you have accounted for all the employers and positions you have held since beginning your full-time, professional career. If you are a recent graduate, list this information for part-time and summer jobs as well.

Go back over the work that you have just completed. Take a few minutes to research your accomplishments and, at the end of the key responsibilities section for each of the positions that you have described, jot down any kind of quantitative information that will be helpful later on in describing the size and scope of your job accountabilities. Include such things as the number of persons managed or supervised, annual budget, sales volume (if in sales or marketing), amount and/or value of goods manufactured (if in manufacturing), capital project costs (if in engineering), and so on. Being able to find this quantitative information quickly during the actual writing of your resume will prove extremely valuable and will save you considerable time.

You now have the basic facts that you will be needing as you begin the writing process. At this point, let's discuss some other things you need to do before you move on to the actual preparation process.

WINNING ATTITUDE

If you don't believe and feel that you are a winner, no one else will! Feelings of uneasiness, apprehension, and insecurity are bound to be reflected in the way you express yourself in the resume. A seasoned employment professional will sense this from the tone and style of your writing. Conversely, if you are confident in your skills and knowledge and feel that you have something of value to contribute to a prospective employer, this positive attitude and enthusiasm is bound to be sensed by the person who reads your resume. It should not surprise you that being in a positive frame of mind is critical to the writing of a good resume. If you are not feeling positive and good about yourself, don't even start!

There are, however, some things that you can do to affect your attitude and self-confidence in a very positive way. The next section should help you considerably.

Developing a Positive Attitude

The key to establishing a positive attitude and improved self-confidence is to take the time to be reflective—to look within yourself for a sense of value. All employers are eager to hire someone who can add value to their organization's bottom-line results! Such "added value" can take many different forms, including the following:

1. Ability to solve key, long-standing problems
2. Ability to bring new, fresh ideas—to bring change and improvement

3. Ability to lead and motivate others to achieve high levels of productivity

4. Ability to spot and realize key cost-reduction opportunities

5. Ability to identify and bring about expansion and substantially improved profits through identification and procurement of key acquisitions

6. Ability to design new, innovative, and profit-generating equipment

These are but a few of the numerous ways that an individual can add value to a prospective employer's organization.

The employment resume and the accompanying cover letter are your only opportunities to prove that you are a valuable commodity, that you have something of great or unique value to contribute to the prospective employer. This is the time to "toot your own horn" in an effective yet inoffensive and tasteful way. This can best be done by citing specific achievements and contributions that you have made to past as well as current employers.

Employment managers are instinctively looking for value in the resume. They are looking for evidence that suggests that the candidate will make a good addition to their company: for example, that they have the capability to make valuable contributions to their employers. Most of these managers believe that the best predictor of future behavior and accomplishment is the behavior and accomplishment of the past. What other evidence does an employment professional have for predicting the candidate's future value?

Thus, in addition to combing the resume for specific education, knowledge, and experience, the professional employment manager is also carefully looking for indications and hard evidence that the candidate will prove to be a good performer—that he or she will get important things done.

One of the biggest mistakes that people make in writing resumes is that they neglect to cite their accomplishments. Frequently the Work Experience section of the resume reads like a job description. It describes what the candidate is responsible for doing but fails to describe what he or she has actually done. Thus many resume writers completely miss the mark. They fail to focus in on their major achievements, leaving the reader guessing how effective they have been in their past positions.

DEFINING YOUR VALUE

It's now time to think about your value to prospective employers. Listed below are several questions followed by blanks to be filled in. Take some time to carefully consider each of these questions and fill in a well-thought-out answer in the space provided. Some of these questions may sound redundant, but the purpose of these exercises is to help you define your value. Asking some of the same questions in a slightly different way may help to stimulate your thinking. One question may not provide much stimulus, but asked in a slightly different way it could serve to trigger a host of ideas and responses.

If you asked a group of five or six of your friends or peers to describe your greatest attributes, what adjectives would they use to describe you? (Use single words only.)

_____   _____

_____   _____

_____   _____

_____   _____

_____   _____

_____   _____

Go back and rank these adjectives from 1 to 12 based upon how you feel these friends would rank them: Number 1 would represent the adjective that your friends would choose to best describe you, with 12 representing the adjective that least describes you.

What positive things are there about your behavior and/or achievements that cause these individuals to describe you in this fashion?

Positive Behavior/Achievements: _____

_____

_____

_____

_____

_____

What are your greatest strengths? Describe these strengths in terms of specific skills and knowledge.

Strongest Skills: _____

_____

_____

_____

_____

Greatest Knowledge: _____

_____

_____

_____

_____

Rank these in order from greatest strength to least strength.

In a business sense, what are those things that you do with greatest proficiency?

Do Best: _____

_____

_____

Reviewing the above list, what is there about you or your skills and abilities that enables you to do these things well? Describe below.

_____

_____

_____

_____

_____

_____

_____

In reviewing your life to date, what do you consider to be your most significant accomplishments and achievements? Of which achievements are you most proud? List three achievements in each of the categories shown.

Education: 1. _____

              2. _____

              3. _____

Business: 1. _____

             _____

2. _____

_____

3. _____

_____

Personal: 1. _____

_____

2. _____

_____

3. _____

_____

Taking each of the employers and jobs that you listed earlier in this chapter, list the three most significant contributions that you made for each position shown.

1. Employer: _____ Job Title: _____

Achievements:

1. _____

_____

2. _____

_____

3. _____

_____

2. Employer: _____ Job Title: _____

Achievements:

1. _____

_____

2. _____

_____

3. _____

_____

3. Employer: _____ Job Title: _____

Achievements:

1. _____

_____

2. _____

_____

3. _____

_____

4. Employer: _____ Job Title: _____

Achievements:

1. _____

_____

2. _____

_____

3. _____

_____

5. Employer: _____ Job Title: _____

Achievements:

1. _____

_____

2. _____

_____

3. _____

_____

6. Employer: _____ Job Title: _____

Achievements:

1. _____

_____

2. _____

_____

3. _____

_____

Take a few minutes to reflect upon the information that you provided in each of the preceding exercises. You have probably been successful in identifying quite a few strengths and accomplishments—things that will be of value to a prospective employer. Having done this, take a minute to answer the following important questions:

Why do I deserve the type of position for which I am applying? Which of my overall strengths and accomplishments best qualifies me for such a position?

You should now be convinced that you have a lot to offer a prospective employer, and you should be confident in your skills and knowledge. The previous exercises should have enabled you to cite a number of key attributes and accomplishments that will add strength and credibility to your resume and your job-hunting campaign as well.

So far in this chapter we dealt with two components of advance preparation. The first was resume content, that is, those dates and facts that you will need at your fingertips as you begin the actual resume-writing process. Second, we developed a series of exercises designed to build a positive, confident attitude. Finally, we deal with the subject of writing style.

WRITING STYLE

Writing style is an extremely important element of the resume-writing process. It is an important aspect from two standpoints. First, style is important in conveying a maximum amount of information in a clear, precise manner that leaves little or no room for misinterpretation or misunderstanding. Second, writing style is critical to the conciseness necessary to condense several years of experience on to a two-page format. If you are going to compete effectively with the thousands of other employment resumes that the employment manager will be reading, your resume must be written in a concise, precise, and forceful way. A sloppy, uninteresting style could cost you interviews! How you say it is as important as what you say.

So that you have a better appreciation for the importance of writing style, take a few moments to consider the following examples. These examples describe identical work experience.

Example A

I worked five years as Manager of Marketing. I was responsible for nationwide sales of all plumbing supplies and managed 15 other sales representatives. I also prepared all marketing plans and strategies. I was responsible for planning all product advertising, including some sizable campaigns. We were very successful and increased sales quite a bit in the second year.

Example B

Marketing Manager. Corporate-wide accountability for marketing and sales for this manufacturer of quality pumps and valves (annual sales $85 million). Developed key marketing plans and strategies which led to a 53% increase in sales in second year. Managed sales force of 15 area representatives.

In reviewing these two examples, I am sure that you would agree that Example B is far more dynamic and interesting than Example A. What makes this difference? What is there about the writing style used in Example B that makes it more effective than Example A? How is this accomplished? Let's take a few moments to examine these two examples more closely. This exercise should give you some pretty strong clues on how to write effectively. Consider the following points:

1. *Job Title.* It is not necessary to repeat the position title in describing job responsibilities. The position title has been listed previously as part of the heading. Listing it again is redundant and adds no new information or increased understanding.

2. *Pronouns.* Note that the pronoun "I" is conspicuously missing from Example B. Since the resume reader is already aware that this is your resume, the "I" is understood.

3. *Complete Sentences.* Since the pronoun "I" is understood, it is not necessary to use complete sentences in writing a resume. Descriptive phrases or clauses are sufficient as long as they convey a complete thought and are clearly understandable.

4. *Brevity.* Note that Example B starts two out of three sentences with a verb followed by a noun or adjective. The practice of starting sentences with a verb will force you to be more concise and precise. This practice will help you to improve your resume-writing style.

5. *Condense and Consolidate.* Where possible, you should attempt to condense related information into a single statement rather than make two separate statements. Note that Example B has combined the "development of marketing plans and strategies" with the "increase in sales in the second year." In Example A, these were treated as two unrelated statements. Where possible, condense and consolidate, eliminating all nonessential information that adds little or no meaning to your employment qualifications.

6. *Quantitative Descriptions.* Where possible, use quantitative terms or descriptions to convey greater understanding of the magnitude or scope of your responsibilities and accomplishments. Example B has made use of this technique—citing $85 million to quantify annual sales volume and 53% to communicate the size of the sales increase. In addition to providing the reader with a more thorough understanding of your qualifications, quantitative terms make the resume considerably more interesting.

The writing style used in the resume is also important from another standpoint. This style is thought by most employment professionals to be reflective of the personal style of the candidate. Thus, if resume style is rambling and verbose, the candidate's personal style is thought to be ranbling and verbose. To the contrary, if the resume is brief, concise, and interesting, it would not be unreasonable to envision an employment candidate who is concise, efficient, and interesting. Thus resume style can sometimes be as important as content and format, if not more so. It is an element that will prove extremely important to the overall effectiveness of your resume.

We have now covered three of the four major elements necessary to preparing you for the actual resume-writing process. These have included positive attitude, resume content, and writing style. The remaining key element is the format, the organization or structure that the resume should take. Chapter 5, The Chronological Resume; Chapter 7, The Linear Resume; and Chapter 9, The Functional Resume, will provide you with step-by-step processes for preparing these three most popular and commonly used resume formats.

4

RESUME WRITING— GENERAL COMMENTS

TYPES OF RESUMES

Generally speaking, there are three conventional styles of employment resumes: the chronological resume, the linear resume, and the functional resume.

Sample resumes at the end of Chapter 5 are examples of the chronological resume. A, B, and C note that the Experience sections of these resumes list jobs in reverse chronological order, starting with the current or most recently held position. The linear resume (see sample resumes D and E at the end of Chapter 7) is a variation of the chronological resume and follows the reverse chronological order as well.

The functional resume (see sample resume F at the end of Chapter 9), on the other hand, is different from the chronological style resume and is organized to give primary emphasis to functional areas in which the candidate has significant experience or particular strengths. Although the functional resume focuses on results or accomplishments, it is somewhat confusing when you attempt to determine in which positions (or with which employer) specific results where achieved. The employment professional is therefore frequently at a loss to effectively evaluate the specifics of the candidate's qualifications with this type of resume.

Thus the functional resume immediately raises some red flags in the mind of the employment professional. For this reason alone, I strongly suggest in most cases that you avoid using this format. Additionally, as mentioned previously, it is difficult for the employment manager to fully understand and evaluate the specific nature of your past positions and accomplishments and relate these to the positions you have held. Many won't even try before they move on to the next resume.

Both the chronological and the linear resumes, by contrast with the functional resume, represent a very straightforward, direct approach to presenting your employment credentials. They leave little doubt in the mind of the employment professional as to where you have been and what you have accomplished. As an employment professional, I can assure you that in almost all cases your chances of securing an employment interview are substantially increased by using these chronological formats as opposed to the functional approach.

Employment authorities estimate that from 90 to 95 percent of all resumes utilize either the chronological or linear format. Choosing these formats, therefore, assures you that your resume will be well understood and well accepted by the majority of employment professionals who will be scrutinizing this document.

PURPOSE OF RESUME

Before proceeding to the actual preparation of your employment resume, it is important to have a clear understanding of the purpose of the resume. Unfortunately, many employment candidates have a rather narrow understanding of the purposes this document serves.

The primary purpose of the employment resume is to convince a prospective employer that you are an outstanding candidate for employment and that it would be well worth his or her time to interview you in person. It must convince the employer that you have something of value to contribute to his or her company—that somehow the company's performance and profitability will be improved by hiring you.

The focus or emphasis of the employment resume must therefore be on your major results, contributions, and accomplishments. It cannot simply state the names of past employers and provide the job titles and descriptions of your past positions. These alone cannot be expected to convince the employer of your value. Your resume must suggest to the employer that you are someone who will bring improvements and make major contributions to the solution of key business problems. Only past contributions and accomplishments will serve to "make the sale."

Although the primary objective of the resume is to help you secure an employment interview, it often serves two additional and very important purposes:

1. It is the road map for your employment interview. The interviewer will frequently use it to structure the employment interview and to focus on the information that you have chosen to emphasize or highlight.

2. After the interview has taken place, the employer will often use the resume as a reference source for recalling and evaluating your specific qualifications and strengths in the light of the credentials of other candidates.

Keeping in mind the several important roles that the resume must play, it should be evident to you by now that you will need to pay particular attention to its sales appeal. If it is to convince a prospective employer to hire you, it must present your qualifications in the most favorable light and must focus on past results and major accomplishments. Additionally, it must continue to remind the prospective employer of your excellent qualifications.

5

THE CHRONOLOGICAL RESUME

A review of the sample chronological resumes provided at the end of this chapter (as well as Chapter 6) reveals that the resume is divided into the following components:

1. Heading
2. Objective
3. Education
4. Experience

Although the order in which these components are arranged on the resume may vary, the sequence presented above is the most commonly used, accepted, and recommended format. The most frequent deviation from this recommended sequence, however, is the positioning of the education and experience components. You will note that the resume on page 59 positions education before experience, while the resume on pages 60–61, lists education after experience. Close examination of these two sample resumes reveals why.

The rule of thumb to be applied in deciding where to position the Education and Experience sections is this: Always position education before experience providing such positioning will not detract from your marketability.

In the case of the first resume, the candidate has very strong educational credentials with very little work experience. Additionally, the schools that the candidate attended are considered prestigious. The candidate is thus best served by placing education first. Conversely, the second resume reveals a candidate with extensive work experience but whose educational credentials might be considered light by some employers' standards. In this case, positioning education first might detract from the candidate's marketability.

In general, younger candidates with good education credentials and little work experience should list education first. Older workers with considerable experience and persons who do not have strong education credentials are generally best served by placing education after experience.

For the older worker, placing education first can often draw attention to his or her age, something that should be avoided. Unfortunately, even though age discrimination is illegal, there are still many companies that practice it. Why then attract attention to your age by placing education first? If you can get the employer to review your work experience and major accomplishments first, and thereby convince him or her that you have something to contribute, perhaps the employer will pay less attention, or, even better, disregard the age issue entirely.

We are now ready to begin the step-by-step process of resume preparation. Our approach will be to examine each component of the employment resume in some detail and provide you with practical exercises that will assist you to expertly develop each of these components. When finished with this section, you will have prepared a logical, professional resume that will effectively portray and market your qualifications to prospective employers.

HEADING

The resume heading consists of three items: your full name, complete address, and home telephone number. Some sample resume headings follow.

JOHN C. SMITH
325 Blue Street
Cleveland Heights
Cleveland, Ohio 39820
Phone: (315) 472-8975

DAVID B. MARKS
126 Lake Road
Windsor, New York 17530
Phone: Home—(212) 744-1965
Office—(212) 658-9712

Your name should be typed in capital letters and set in bold type so it stands out from the rest of the heading. Address and telephone number are typed in lower case. Although there are acceptable alternatives, generally the heading should be centered on the page.

It is usually not advisable to include your office telephone number on the resume unless you feel confident that you can accept employment-related phone calls with adequate privacy. Additionally, if the office number is listed on the resume, it may serve to raise some suspicion on the part of prospective employers that your current employer is aware that you are job hunting and may even be eager to have you depart. The rule of thumb is to avoid listing your office phone number on the resume unless prospective employers will otherwise have difficulty in reaching you. Having an answering machine on your home phone provides an effective solution, and allows you to easily access calls at will with the assurance of absolute privacy.

Most employment managers are willing to call you at home in the evening if you ask them to do so in your cover letter. In the absence of an answering machine, another way to get around the telephone-contact hurdle is to include a statement similar to the following in the cover letter that accompanies your resume:

I can normally be reached at my home telephone number after 7:00 P.M. In the event that you find it necessary to contact me during business hours, my wife, Sally, will be pleased to relay your message. Sally can be reached at (212) 947-3015.

Keeping in mind the above instructions for developing your resume heading, try to write your own heading.

OBJECTIVE

In developing the Objective section of your resume, take care that your objective is neither too narrow nor too broad. Consider the following statements of job objective:

1. *Objective.* Senior level Accounting or Financial position with broad responsibility for achievement of company's financial objectives.
2. *Objective.* Overall direction of the Financial Planning function with advancement opportunities to senior level management position.

You will note Objective 1 is worded very broadly and suggests that the candidate is receptive to a wide range of financial and accounting positions (including Financial Planning). By contrast, Objective 2 is very specific and suggests to the prospective employer that the candidate will only consider positions in Financial Planning.

Unless by specific intent, care should be taken not to word your objective too narrowly or it could cause the employer to screen you out from positions that could be of real interest to you. As a case in point, in our example above, the narrow statement of Objective 2 could easily cause a prospective employer to screen you from consideration for such positions as:

Director of Corporate Accounting

Director of Manufacturing Accounting

Director of Financial Analysis

These three positions may well be of interest to you.

On the other end of the spectrum, it is also possible to be too general in your statement of objective. Some examples are:

3. *Objective.* A good job with a good company.

4. *Objective.* A good accounting position.

Vague objectives of this type will suggest to prospective employers that you have given little thought to your career objectives. Such statements of objective may also imply that you lack the ability to plan ahead or that you lack the ability to analyze your qualifications and career direction. Either way, the employer will probably not be very impressed with your objective and will likely decide not to extend an invitation for an employment interview.

Carefully study Objectives 1 and 2 above as well as the objectives presented on the sample resumes at the end of this chapter. Note the brevity, conciseness, and clarity with which these objectives are stated. Try writing your own employment objective. Remember to guard against being too specific or too general.

EDUCATION

The Education section of the employment resume should include the following facts: (1) degree awarded, (2) schools attended, (3) year graduated, (4) major field of concentration, and (5) honors. Some sample education statements have been provided below for your reference.

1. <u>Education:</u>   Ph.D., University of Michigan, 1985
   Major: Mathematics

> M.S., University of Michigan, 1983
> Major: Economics
>
> B.S., Michigan State University, 1981
> Major: Economics
> Magna Cum Laude

2. <u>Education:</u>   M.S., Un. of Southern California, 1990
Major: Mechanical Engineering
Sloan Engineering Scholarship

B.S., University of Florida, 1988
Major: Mechanical Engineering
Tau Beta Pi (Engineering Honorary)

3. <u>Education:</u>   B.A., Bucknell University, 1989
Major: Business Administration

Generally, unless you are a recent college graduate, very little space should be allocated to the Education section of your employment resume. The general axiom to be followed in developing this section of your resume is "The further along you are in your professional career, the less important are your educational credentials and the more important are your work experience and specific accomplishments." Correspondingly, the more experienced you are, the more you should seriously consider positioning education following experience in the resume.

If you graduated from college in the last few years, you may want to highlight your educational credentials by positioning them early in the resume. If, however, you have only a bachelor's degree and most employers strongly prefer a master's degree for work in your career area or professional discipline, it is best to position education after experience.

Now try to develop the education portion of your resume using the instructions previously provided.

EXPERIENCE

The Experience section of your resume is probably its single most important component. It is this section that must convince prospective employers that you are worth invest-ing their time in an employment interview. Therefore, you should spend the most time and devote the most attention to developing this portion of your resume. This will be time well spent and can be expected to yield appropriate rewards in the form of both more job interviews and better employ-ment opportunities.

An important benefit to be derived from careful develop-ment of this section of your resume is that it will force you to thoroughly review your work history and accomplishments. In essence, it will serve to provide you with a thorough men-tal rehearsal of your background and qualifications prior to the actual job interview. This will go a long way toward in-creasing your overall interview effectiveness.

Careful review of the sample resumes provided at the end of this chapter and in Chapter 6 will reveal that each job listed in the Experience section has a description that in-cludes the following:

1. Dates of employment
2. Employer
3. Division or location of position
4. Job title
5. Brief statement of major job accountabilities and scope
6. Brief statement of major contributions and accom-plishments

A good general rule to follow in preparing this section of your employment resume is to devote the greatest amount of space to your most recent and most responsible jobs. Little space should, conversely, be devoted to positions held 20 or 30 years ago or to positions that have little bearing on your current employment objective. Most employers care very lit-tle about the jobs you held several years ago. Of great inter-est, however, are the positions held and contributions made to employers in recent years.

Review of the sample resumes contained at the end of this chapter and in Chapter 6 will also reveal that there are rarely any pronouns (I, you, they, he, etc.) or articles (a, the, an, etc.) used. Additionally, many sentences begin with verbs or action words which lend both brevity and a sense of "results orientation" to the resume. You will find that by starting most sentences of your resume with a verb or action word you will be forced to be brief and concise in your statements. Additionally, you will be forced to state specific results achieved and contributions made.

Starting almost every sentence with a verb or action word is probably the *greatest secret of effective resume writing!*

To assist you in getting started with this effective resume-writing technique, a list of key verbs or "action words" is provided at the end of this chapter. You are encouraged to refer to and make use of this list while developing this section of your employment resume.

Another effective technique to employ in developing the Experience section of your resume is to use quantitative descriptions when these serve to highlight your experience and contributions. Consider the following:

Wrong	I managed a Corporate Accounting Department.
Right	Managed Corporate Accounting Department of 50 professionals with $1.5 million budget accountability.
Wrong	I developed a new equipment design that saved the company a lot of money.
Right	Developed new wrapping equipment design resulting in $2 million company savings in 1995 alone.
Wrong	I helped to develop a new shipping system that saved a lot of shipping time.
Right	Participated in development of new shipping system saving over 500,000 hours of labor annually ($1.5 million annual savings).

You are now ready to develop the experience section of your resume. Remember to begin your sentences with action words and to use quantitative descriptions where possible.

Start with your current or most recent job first and continue in reverse chronological order. An example is provided below for your reference.

Employment dates	From 1990 to present
Employer	National Knitting Corporation
Division/location	Corporate Offices
Job title	Engineering Manager
Job description	Manage 50-employee engineering department for this Fortune 200 manufacturer of knitting equipment (annual sales $4 billion). Direct development, design, installation, and startup of advanced technology, computer-controlled knitting machines.
Major accomplishments	(1) Developed three revolutionary knitting machines increasing company sales by 25% in last two years accounting for $50 million annual profit improvement. (2) Restructured Engineering Department with resultant labor-cost reduction of 10% and simultaneous 25% productivity increase. (3) Maintained high level of employee morale with annual employee turnover of less than 1%.

Try to list at least three major accomplishments for each position held.

REFERENCES

It is strongly recommended that references not be provided on the resume. The danger in providing references is that the prospective employer may elect to check these references prior to inviting you for an employment interview. The slightest bit of negative information uncovered by the employer may result in a decision against an interview. This places you at a decided disadvantage, since you will never have the opportunity to counter this negative impression.

Additionally, references are not really needed by the employer until you have been interviewed and there is interest in making an offer of employment. Why waste valuable resume space when this space could be better used to present job-relevant qualifications? Instead, have a separate list of references available in case the employer requests them. Do not volunteer this list unless the employer specifically asks for this information.

MISCELLANEOUS

Extracurricular activities and hobbies also have no place on the modern employment resume unless they are directly related to your qualifications for the position you seek. There may occasionally be some advantage to listing extracurricular activities on the resume, however, if it serves to accomplish some specific objective such as to substantiate leadership ability—president or vice-president of a related professional society or other well-known organization. Likewise, hobbies seldom add anything of real value when it comes to important job qualifications.

Technical professionals may wish to list key publications, papers, and patents that are job relevant. These could have direct bearing on their qualifications for employment and increase their marketability to prospective employers. List only those items that are truly important and meaningful, however; do not list minor or insignificant publications.

Sample Resume A

DAVID C. BROOKS
315 Fawn Avenue
Riverside, NY 32715
Phone: (516) 734-9215

OBJECTIVE

Responsible management position in Corporate Finance or Accounting offering advancement to senior management.

EDUCATION

M.B.A., Wharton School, University of Pennsylvania, 1993
Major: Finance
President Beta Gamma Sigma Honorary ·

B.A., Business Administration, Harvard University, 1991
Major: Accounting
Magna Cum Laude

C.P.A., May 1995

PROFESSIONAL EXPERIENCE

1995
to
Present

DAVIDSON ELECTRONICS, INC. (Corporate Offices)

Assistant Corporate Controller
Direct Cost Accounting, Tax Accounting and Information Services functions (36 employees) for this Fortune 500 manufacturer of cable T.V. components (annual sales $1.2 billion). Provide guidance to six Plant Controllers in cost accounting and tax practices. Major accomplishments include: implemented new equipment asset valuation program (annual tax savings $1 million), developed inventory cost accounting system (annual savings $750,000), installation/start-up of new on-line, real-time computer order entry system.

1993
to
1995

DAVIDSON ELECTRONICS, INC. (T.V. Components Division)

Assistant Division Controller (1994 - 1995)
Reported to division Vice President of Administration with full accountability for all Accounting, Financial and Information Services functions for this 1200 employee Division (annual sales $500 million). Revamped brand manufacturing cost accounting system resulting in substantially improved managerial cost control. Developed and installed computerized brand costing system resulting in elimination of 12 positions and annual payroll savings of $480,000.

Brand Cost Analyst (1993 - 1994)
Responsible for development and maintenance of brand costing system.

Sample Resume B

JOHN R. SIMPSON
819 Snow Hill Circle
Cedar, Washington 89047
Phone: (615) 943-7716

OBJECTIVE

Senior level Human Resources position with broad responsibility for contributing to Company's strategic business objectives.

PROFESSIONAL EXPERIENCE

1992
to
Present

NATIONAL GLASS, INC. (Corporate Offices)

Corporate Staff Human Resources Manager (1994 - 1997)
Manage staff of 20 employees with responsibility for providing full range of human resources services to Corporate Staff (900 employees) of this Fortune 200 manufacturer of glass specialties (annual sales $2.5 billion). Functions managed include: human resource planning, staffing (internal & external), salary administration, employee relations, organization development, safety and security. Accomplishments include: development/implementation of employee profit-sharing program resulting in 30% increase in employee productivity, installation of human resources information system (clerical savings $200,000 annually) and development of first Human Resources Policies and Procedures Manual.

Corporate Employment Manager (1992 - 1994)
Corporate-wide employment responsibility for the recruitment and employment of exempt administrative, marketing and technical employees (annual budget $1.2 million). Managed staff of six professionals with responsibility for annual employment volume of 500-600 new hires at all levels from college entry to corporate vice president. Creative recruiting methods reduced annual hiring costs by $250,000 with simultaneous reduction in average "fill time" from five to three months. Awarded *President's Bonus* in 1993 for unique contribution to the Business.

1980
to
1992

AMERICAN MANUFACTURING COMPANY (Plastics Division)

Division Human Resources Manager (1986 - 1992)
Division-wide accountability for broad range of human resources services for this 1500 employee profit center involved in the manufacture of custom plastic materials. Directed staff of 16 with responsibilities including: salary administration, staffing, training and development, organization design, benefits, labor relations, safety and security. Contributions included: implementation of new job evaluation (Hay) system, total revision of employee benefits program (25% increase in benefits with simultaneous $50,000 annual savings), successful negotiation of three labor contracts (no strikes, settlements averaged 10% below budgeted level), reduced engineering manpower turnover from 20% to less than 1% per year.

60

<u>Assistant Human Resources Manager</u> (1982 - 1986)
Assisted Division Human Resources Manager in providing full range of human resources services to Division clients. Major focus was staffing (internal & external), benefits administration and salary administration.

<u>Human Resources Assistant</u> (1980 - 1982)
Implemented numerous special studies covering broad range of human resources topics. Managed hourly job evaluation and Division safety program.

EDUCATION

B.A.,   Business Administration, Anderson College, 1980
Major: Human Resources Management

SANDRA M. DUNCAN
120 Padre Avenue
Ocean Side, California 80716
Phone: (712) 877-9412

OBJECTIVE

Senior operations management position at the plant, division or corporate
level with P&L responsibility.

PROFESSIONAL EXPERIENCE

1994
to
Present

DOBBER TOY MANUFACTURING, INC. (Ocean Side Plant)

Plant Manager
Manage staff of five with full P&L responsibility for this 500 employee toy
manufacturing plant (annual value of goods manufactured - $30 million). Hired
in 1981 to engineer plant turnaround (1980 loss was $3.2 million). Conducted
exhaustive study of operations methods and manufacturing costs, pinpointing key
cost improvement opportunities. Reorganized, trained and motivated plant staff.
Successfully directed ambitious profit improvement program resulting in 1995
profit of $3 million (200% improvement).

1983
to
1994

TYLER PUMP COMPANY (Corporate Offices)

Brand Manager - Valves (1990 - 1994)
Corporate-wide profit responsibility for the full line of Tyler valves for this 5,000
employee manufacturer of specialty industrial pumps and valves (annual sales
$125 million; profit $18 million). Led multi-discipline (R&D, manufacturing,
sales) profit improvement task force in the development and implementation of a
profit improvement plan to achieve increased annual profitability of the Valve line
from $6 to $9 million in two years. Goal was achieved in one year with an
additional $2 million of cost savings realized by end of second year.

Department Manager - Specialty Valves (1988 - 1990)
Managed Specialty Valve Department (four shift supervisors; 200 hourly
employees) with responsibility for the profitable manufacture of some $50 million
of specialty valves annually. Exceeded manufacturing cost and profit objectives
for three consecutive years.

Project Engineer - Valves (1983 - 1988)
Responsible for the design, installation and start-up of a wide range of specialty
valve manufacturing equipment. Major project completed was $40 million
expansion of the Denver Valve Plant. Project was completed four months ahead
of schedule and $1 million under budget.

1980   **JOHNSON MACHINERY COMPANY** (Corporate Offices)
to
1983   Research Engineer
          Developed new technology valves and related products from concept through pilot
          plant testing.

EDUCATION

M.B.A.,   Purdue University, 1980
Major: Production Management

B.S.M.E.,   University of Michigan, 1978

6

SAMPLE CHRONOLOGICAL RESUMES

This chapter contains 20 sample chronological resumes for your review and easy reference. You will note in reviewing these samples that there are 10 separate business disciplines or functions represented. These 10 disciplines represent a logical, functional breakdown of a typical manufacturing company and thus provide an excellent cross section of business functions. For each of these 10 functions you will find two sample resumes. The first is the resume of an experienced senior individual; the second resume represents a less experienced person.

The following Resume Locator should prove helpful in locating those sample resumes that are of greatest interest to you.

Resume Locator

Experience Level

Field or Discipline	*Senior Person*	*Junior Person*
	(Pages)	(Pages)
Accounting	66	68
Engineering	69	71
Finance	72	74
Human Resources	76	78
Information Services	80	82
Logistics	83	85
Marketing and Sales	87	89
Operations	90	92
Procurement	93	95
Technology	96	98

JOHN R. SMITH
225 Fair Oaks Avenue
Cleveland, Ohio 87953
Phone: (315) 857-2345

OBJECTIVE

Senior level Controllership position with broad responsibility for achievement of company's financial objectives.

PROFESSIONAL EXPERIENCE

1996
to
Present

SMITH DAVIDSON CORPORATION (Corporate Offices)

Assistant to Corporate Controller

Report to Corporate Vice President of Finance with full accountability for management of the Corporate Accounting and Bickford Division Accounting functions (32 employees) for this multi-division manufacturer of computer hardware (annual sales $320 million). Corporate responsibilities include: preparation of capital and operating budgets, financial statements for SEC and shareholder reporting, federal and state tax filings, external auditor coordination, consolidation and analysis of monthly financial statements, and accounting policy development. Division functional responsibilities include: general and cost accounting, accounts receivable, accounts payable and credit. Major accomplishments include: computerization of standard product cost build-up (500 hours labor savings annually), purchase/implementation of fixed assets computer software (optimizes tax depreciation), and operational efficiencies estimated to produce annual savings of $250,000 to $300,000.

1993
to
1996

ZEBAR METAL CONTAINER CORPORATION (Corporate Offices))

Manager of Corporate Accounting (1994 - 1996)

Managed staff of 14 professionals with full responsibility for the Corporate Accounting function of this $150 million manufacturer of overseas shipping containers. Reported to Chief Financial Officer with management responsibility for preparation & monitoring of budgets ($130 million), monthly and year-end financial statements, accounting system development/implementation, internal audit and payroll. Key accomplishments included: design/implementation of cost accounting system (annual savings $1.2 million), revamped department operating procedures (estimated annual savings 1,500 manhours), improved audit procedures capturing some $120,000 in unauthorized expenditures.

Senior Accountant (1993 - 1994)
Reported to Manager of Corporate Accounting with full responsibility for
consolidation, review and analysis of Company's monthly and year-end financial
statements.

1983
to
1993

BARLEY & JOHNSON, INC.

Senior Accountant (1988 - 1993)
Provided wide range of consulting and auditing services to client companies for
this public accounting firm. Major areas of concentration were cost accounting
and taxation. Clients ranged in size from $50 to $150 million.

Accountant (1983 - 1988)
Duties similar to those of Senior Accountant. Focus was on clients with annual
sales under $50 million.

1979
to
1983

JORDAN ELECTRONICS, INC. (Kirkwood Plant)

Senior Cost Accountant (1981 - 1983)
Performed wide range of cost studies for this $4.5 million manufacturer of cable
T.V. components.

Cost Accountant (1979 - 1981)

EDUCATION

M.B.A., University of Northern Ohio, 1979
Major: Accounting/Finance
            Bettinger Scholarship

B.A.,   Business Administration, Cannon College, 1977
Major: Accounting
            Magna Cum Laude

C.P.A., May 1985

DAVID P. BERRINGTON
39 Fowler Place, Apt. 4-C
Syracuse, New York 09872
Phone: (814) 972-4454

OBJECTIVE

Leadership position in general or cost accounting field with opportunity for advancement to department management based on demonstrated results.

EDUCATION

M.A.,	Business, Luster University, 1991
Major:	Accounting
	Syracuse Businessman Fellowship
B.A.,	Business Administration, Syracuse University, 1989
Major:	Accounting G.P.A. 3.4/4.0
Minor:	Finance G.P.A. 3.75/4.0
	Magna Cum Laude
	Davidson Scholarship (4 years)
Activities:	President, Student Government Association
	President, Accounting Honorary Society
	Captain, Varsity Football
	Captain, Varsity Track

PROFESSIONAL EXPERIENCE

1991
to
Present

MINUTEMAN ELECTRONICS, INC. (Syracuse Plant)

Senior Cost Accountant (1993 - Present)
Report to Cost Accounting Manager with full cost accounting responsibility for the Biostar electrical harness (annual manufacturing cost of $45 million). Provide day-to-day guidance to two Cost Accountants in the application of cost accounting standards and procedures. Responsible for researching and developing new cost standards and approaches. Major accomplishments include: development/implementation of computerized cost tracking system for early detection of negative cost trends (estimated six months savings $125,000), breakout of Rocker Assembly material costs (better material control with annual savings potential of $50,000), improved labor cost estimates for retrofits.

Cost Accountant (1991 - 1993)
Application of established cost accounting practices and procedures in the cost accounting and analysis of sophisticated electronic harnesses. Credited with $115,000 in material cost savings through unique cost tracking approach.

PETER B. JOHNSON
1835 Linwood Place
Linwood, NJ 45973
Phone: (312) 447-2424 (H)
(312) 447-8842 (O)

OBJECTIVE

Senior level engineering management position.

PROFESSIONAL EXPERIENCE

1984
to
Present

BERRINGTON MANUFACTURING COMPANY, INC. (Corporate Engineering)

Vice President of Engineering (1996 - Present)
Direct 250 employee engineering department in the engineering of new facilities for this Fortune 200 manufacturer of residential and commercial air conditioning and heating equipment. Successfully managed two-year, $850 million expansion program including the installation and start-up of two new residential air conditioning manufacturing plants (largest single capital program in company's history). Projects were completed three months ahead of schedule and 20% under budget. Directed wide range of engineering disciplines including Mechanical Engineering, Civil Engineering, Electrical Engineering, Systems Engineering and Chemical Engineering.

Director, Mechanical Engineering (1992 - 1996)
Provided direction to 160 employee engineering section with full responsibility for all mechanical project engineering associated with capital facilities projects (annual budget of $250 million). Major projects included installation of computer controlled Ram Shear, high speed commercial heating equipment line (project budget $245 million), complete rebuild of two obsolete Pennington residential heating equipment lines (budget of $185 million), and installation and start-up of $110 million commercial air conditioning manufacturing line. All projects were completed ahead of schedule and averaged 10% under project budget.

Manager, Systems Engineering (1986 - 1992)
Managed department of 20 electrical instrumentation and systems engineers in the application of instrumentation and control systems to manufacturing operations. Successfully managed numerous projects involving the first-time application of mini-computer and microprocessor systems to heating and air conditioning assembly lines. Average projects were in the $5-10 million range.

Senior Project Engineer, Heating (1984 - 1986)
Led project engineering teams in the design, installation, start-up and debugging of high speed, automated commercial heating system manufacturing assembly lines.

69

1982   **WILCOX ENGINEERING SYSTEMS, INC.** (Corporate Engineering)
to
1984   <u>Project Engineer</u>
          Design, installation and start-up of large-scale biomass boiler power generation systems.

EDUCATION

M.S.   University of Michigan, 1982
Major: Mechanical Engineering
          Wainwright Scholarship

B.S.,   University of Michigan, 1980
Major: Electrical Engineering
          Magna Cum Laude

          President, Tau Beta Psi
          Shearson Scholarship (4 years)

MARTIN S. SAMPSON
17 Beechwood Lane
Fort Wayne, Indiana 37655
Phone: (513) 556-7720

OBJECTIVE

Senior Project Engineering position in Corporate Engineering Department with major responsibility for multi-million dollar projects involving design, installation and start-up of new facilities and equipment.

PROFESSIONAL EXPERIENCE

1990
to
Present

ARROW ALUMINUM COMPANY, INC. (Corporate Engineering)

Senior Project Engineer (1992 - Present)
Report to Manager of Mechanical Engineering with responsibility for design, installation, start-up and debugging of aluminum and magnesium production facilities with emphasis on furnace complexes, flash calcining facilities and conveyor material handling systems. Successfully managed the mechanical design of $20 million furnace complex including coordination with Electrical Engineering Department (project on time and 5% under budget). Redesigned refractory lining in flash calciner resulting in 35% reduction in heat loss from existing units and 50% from new units. Responsible for design, installation and start-up of $12 million furnace complex. Project currently on time and under budget.

Project Engineer (1990 - 1992)
Reported to Senior Project Engineer with responsibility for design, installation, start-up and debugging of aluminum manufacturing furnace complexes and material handling equipment. Assisted in the design and start-up of $18 million furnace complex and associated material handling systems.

EDUCATION

B.S.,   Drexel University, 1990
Major: Mechanical Engineering
         Cum Laude Graduate

         Member Tau Beta Psi
         Vice President, American Society of Mechanical Engineers

AFFILIATIONS

American Society of Mechanical Engineers
Association of Aluminum Manufacturing Engineers

Sample Chronological Resume—Finance

STEPHEN C. TEMPLE
600 Ferrington Road, NW
Chicago, Illinois 55733
Phone: (513) 772-6464

OBJECTIVE

Senior Financial Officer

PROFESSIONAL EXPERIENCE

1986
to
Present

TEXTRON INTERNATIONAL CORPORATION (Corporate Offices)

Vice President and Treasurer (1996 - Present)
Report to Executive Vice President, Finance and Planning for this $4 billion, Fortune 100 manufacturer of earth moving and excavation equipment. Direct staff of 48 professionals with responsibility for anticipating and providing the financial resources for short and long-term funding of all domestic and international operations. Annual financing requirements average $400 to $600 million. Functions directed include: Domestic Finance, International Finance, Money & Banking, Insurance and Pension Funding. Developed five-year funding strategy to finance $3.1 billion capital expansion plan with interest rates averaging 2% below market. Maintained top financial ratings through carefully orchestrated investor relations strategy despite substantial increase in long-term debt.

Director of Corporate Finance (1992 - 1996)
Reported to Vice President and Treasurer with responsibility for anticipating, planning and execution of effective financing for the Company on best terms and conditions available. Accountable for keeping abreast of the domestic and international capital markets to assure that financial needs were effectively accommodated. Managed departments of five Analysts with annual financing requirements averaging approximately $300 million. Developed five-year financial planning computer model permitting more accurate long-range planning of international operations' financial requirements. Secured $185 million financing for Italian affiliate at exceptionally good terms. Became major consultant to international operations in their financial planning work.

Senior Analyst, Corporate Finance (1989 - 1992)
Reported to Director of Corporate Finance. Responsible for identifying, analyzing and recommending alternative financing methods and sources for a wide range of domestic clients. Assisted top management in 5 major domestic divisions to build five-year plans. Developed and implemented user friendly computer models allowing management to forecast long range financial requirements with greater accuracy. Provided key consultation in the formulation of long-term financial strategy and analyzed and recommended a wide range of funding alternatives.

<u>Analyst, Corporate Finance</u> (1986 - 1989)

Reported to Senior Analyst with responsibility to assist in the identification, analysis and recommendation of a wide range of business opportunities and financing options.

EDUCATION

M.B.A.,   Wharton School, University of Pennsylvania, 1986
Major: Finance

B.A.,   Pennsylvania State University, 1984
Major: Financial Management
Minor: Economics
        Magna Cum Laude

JANET N. MORSE
300 Mocking Bird Lane
Newtown Square, PA 19073
Phone: (610) 775-5757

OBJECTIVE

Responsible Financial Management position in corporate offices of growth-oriented manufacturing company.

PROFESSIONAL EXPERIENCE

1992
to
Present

DELTRON AEROSPACE INCORPORATED (Corporate Offices)

Senior Financial Analyst (1995 - Present)
Report to Manager of Corporate Financial Planning of this $2 billion federal contract supplier of missile guidance systems. Work with government scientists, engineers and procurement officers in developing manufacturing cost estimates for sophisticated missile guidance systems based on prototype costs. Develop program funding requirements and determine best available funding sources and options. Have developed funding estimates and recommendations for several programs in the $200 to $400 million range. Recipient of six federal commendations for outstanding service in financial planning work.

Financial Analyst (1994 - 1995)
Reported to Senior Financial Analyst and assisted in the development of funding requirements and financial strategies to support full-scale manufacture of sophisticated missile guidance systems. Researched wide range of funding options and sources recommending those with most favorable rates and terms.

Analyst (1992 - 1994)
Studied various methodologies for calculating manufacturing costs of missile guidance systems. Required conceptual scale-up from lab prototype to full-scale production model. Developed computer model which reduced time required to calculate cost estimates by 80%.

1991
to
1992

SEPTRAM INTERSCIENCE, INC. (Corporate Offices)

Planning Analyst
Reported to Manager of Corporate Planning. Developed computer models to support long-range financial planning process.

74

EDUCATION

M.B.A.,   Harvard University Business School, 1991
Major: Financial Planning

B.S.,   Cornell University, 1987
Major: Management Science
    Cum Laude
    Torrington Computer Scholarship (4 years)

DAWN M. MARKS
300 Ollinger Avenue
Richmond, Virginia 23375
Phone: (314) 872-4467

OBJECTIVE

Senior level position with corporate-wide responsibility for management of the
Human Resources function.

PROFESSIONAL EXPERIENCE

1991
to
Present

CARSON MANUFACTURING COMPANY, INC. (Corporate Offices)

Director of Human Resources (1995 - Present)
Report to Corporate Vice President, Human Resources of this $1.5 billion manufacturer
of residential and commercial furniture. Direct staff of 25 professionals in providing
full range of Human Resource services to the Corporate Staff Headquarters complex of
1,000 professional employees. Functional responsibilities include: Human Resource
Planning, Internal Staffing, External Staffing, Organization Design, Performance
Evaluation, Salary Administration and Training & Development. Major
accomplishments include: design and implementation of computerized human resource
information system estimated to save $500,000 per year in time and increased
productivity, development of computer model which ties in human resource planning
with overall business strategic and operations planning, development of a management
incentive plan credited with a dramatic increase in productivity, and direction of major
hiring effort requiring the employment of 90 engineers to support major capital
expansion effort.

Manager Corporate Staffing (1993 - 1995)
Reported to Director of Human Resources with full responsibility for all staffing, both
internal and external. Managed staff of 12 professionals and 13 support personnel,
with annual budget of $2.1 million. Typical annual volume included 250 new hires and
350 internal placements. Worked closely with top management in handling search
assignments at both the director and staff vice president levels. Confidentially
orchestrated searches involving highly sensitive organizational changes at the corporate
vice president level. Reduced average time to fill positions from six to four months.
Through implementation of improved prescreening techniques, reduced the interview-
to- offer ratio from six to one to a ratio of two to one. Offer-to-acceptance ratio was
also improved to an 80% acceptance rate. Average cost-per-hire was reduced 45%
(annual savings of $750,000).

Manager of Administrative Staffing (1991 - 1993)
Reported to Manager of Corporate Staffing with responsibility for internal and external
staffing of administrative positions. Clients included Human Resources, Accounting,
Finance, Law, Information Services, Logistics and Procurement. Developed and
implemented internal professional level posting system which now serves as the
primary source for filling most internal openings (excludes director level and above).
Developed and implemented candidate assessment process credited with substantial
improvement in quality of candidates selected.

1983
to
1991

BARSOM, CLIFFORD AND JANSEN, INC. (Corporate Offices)

Senior Consultant (1987 - 1991)
Provided services to client companies in the design and development of employee
evaluation programs for this major consulting firm in the field of Human Resources.
Successfully designed and installed three major performance evaluation systems, each
tailored to client company's unique requirements.

Consultant (1983 - 1987)
Performed research work in support of development of employee evaluation systems.

EDUCATION

M.B.A., Michigan State University, 1983
Major: Human Resource Management
Thesis: "The Role of Performance Feedback in the Motivation of Professional
           Employees"

B.A.,   Michigan State University, 1981
Major: Human Resource Management
           Cum Laude
           Salem Scholarship (4 years)

DAVID R. JEFFRIES
36 Tartan Road, SW
Birmingham, Alabama 75663
Phone: (314) 872-5533

OBJECTIVE

Overall direction of Corporate Staffing function with advancement
opportunities to senior level Human Resources position.

PROFESSIONAL EXPERIENCE

1989
to
Present

COMSTAR MANUFACTURING CO., INC.

Corporate Manager - Operations Employment (Corp. Offices) (1994 - Pres.)
Corporate-wide accountability for the employment of exempt operations and
technical personnel for this 13,000 employee corporation (annual sales $1.6
billion). Direct responsibility for recruitment and employment of all operations
and technical personnel (through vice president level) for corporate office
complex. Additionally, provide overall staff guidance and support to
decentralized employment functions of six profit centers and 14 manufacturing
plants. Developed strategy and successfully directed multi-location recruiting
effort to staff $1 billion capital expansion program. All critical positions filled
and deadlines met. Project delivered below budget.

Manager of Employment Services (Vanstar Division) (1991 - 1994)
Responsible for all levels of salaried recruiting and employment --
administrative, technical and operations -- for this 2,500 employee division
involved in the precision chemical coating of space vehicle parts. Position
required ability to apply innovative, creative techniques to identify and recruit
exceptionally hard-to-find, highly-specialized research scientists. Used
combination of patent computer data base and search techniques to successfully
locate and recruit two key scientists in the field of electronic scanning imaging.
Developed outstanding reputation for "doing the impossible".

Plant Human Resources Manager (Melville Plant) (1989 - 1991)
Responsible for providing full range of human resources services to this missile
nose cone manufacturing plant of 450 employees. Areas of responsibility
included: employment, employee relations, wage and salary administration,
training, benefits, safety, security, medical, communications and public
relations. Successfully stayed-off two attempted union drives through development and implementation of highly effective organization effectiveness program.

1985   **JOHNSON AND BARTON, INC.** (Westerly Plant)
to
1989   <u>Assistant Human Resources Manager</u>
            Reported to Plant Human Resources Manager of this 800 employee clothing
            manufacturing facility. Responsible for assisting manager in providing full
            range of human resources services.

1985   **BILTMORE ELECTRONICS, INC.** (Westerly Plant)
to
1981   <u>Human Resources Assistant</u>
            Entry level human resources position for this 300 employee manufacturer of
            electronic equipment.

EDUCATION

B.A.,   University of Alabama, 1981
Major: Business Administration

Sample Chronological Resume—Information Services

JEFFREY A. MORSE
225 Highland Road
Clifton, NJ 18337
Phone: (609) 377-9787

OBJECTIVE

Senior executive position in Information Services.

PROFESSIONAL EXPERIENCE

1986
to
Present

CORBOTT MANUFACTURING COMPANY, INC. (Corporate Offices)

Director of IS (1996 - Present)
Report to Executive Vice President of Administration for this $2 billion, Fortune 200 manufacturer of pumps, valves and fittings. Direct 110 employee department and $8 million budget in the development, maintenance and control of corporate-wide information systems. Direct the activities of the Corporate Information Services Center and manage the corporate-wide data communications network. Provide systems development support to four divisions and 16 manufacturing facilities. Developed and implemented first five-year corporate plan for information systems development and utilization. Successfully installed $7 million system providing computerization of the sales forecasting, production scheduling and materials control functions estimated to save Company $5 million annually. Project completed three months early and 20% under budget.

Corporate Project Manager (1994 - 1996)
Managed the activities of 8 to 12 project managers in the design, installation and start-up of a wide range of management information projects. Annual budget of $5 million. All projects were completed on or before deadline with 95% of projects under budget. Major projects successfully completed include: Human Resources System, Payroll System, Order Entry System, Credit Control System, Production Scheduling System, Finished Goods Inventory Control System, Raw Materials and Vital Supplies Control Systems.

Manager of Client Planning Services (1990 - 1994)
Managed department of six professionals responsible for planning the future information systems needs of functional clients. Reviewed clients' strategic and operating plans to determine management information needs necessary for meeting plan objectives. Identified computer systems applications and developed long-range information systems plans by client area. Identified major cost savings opportunities and assisted Director of IS in establishing corporate priorities. Completed long-range plans for five functional areas including: Industrial Relations, Controllers, Finance, Manufacturing and Procurement.

80

Senior Programmer Analyst (1986 - 1990)
Directed the activities of Analysts and Programmers in the development of numerous systems and programs covering a wide range of client information requirements.

1984   **MONTGOMERY CORPORATION** (Corporate Offices))
to
1986   Programmer Analyst
Developed numerous programs to meet the information requirements of several clients.

EDUCATION

Ph.D.,   Cornell University, 1984
Major: Computer Science

M.S.,   Cornell University, 1982
Major: Computer Science
         Data Resources Scholarship (2 years)

B.S.,   Lawrence University, 1980
Major: Mathematics
         Pennington Scholarship (4 years)

SANDRA D. THOMPSON
32 East March Street
Thornton, Michigan 77599
Phone: (817) 552-9494

OBJECTIVE

Position as Programmer Analyst in Data Communications R&D
for major systems engineering company.

EDUCATION

M.S., Massachusetts Institute of Technology, 1994
Major: Computer Science
Ransin Laboratory Fellowship (2 years)

B.S., Massachusetts Institute of Technology, 1992
Major: Computer Science   G.P.A. 3.85/4.0
Minor: Mathematics   G.P.A. 3.78/4.0
Mattson Foundation Scholarship (4 years)

President, Computer Science Society
Vice President, Mathematics Honorary

PROFESSIONAL EXPERIENCE

1994
to
Present

TRANSCON SYSTEMS LABORATORIES, INC. (Corporate R&D)

Programmer Analyst
Provide programming support to the development of state-of-the-art data
communications system for major systems engineering research firm.
Responsible for the SNA/ACP/NCP functions of the Communications
Controller in a PEP environment. Responsibiiities include: maintaining the
ACP/NCP system requirements, diagnosing software problems, and
participating in network tuning, troubleshooting, testing and studies.

KEVIN P. BURTRAM
32 Worrington Lane, SW
Dallas, TX 33755
Phone: (719) 377-2424

OBJECTIVE

Senior level Logistics Management position with progressive company that encourages use of state-of-the-art concepts and values bottom line results.

PROFESSIONAL EXPERIENCE

1996
to
Present

HERRINGER FOOD PROCESSING. INC. (Corporate Offices)

Director of Logistics
Report to Senior Vice President - Operations for this $1.4 billion, Fortune 500 food processing corporation. Direct the development and implementation of both strategic and operating operation plans for the Warehousing and Transportation functions on a corporate-wide basis (eight plants, 750 employees, annual budget of $125 million). Responsible for maximum use of Logistics resources (budget, people, equipment) in assuring high level of customer service satisfaction at lowest possible cost.

Directed the development and installation of computerized order entry and distribution planning system which allows advanced planning of transportation requirements and returns $18 million in freight cost savings per year. Saved $4.7 million per year in warehouse handling costs through installation of automatic palletizers and computer controlled conveyor system. Negotiated corporate-wide rail carrier rates resulting in annual savings of $3.9 million.

1987
to
1996

THE BOSTON BEVERAGE COMPANY (Corporate Offices))

Logistics Manager (1993 - 1996)
Reported to Executive Vice President - Operations for this $850 million bottler of carbonated beverages. Managed the Corporate Distribution Department (250 employees, budget $85 million) with nation-wide distribution through network of company owned and leased warehouses. Responsible for development and execution of strategic and operating plans for all warehousing and transportation operations to achieve lowest possible cost consistent with customer service requirements. Consolidated all field warehousing facilities into large regional leased warehouse operations with annual savings of $10.2 million. Designed and installed computer model for determination of best shipping point and mode of transportation with resultant savings of $5 million annually.

Senior Distribution Analyst (1990 - 1993)
Reported to Distribution Manager with responsibility for conducting a wide range of
studies to determine maximum use of overall Distribution resources to achieve
customer service and cost objectives. Areas studied include: site selection for new
distribution facilities, loading patterns for various modes and types of shipments
(carriers and equipment), warehouse layout and storage patterns, warehousing
operations analysis, etc. Introduced the use of computer models in Distribution
analysis work. In three years, designed six key computer models now used in decision
analysis on a daily basis and estimated to save approximately $3 million per year.

Distribution Analyst (1987 - 1990)
Provided support to Senior Distribution Analyst and Distribution Manager in the
analysis and study of a wide range of Distribution planning problems requiring
quantitative solutions. Extensive use of statistical methods and computer techniques.

EDUCATION

M.S.,   Georgia Institute of Technology, 1987
Major: Industrial Engineering
           Weller Scholarship (2 years)

B.S.,   Texas A&M, 1985
Major: Industrial Engineering
           Hanson Oil Company Scholarship (4 years)

PETER B. DIRKSON
18 Ocean View Road
Clearview Beach, California 77533
Phone: (714) 377-2525

OBJECTIVE

Corporate level position in Logistics Management.

PROFESSIONAL EXPERIENCE

1995
to
Present

ROVER DOG FOOD COMPANY, INC. (Corporate Offices)

Manager of Warehousing
Manage Corporate Warehousing function for this $300 million manufacturer of dog food. Scope of responsibility includes 150 employees (35 salaried, 115 hourly), Corporate Distribution Center and 12 field warehouses (eight leased, four owned) and annual budget of $32 million. Accountable for development and execution of strategic and operating plans for use of all warehousing resources (capital, equipment, facilities and people) to achieve lowest storage and shipping costs consistent with customer service objectives.

Implemented palletized railcar loading resulting in $2 million annual savings. Worked with Corporate Packaging in redesign of shipping container size allowing 10% more product to be shipped per railcar (annual savings $450,000). Successfully renegotiated warehouse leases at 5% below preceding year's cost (annual savings $320,000).

1987
to
1995

HORSHAW FASTENER MANUFACTURING CO. (Fairfield Plant)

Distribution Center Manager (1993 - 1995)
Reported to Plant Manager with responsibility for management of plant Distribution Center for this $120 million manufacturer of metal fasteners. Directed staff of 65 employees in the daily storage and shipment of finished products.

Installed extendable powered conveyers for truck loading resulting in reduced labor costs of 10% ($300,000). Redesigned warehouse storage pattern substantially reducing product handling costs (estimated annual savings $135,000). Initiated crew training in proper product handling techniques, reducing product damage by 75% (annual savings $115,000).

Shipping Manager (1987 - 1993)
Reported to Distribution Center Manager with responsibility for managing the
loading and shipment of all plant finished product. Through increased use of
"gypsy carriers", was able to reduce annual shipping costs by 20% for truck
shipments (savings $2.1 million)

1984
to
1987

DEITRICK TRUCKING COMPANY (Fairfield Terminal)

Dispatcher
Accepted and placed orders for truck shipments with responsibility for allocation
and dispatch of all trucking equipment.

EDUCATION

B.A.,   Anderson College, 1984
Major: Business Administration

SCOTT M. BEATTY
900 Lordon Avenue, SW
Atlanta, Georgia 57994
Phone: (912) 774-3434

OBJECTIVE

Executive level position in Marketing and Sales Management.

PROFESSIONAL EXPERIENCE

1994
to
Present

CORRDIGAN CHEMICALS, INC. (Corporate Offices)

Director of Marketing
Direct marketing and sales organization of 185 employees with annual budget of
$225 million for this leading manufacturer of specialty products (annual sales
$725 million). Functions managed include Market Research, Market Planning,
New Market Development, Advertising & Promotion and Field Sales. Principle
products include specialty solvents and resins. Established company as the
leading marketer of solvents in the European Market through the establishment
of a sophisticated marketing and dealer network which increased company's
export business by 75% ($225 million) in two years. Worked with R&D in the
development and test market of new low-viscosity resin product for use in the
manufacture of polyurethane foams. National roll-out of this product has
accounted for $150 million in new sales in first year.

1986
to
1994

STANTON CHEMICAL SPECIALTIES, INC. (Corporate Offices)

Director of Marketing and Sales (1990 - 1994)
Reported to President with full accountability for all domestic and international
marketing and sales for this specialty chemical manufacturing company (annual
sales $525 million). Responsibilities included Market Research and Planning,
Brand Management, Advertising and Sales. Managed sales force of 125
employees with annual budget of $130 million. In less than four years,
successfully introduced eight major new products accounting for an increase in
total sales of 40% ($210 million). During this same period, expanded sales
force hiring and training 60 new sales representatives.

Marketing Brand Manager (1988 - 1990)
Reported to Director of Marketing and Sales with responsibility for management
of company's *Darcell* brand. Worked closely with Market Research and
Advertising to give this brand a new image and repositioned it in the
marketplace as a low-priced, high quality product. In less than two years,
Darcell rose from number five to number one in the marketplace and
experienced a 225% increase in sales volume.

<u>Associate Brand Manager</u> (1986 - 1988)
Reported to Marketing Brand Manager with responsibility for coordination of all market research and test markets for the company's *Tetron* brand. Designed and implemented test market studies that proved that customers could not distinguish the difference between *Tetron* (second lowest priced product on the market) and two of our competitor's high-priced brands. Recommended price rise increasing revenues by 20% with no loss in volume.

1981 to 1986	**CRISWELL CHEMICALS CORPORATION** (District Sales Office) <u>Senior Sales Representative</u> (1985 - 1986) Responsible for sale of chemical specialties to the pharmaceutical industry in the states of New York, New Jersey, Pennsylvania and Delaware. Increased territory sales volume by 15% in one year. <u>Sales Representative</u> (1981 - 1985) Sold chemical specialties to the pharmaceutical industry.

EDUCATION

M.B.A.,   University of Chicago, 1981
Major: Marketing

B.S.,   Syracuse University, 1979
Major: Chemistry
           President of Chemical Society

ALLAN D. MARKS
100 Cedar Road
Clinton, Michigan 77229
Phone: (713) 559-0085

OBJECTIVE

Responsible Sales Management position with growth-oriented company in
the equipment field.

PROFESSIONAL EXPERIENCE

1990
to
Present

MICRO GRAPHICS, INC. (Detroit Regional Office)

District Sales Manager (1995 - Present)
Manage five employee sales force in the application sales of sophisticated
computer microfilm record recording, storage and retrieval system in the states of
Michigan, Ohio and Indiana. Successfully launched and marketed world's first
updatable computer microfilm record keeping system to municipalities, colleges,
universities, libraries, banks and insurance companies accounting for $30 million
sales in first year. Creative sales strategy and strategic selling skills have
accounted for over 300% sales increase in last two years, with annual sales now
approaching $100 million.

Senior Sales Representative (1992 - 1995)
Worked closely with venture team in the test marketing of computer updatable
microfilm record keeping system. Primary focus was on banking industry
applications. Was successful in selling, installing and starting up first banking
application for new system. Sale proved the viability of this application and
paved the way to $330 million in third year sales.

Sales Representative (1990 - 1992)
Successfully sold wide range of microfilms and other specialty films through
network of film dealerships. Selected and trained new dealers. Increased sales in
the Greater Detroit market form $1.8 million to $5.2 million in two years.

EDUCATION

B.A.,   University of Michigan, 1990
Major: Marketing

President, Student Government
President, Delta Upsilon Fraternity
Captain, Varsity Track Team

CHRISTOPHER T. BEATTIE
106 Summit Avenue
Reading, Pennsylvania 19330
Phone: (215) 775-0978

OBJECTIVE

Senior level Operations management position to include functional responsibility for Manufacturing, Engineering, Procurement and Distribution in medium-size manufacturing organization.

PROFESSIONAL EXPERIENCE

1989
to
Present

STERLING TUBE CORPORATION

Vice President Operations (Corporate Offices) (1994 - Present)
Report to President with full P&L responsibility for two copper refineries and tube manufacturing plants for this leading producer of copper tubing (annual sales $500 million). Direct the activities of two Plant Managers, 300 salaried and 5,000 hourly employees with annual budget of $300 million. Organized and directed multi-discipline cost reduction task force which identified and implemented cost reduction opportunities resulting in 20% decrease in overall manufacturing costs in last three years (current estimated annual savings of $110 million). Directed investigation and implementation of sophisticated computerized materials management scheduling and control systems which cut raw materials inventories by 30% (annual savings $15 million).

Plant Manager (Norfolk Plant (1989 - 1994)
Reported to Vice President of Manufacturing with P&L responsibility for this 2,800 employee copper refinery and tube manufacturing plan ($375 million annual production). Functions reporting included Manufacturing, Materials Management, Distribution, Maintenance & Engineering, Accounting and Human Resources. Successfully directed two-year, $125 million plant expansion program designed to double plant's annual production capacity. (All engineering done at plant level.) Project completed three months ahead of schedule and 10% below budget. In preparation for plant start-up, transferred 75% of hourly workers to new jobs in two months with no loss in plant productivity. Set plant production and safety records for four out of five years.

1979   **BRADFORD COPPER COMPANY, INC.**
to
1989   Manager of Engineering (Corporate Offices) (1984 - 1989)
          Managed 150 employee central engineering function for this manufacturer of
          refrigeration tubing (annual sales $300 million). Directed engineering
          organization in all capital project expansion programs to include design,
          installation, start-up and debugging of copper tube manufacturing facilities and
          refineries. Successfully engineered major $250 million capital program (largest
          in company's history) including installation and start-up of state-of-the-art,
          computer controlled, integrated refinery and tube mill. Project delivered four
          months ahead of schedule and on budget.

          Department Manager, Drawing Operations (Bradford Plant) (1982 - 1984)
          Managed 100 employee tube drawing operation with annual production valued at
          $85 million. Increased production by 18% with simultaneous 15% reduction in
          manufacturing costs in two-year period.

          Project Engineer (1979 - 1982)
          Responsible for design, installation and start-up of major capital projects in
          furnace and drawing operations. Independently handled projects in the $40-50
          million range.

EDUCATION

          M.S.,   Pennsylvania State University, 1979
          Major: Mechanical Engineering

          B.S.,   Pennsylvania State University, 1977
          Major: Mechanical Engineering
                   Tau Beta Psi

MARGARET R. TEMPLE
200 Remmington Drive
Springfield, Ohio 75332
Phone: (315) 772-6767

OBJECTIVE

Manufacturing management position with medium-size company offering opportunity for advancement based upon demonstrated performance.

PROFESSIONAL EXPERIENCE

1993
to
Present

REED MANUFACTURING COMPANY (Linwood Plant)

Assistant Plant Manager (1996 - Present)
Report to Plant Manager of this 1,000 employee manufacturer of silicone-based waxes and polishes ($325 million annual sales). Manage the Can Finishing and Warehousing Departments with full management responsibility for 210 employees (40 salaried, 170 hourly) and an operating budget of $130 million. Introduced automatic palletizers and palletized railcar loading, cutting warehouse operating costs by 25% (annual savings $15 million). Initiated absenteeism control program reducing absenteeism from 11% to less than 4% in one year. Reduced union grievances from 185 to 62 in two years through effective employee relations practices.

Department Manager, Formulations (1993 - 1996)
Reported to Manufacturing Manager with accountability for the formulations and mixing operations. Managed 50 employee (five salaried, 45 hourly) department with annual budget of $75 million. Organized and led hourly employee cost reduction task force implementing several programs resulting in total annual savings of 10% ($7.5 million) in one year. Increased department production by 18% in two years through employee job rotation and enrichment program. Awarded annual safety award for best departmental safety record in both 1993 and 1994.

1991
to
1993

CLOVER WAX COMPANY (Radley Plant)

Supervisor, Formulations
Supervised 15 employee wax formulations department for this leading manufacturer of shoe polish and furniture wax (annual sales $150 million).

EDUCATION

B.S.,   Bradley College, 1991
Major: Industrial Technology   G.P.A. 3.5/4.0
          Cum Laude

BRUCE B. PARSONS
32 Roam Avenue
Utica, NY 79443
Phone: (319) 447-2242

OBJECTIVE

Executive level position with major company offering opportunity for corporate-wide management of Procurement function.

PROFESSIONAL EXPERIENCE

1996
to
Present

CARSON MANUFACTURING COMPANY, INC. (Corporate Offices)

Director of Procurement
Direct staff of 15 professionals in the corporate-wide management of the procurement function for this $1.2 billion manufacturer of consumer food products. Direct the purchase of all raw materials, equipment, vital supplies and services for corporate offices and eight manufacturing plants with annual budget of $580 million. Develop, implement and control all procurement strategies and policies including centralized procurement programs on all consolidated purchases.

Implemented computerized raw materials inventory tracking and forecasting system allowing substantially reduced inventory levels (annual savings $26 million). Consolidated purchase of packaging supplies with resultant savings of $22 million. Reduced fuel costs by 20% through conversion to bio-mass boilers and long-term contracts with bio-mass fuel suppliers ($18 million annual savings).

1988
to
1996

WILSON BAKING CORPORATION (Corporate Offices)

Manager of Corporate Procurement (1990 - 1996)
Directed the procurement function on a corporate-wide basis for this $850 million manufacturer of cookies, crackers and breads. Managed a staff of eight, with annual budget of $325 million and full centralized purchasing responsibility for five plants. Centralized procurement function with net headcount reduction of ten and annual savings of $300,000. Centralized purchasing and consolidated purchases of hundreds of items with first year's savings of $16.5 million.

Senior Buyer - Vital Supplies (1988 - 1990)
Managed department of two professionals and two non-exempts with responsibility for procurement of all packaging and vital supplies ($200 million budget). Developed computerized vital supplies and packing forecasting system based upon sales forecasts which permitted more efficient control of purchases and inventories (annual savings $3.2 million). Negotiated two-year contract on purchase of shipping cartons resulting in annual savings of $1.3 million. Consolidated flour and sugar purchases with estimated savings of $850,000.

1982
to
1988

JOHNSON FOODS, INC. (Corporate Offices)

Manager of Procurement (1985 - 1988)
Managed department of three (annual budget of $50 million) for this $150 million snack foods manufacturer. Credited with $3 million in annual savings through better inventory control and procurement practices.

Buyer (1982 - 1985)
Reported to Manager of Procurement with responsibility for purchase of all packaging materials and supplies.

EDUCATION

B.A.,   Syracuse University, 1982
Major: Business Administration

President of Business Club
Captain, Varsity Baseball

JAMES R. WINDTHROPE
18 Bay View Place, Apt. 4-D
Briney Beach, California 32775
Phone: (415) 773-4424

OBJECTIVE

Management position in Procurement with progressive company offering opportunity for advancement based upon achievement and bottom-line contribution.

PROFESSIONAL EXPERIENCE

1995
to
Present

HILTON PAPER COMPANY, INC. (Corporate Offices)

Senior Purchasing Agent - Vital Supplies
Report to Manager of Procurement for this $350 million manufacturer of printing and converting grades of paper. Responsible for purchase of all vital supplies including: knock-down containers, poly wrap, shrink packages, etc. Annual purchase volume $18 million. Accountabilities include procurement, delivery, storage and distribution to manufacturing departments as needed. Negotiated two-year contract for knock-down containers 20% under normal purchase cost (annual savings $1.3 million). Developed and successfully installed computer system for forecasting changes in demand for vital supplies based upon changes in the sales forecast. Resultant inventory adjustments have saved estimated $575,000 annually.

1992
to
1995

BRANDON PAPER COMPANY (Corporate Offices)

Vital Supplies Buyer
Reported to Manager of Procurement for this $110 million converter of consumer paper products. Responsible for $4 million budget in the purchase of vital supplies in support of manufacturing operations. Managed the purchase, delivery, storage and in-plant distribution of all supplies purchased. Supplies included: knock-down cartons, poly wraps and shrink wraps. Negotiated new poly wrap contract with 10% reduction in cost (annual savings $200,000). Through use of computer forecasting, reduced vital supplies inventories by 20% with net savings of $125,000 per year.

EDUCATION

B.A.,   University of Southern California, 1992
Major: Business Administration G.P.A. 3.8/4.0
            Cum Laude
            Janzen Scholarship (4 years)

            President, Delta Upsilon Fraternity
            President, Student Government Association

CAROLYN B. TABOR
25 Reedsville Road
Sampson, Oregon 77033
Phone: (409) 357-2999 (O)
(409) 357-5673 (H)

OBJECTIVE

Senior level R&D management position with responsibility for achievement of company's technology objectives.

SUMMARY

Over 20 years dynamic, innovative management and leadership in Fortune 500 companies. Demonstrated capability to achieve business goals through innovative technology. Broad range of technical expertise coupled with highly effective communications and interpersonal skills.

PROFESSIONAL EXPERIENCE

1994
to
Present

OREGON PAPER COMPANY (Corporate Research Center)

Vice President of Technology
Manage 500 employee Corporate Technology Center for this Fortune 100 paper and packaging manufacturer ($4.2 billion sales). Annual Technology budget of $32 million. Major accomplishments include development and successful reduction-to-practice of new, innovative magnetic fiber forming device imparting unique characteristics (softness and absorbency) to consumer tissue-based product. Process permits 30% reduction in fibers (estimated savings of $300 million annually) with enhanced product quality. Successfully developed and introduced five new products accounting for a 15% increase in total sales. Two additional major consumer products now ready for test market.

1986
to
1994

STRATTON FIBER CORP. (Packaging & Materials Laboratory)

Research Director, Packaging & Materials
Managed 135 professionals and technicians in the research and development of all packaging, non-wovens, plastic materials and photographic film (annual budget $12 million). Developed new technology allowing synthetic fibers to be run on a wet lay technology paper machine. Resultant web has unique strength and appears to have wide application to commercial products. Estimated five-year potential is $125 million in new sales. Developed new frozen food packaging material that prolongs thawing time by 300% at room temperature. Food processors to experience estimated 30% reduction in spoilage, providing Stratton with substantial competitive advantage.

96

1977
to
1986

BARTON INTERNATIONAL FIBER, INC. (Corporate Research)

Research Manager, Synthetic Fibers (1981 - 1986)
Managed Research Department of 38 professionals in the development and application of novel synthetic fibers to packaging and consumer paper webs.

Senior Research Scientist, Polymer Research (1977 - 1981)
Pioneered and accelerated the development of proprietary polymeric materials through experimental and theoretical studies including computer modeling.

1975
to
1977

VELSTAR ELECTRONICS & SPACE LABORATORY

Research Specialist
Pioneered development of proprietary materials for Velstar communications satellite heat shield. Conducted re-entry simulation tests and qualified materials for use in treating the surface of the heat shield for first satellite launch.

EDUCATION

Ph.D., University of Michigan, 1975
Major: Chemical Engineering
Pennington Fellowship

M.S., Rochester Institute of Technology, 1973
Major: Materials Engineering

B.S., Rochester Institute of Technology, 1971
Major: Chemical Engineering
Cum Laude
Barlow Scholarship (4 years)

President, Chemical Engineering Society

PUBLICATIONS

46 professional publications and papers (1973 - 1994)

AFFILIATIONS

American Society of Chemical Engineers
American Chemical Society
American Physical Society
Technical Association of Pulp & Paper Industry

J. WALTER LOFTEN, Jr.
315 Post Road, South
Benton Harbor, Michigan 45776
Phone: (917) 472-3927

OBJECTIVE

Research and Development position requiring creativity and innovation in the development of novel polymer-based products and processes.

PROFESSIONAL EXPERIENCE

1994
to
Present

NORWOOD CHEMICAL SPECIALTIES, INC. (Corporate Technology)

Senior Research Engineer, Polymers (1996 - Present)
Provided technical leadership to research team in the development of new polymer-based material for use in the manufacture of boat hulls. Developed Sampson TM, a revolutionary new polymeric material having twice the strength of conventional fiberglass at half the cost and representing an annual projected market value of $300 million. Three patents awarded.

Research Engineer, Polymers (1994 - 1996)
Developed new synthetic fabric including all process steps from innovative polymerization process through fabric finishing. Transferred process from laboratory bench scale to pilot plant scale two months ahead of schedule and 30% under research budget. Awarded four patents and presented Norwood's "Inventor of the Year" award.

1991
to
1994

HAWTHORNE CHEMICAL COMPANY (Central Research)

Polymer Chemist
Developed high temperature resistant molding polymers and inherent fire retardant plastics. Awarded two patents for creative product development work associated with phenolic molding compounds.

EDUCATION

Ph.D.,   Massachusetts Institute of Technology, 1991
Major: Polymer Engineering
Thesis: "Copolymerization of Diamond Polymers"
         Hawthorne Fellowship

M.S.,   Rochester Institute of Technology, 1989
Major: Chemical Engineering
         Ludwig Scholarship

B.S.,   Rochester Institute of Technology, 1987
Major: Chemical Engineering
           Magna Cum Laude
           Stanton Scholarship (3 years)

           President, Polymeric Society

PATENTS

Awarded 10 U.S. patents since 1991.

AFFILIATIONS

American Society of Polymer Scientists
American Society of Chemical Engineers
National Institute for Polymer Research

7

THE LINEAR RESUME

Throughout the later part of the 1980s, and well into the 1990s, there has been considerable focus on corporate downsizing, with many U.S. employers continuing to strip away at employee headcount in an effort to become more cost-effective and competitive both domestically and internationally. This trend is expected to continue well into the 1990s and perhaps beyond as employers increasingly feel the pressure to further cut operating costs in the face of ever stiffening competition from the Pacific Rim countries and other invigorated Third World Markets.

Along with these mass employee headcount reduction programs has come the emergence of the popular linear resume format, which continues to grow rapidly in both use and popularity. This resume format has been developed and greatly promoted by many of the nation's leading outplacement consulting firms.

The linear resume format, propelled by the big push from these professional outplacement consultants, has today, by far, become the most widely used and accepted resume style. This chapter, therefore, is committed to a full discussion of the linear resume; it provides complete step-by-step instructions for preparation of this highly popular and effective resume format.

TECHNICALLY A CHRONOLOGICAL FORMAT

A close study of the sample resumes at the end of this chapter, will reveal that the linear resume is technically a variation of the "classical" chronological resume format described in Chapter 5. What classifies it as a chronological resume is the treatment of the Experience section of the resume. You will note, as with the "classical" chronological resume samples provided in the previous chapter, the linear resume presents employers and positions held in reverse chronological order. The current (or most recent) employer and job are listed first, with each subsequent employer and job listed in reverse chronological order, ending with the candidate's first professional position held.

Although technically a chronological resume, the linear resume format has some distinct characteristics that set it apart from the "classical" chronological approach. In particular, the main feature that distinguishes it from its "classical" relative, and accounts for the name "linear," is the manner in which the Experience section of the resume is written. Comparison of the linear resume samples at the end of this chapter with the "classical" chronological resumes presented in the two previous chapters will show that the "classical" chronological resume uses a "literary" style when describing work experience. In contrast, the linear resume uses a "linear" approach when presenting much or all of this data. That is, each specific job responsibility and/or accomplishment is presented on a line-by-line (linear) basis, thus setting this data apart from the balance of the text and serving to highlight it for ease of reading.

An informal survey of several hundred linear resumes received by my company, Brandywine Consulting Group, establishes that there are some additional differences between the "classical" and linear chronological resume formats. Specifically, the linear resume:

1. Lacks a "job objective" section
2. Includes a "qualifications summary" section

Otherwise, the two chronological formats are substantially the same.

ADVANTAGES OF THE LINEAR FORMAT

The advantages of using the linear chronological resume format over the functional resume (see Chapter 9) are several. As with the "classical" chronological resume, the key advantages of the linear chronological format are:

1. Since it is the most commonly used format, the chronological resume (including the "classical" and "linear" variations) is the format with which employers are most familiar and feel most comfortable.
2. It provides for a logical, easy-to-read flow, with point-to-point continuity from one employment position and employer to the next.
3. This same logical flow makes the linear chronological format one of the easiest resume styles to prepare.
4. This format allows the job hunter to emphasize career growth and progression (where the candidate has experienced such)—two factors viewed favorably by most employers.
5. The linear chronological format, likewise, serves to highlight continuity of employment (employer and job stability) and career continuity (growth)—both felt to be desirable factors by the majority of employers.
6. By contrast with the functional resume, this approach serves to highlight names of past employers—an advantage when these are well-known, prestigious companies.

Further, when compared to the "classical" or traditional chronological resume format discussed in the two previous chapters, the "linear" chronological resume has the following advantages:

1. The line-by-line itemization of job responsibilities and/or accomplishments greatly facilitates ease of reading (when compared to the literary approach used in the "classical" format), thus increasing the probability the resume will be read.

2. Most resume writers find it easier to delineate job responsibilities and accomplishments on a line-by-line basis as opposed to a literary format, making the linear resume easier to write.

3. The clear, separate delineation of accomplishments serves to highlight these achievements in the mind of the reader/employer.

4. Elimination of the "objective" section of the resume saves valuable space, thus providing increased room to cite more important information such as job accomplishments.

DISADVANTAGES OF THE LINEAR FORMAT

Since it is a variation of the chronological format, the linear resume is not the "resume of choice" in all cases. As with the "classical" chronological resume, the linear chronological resume can sometimes have certain disadvantages when contrasted with the functional resume format (see Chapters 9 and 10). Such drawbacks can include the following:

1. This format can serve to highlight obvious employment handicaps (where these exist), including:
   a. Job hopping
   b. Employment gaps
   c. Underemployment
   d. Lack of career progress

  e. Little or no job-related experience

  f. Age

2. It focuses attention on career progression rather than specific functional skills or personal strengths.

3. It tends to highlight most recent experience when certain earlier experiences may, in fact, be more relevant to the current job objective.

4. It may serve to shortchange certain key accomplishments when these achievements occurred earlier in one's career.

Where these shortcomings are evident and could negatively affect the presentation of your qualifications, you should likely be using the functional resume format described in Chapter 9. Use of the linear chronological format, in such cases, would no be to your advantage.

In addition, when compared to the "classical" chronological format described in Chapter 5, the linear chronological format can have the following disadvantages:

1. Inclusion of the "qualifications summary" at the beginning of the resume takes up valuable space and can be viewed by some readers/employers as unnecessarily redundant because most of this information is already self-evident from the rest of the resume text.

2. Lack of an "objective" statement at the beginning of the resume may leave the reader/employer uncertain about the level and type of position acceptable to you. (This may prove a problem if you are willing to consider a lateral or even a downward career move.)

3. The line-by-line itemization of job responsibilities and/or accomplishments, although more easily read, takes up more room than the literary approach employed in the "classical" format. Thus, use of the linear approach will increase resume length.

In my judgment, exclusion of an "objective statement" by the linear resume is not a serious flaw. Also, the additional space consumed by the line-by-line approach of the linear resume is not particularly objectionable, since the additional resume length is usually more than offset by the substantially improved ease of reading achieved by the linear format.

If space is truly a critical consideration, in my opinion, the resume author could consider the elimination of the "qualifications summary" of the resume since, as previously mentioned, this information is frequently self-evident and redundant to the information presented in the body of the resume. To reiterate, however, it should not be necessary in most cases to eliminate the summary section since, due to the easy readability of the linear resume format, lengthening the resume would not be found to be particularly objectionable to most readers/employers.

Two Variations of the Linear Format

Review of the numerous linear resumes received by our company reveals that there are two basic variations of the linear resume. These are:

1. The narrative linear format
2. The straight linear format

Use of these format variations is unevenly divided between the two, with the narrative linear approach now clearly representing the lion's share of usage.

Sample Resume D, presented at the end of this chapter (pages 116–117), is an example of the straight linear approach; Sample Resume E (pages 118–119) exemplifies the narrative linear format. Comparison of the two will distinguish the basic differences.

You will note that in the "experience" section of the resume, the narrative linear format (see Sample Resume E) makes use of literary or narrative approach when describing the job (that is, company description, reporting relationship, job scope, and key functional accountabilities). Key accomplishments, on the other hand, are presented on a line-by-line, linear basis.

In contrast, the straight linear format (see Sample Resume D) uses *only* the linear approach to describe both the job and related key achievements. You will also note that with the straight linear approach there is no physical separation between job description factors and key achievements. The line items presented by the resume author simply flow from job description straight to achievements, with no physical demarcation between these two categories. In fact, descriptions of key job accountabilities are written much the same as if they were achievements.

Although both approaches (narrative and straight linear) to the linear resume are certainly acceptable, I personally feel that the narrative linear approach has the distinct advantage of ease of reading. The physical separation between job description and accomplishments makes this distinction evident, and the reader does not have to wrestle with where the job and company descriptions end and key accomplishments begin. It also serves to highlight key accomplishments, which could prove advantageous during the interview process.

Additionally, the narrative format will allow you to accommodate more information in the same amount of space. For example, note how, although the sample resumes at the end of the chapter are resumes of the same person, the second resume (narrative format) permits the inclusion of the "professional affiliation" section at the end of the resume. In contrast, the first resume (straight linear format) does not allow sufficient space to accommodate this information. There is thus some loss of resume space when electing to use the straight linear format.

Although I have a slight preference for the narrative linear approach, it is important to emphasize that both the narrative and straight linear approaches are quite acceptable for writing a linear resume. Either can be used to present your credentials to a prospective employer in an effective manner. Basically, the choice is yours.

RESUME COMPONENTS

Review of the sample resumes contained at the end of this chapter and in Chapter 8 will reveal that the linear resume format is divided into the following key components:

1. Heading
2. Summary
3. Experience
4. Education
5. Military (optional)
6. Other (optional)

My study of several hundred linear resumes has shown that the "other" section of the resume is highly variable as used by different resume authors. Alternate titles for this section of the resume may include the following:

1. Professional Affiliations
2. Patents and Publications
3. Community Leadership
4. Activities

We will now start the step-by-step process of constructing a linear resume. We will examine each resume component in detail and provide practical examples so that you can tailor your own resume component accordingly. Should you follow this process, by the time we have completed this chapter, you will have prepared a highly professional looking linear resume that should serve your needs rather well.

Heading

As described in Chapter 5, the resume heading consists of three items. These are your full name, complete address, and home telephone number. Under certain circumstances, your office telephone number can also be provided. Some sample resume headings follow:

SAMUEL B. SWANSON
518 Barrowcroft Road
Clear Lake, WI 19847
Phone: (812) 473-9871

KAREN W. WHAITLLEY
814 Yellow Duck Lane
Meadowview Farms
Portland, OR 27895
Phone: Home (716) 386-9837
Office (716) 875-2835

Your name should be typed in capital letters, with the remainder of the heading presented in lower case. Bold type should be used to highlight your name.

As discussed in detail in Chapter 5, inclusion of your office telephone number on your resume might create sensitive situations. Listing the office number can suggest that you are "at odds" with your current employer and that you are being encouraged to leave. Although this may well be untrue, use of the office phone number could nonetheless trigger unnecessary suspicion concerning your employment status on the part of prospective employers.

Summary

The intent of the Summary section of the resume is to provide the reader/employer with just enough information about your credentials to compel reading of the rest of the resume document. Generally, this is accomplished by providing a brief statement that describes the depth and breadth of your experience in your field of expertise, followed by a statement that highlights certain key strengths in relevant areas likely to interest prospective employers.

Review of the sample resumes contained at the end of this chapter and in Chapter 8 show that these "summary" sections have some similarities. You will notice that the first sentence of most summary statements cites the candidate's career or professional field and states the years of experience. The second sentence is normally used to market key job-related strengths. Finally, the third sentence (which is optional) is normally used to either further describe the breadth of the candidate's experience or, alternately, to further market some unique skill or fact that would likely be perceived as valuable to a prospective employer.

If age is a potential barrier to employment, you may want to think twice about stating the precise number of years of experience in the summary section. For example, stating that you have 40 years' experience in the electronics industry may be a dead giveaway that you are no longer a spring chicken. In such cases, you may want to be a little less specific. For example, as an alternative, you could state that you have "over 20 years" experience. In this way, the employer can't tell whether you are age 40 or age 60. Should you be concerned about how to handle age in the resume, let me suggest that you review Chapter 11, Problem Resumes, which discusses this subject in detail.

The "summary" section of the resume should be concise and to the point. It should not be a lengthy, rambling epistle. Component statements need not be written in complete sentences. Instead, they may be written as simple, descriptive phrases that are intended to be crisp, hard-hitting, and concise—much the same as the copy used in advertising. One trick to achieve this is to begin each statement with an adjective followed by a noun (or adverb followed by a verb). This will force you to be brief and to the point.

The following are a few sample summary statements for use in modeling your own resume summary section.

1. *Summary.* Seasoned executive with over 20 years solid career progression in Information Services field. Excellent reputation for directing development of effective systems in response to key management information needs. Known for strong interpersonal and motivational management skills.

2. *Summary.* Highly motivated Senior Financial Analyst with outstanding educational credentials and five years' experience with top 10 consulting firm. Demonstrated ability to effectively manage key financial projects, from cost estimate to final funding, for programs in the $500 to $800 million range.

3. *Summary.* Senior manufacturing executive with 15 years' responsible line and staff experience in electronics manufacturing. Excellent record of fast track career growth earned through solid contributions to

bottom-line results. Outstanding reputation as organizer and leader who consistently achieves committed objectives.

Experience

For the experienced person, the Experience or Work History
section is undoubtedly the single most important component of the employment resume. It is this section on which
the employer generally focuses to determine whether or not
you have the specific experience, knowledge, and skills to
effectively perform the duties of the position for which you
are being considered. It is very important, therefore, that
you invest the needed time and effort to do an unusually
good job of describing these critical factors in your background summary.

The prework that you have done in Chapter 3, Preparing
to Write, should serve you very well at this point in providing the data needed to construct this important section of
your resume. You are encouraged to retrieve this prework
and keep it handy for easy reference during development of
this section of the linear resume format.

Essentially, information in the Experience section of
your resume falls into three parts, as represented by the
following outline:

I. Employer Descriptors
   A. Dates of employment
   B. Name of employer
   C. Location employed
   D. Company size, products, or services
II. Position Descriptors
   A. Position title
   B. Dates position held (from . . . to)
   C. Reporting relationship (title of boss)
   D. Position size/scope (quantitative description of po-
      sition—people and budgets managed, dollars im-
      pacted, and so on)

    E. Functional responsibilities (functions performed/
       managed, titles of those managed)

III. Key Accomplishments (quantitative descriptions)

    A. Results achieved

    B. Dollars saved

    C. Efficiencies gained

    D. And so on

As discussed earlier in this chapter, the linear resume follows a chronological resume format. It is for this reason, as you will note in reviewing the sample linear resumes provided, that the entire "experience section" of the resume is arranged in reverse chronological order. Thus, the "experience section" begins with your most recent (or current) employer (and position held) and then continues through previous employers (and positions held), in reverse chronology, ending with your very first employer (and position held) at the beginning of your career.

Study of the sample linear resumes provided will reveal that dates of employment are displayed on the extreme right side of the resume page. This is a deviation from older resume styles, where employment dates were positioned at the left hand margin. By positioning these dates at the right, this modern resume format saves considerable space by allowing you to move the full resume text to the left margin. Company name is presented in capital letters and is set in bold type. Location is presented in lower case letters and parentheses, and is positioned to the right of company name. Location is also set in normal rather than bold type.

Title of position held is presented on the next line. With the exception of initial capitals, this information is presented in lower case letters, and the full title is underlined. You will note the spacing between the line containing the company name and line displaying position title. This is not only aesthetically pleasing but provides for good visual separation of the material presented, greatly enhancing resume readability. Information is presented in readable "chunks" which are of a size that can be readily assimilated with a single glance.

If more than one position has been held with a single employer, each position is separated from the previous position description and key accomplishments by a line of spacing. With the exception of initial letters, position titles are always set in lower case type, and the title is fully underlined.

In the case of multiple positions with the same employer, you will also note that the dates of employment for each position are displayed in parentheses to the immediate right of position title. Placing these "position" dates just to the right of the job title, rather than at the far right margin, prevents any possible confusion with "employer" dates, which are presented at the right margin of the resume. This clear separation eliminates any possible confusion about employment stability, since there has been a clear separation between general employment dates and the dates during which the resume author held specific positions with that same employer.

In the case of the "narrative" linear format, the next line following the job title contains a brief narrative description of both the employer and position. Examination of this section will reveal that this description begins with a statement of the position's reporting relationship, followed by a description of the position's principal accountability and the employer's business (including size and products produced or professional services provided). Sometimes an additional statement is included that further outlines the position's major functional responsibilities. This is optional, but such a statement can sometimes be helpful in more fully conveying the nature and scope of the position and its accountabilities.

By contrast, as Sample Resume D illustrates, the "straight" linear format does not provide this position and employer description in a literary or narrative form. Instead, this information is presented in a line-by-line (linear) format. Typically, however, the first line of this format, as with narrative format, describes the reporting relationship and provides a brief description of the employer's business (including size, products, and/or services). The subsequent line is then normally used to describe the job's principal functional accountability along with some quantitative description of the position's principal dollar impact (that is, sales volume, operating budget, and so forth). Sometimes a third statement follows, offering a broader description of the position's functional responsibilities. This may, for example, detail positions reporting, subfunctions managed, and so on.

In the case of both the "narrative" and "straight" linear resume formats, the next section of the resume (following both the employer and position descriptions), details key accomplishments. Usually three or four major accomplishments (where appropriate) are cited for each position held. The resultant resume length will prohibit individuals with many years of experience from listing key accomplishments for all positions they have held. For such people, it is not necessary to list accomplishments in positions held earlier in their career, and a simple statement of key job accountabilities or job title alone will suffice. (Note how this has been handled on the second pages of the sample resumes at the end of this chapter.)

In reviewing these sample resumes, you will also note that each accomplishment statement is highlighted by a bullet and offset by double spacing. This makes the accomplishment stand out; it thus has a greater impact on the reader/employer and greatly enhances the resumes's readability. This is the major advantage of the linear approach to resume writing that sets it apart from other forms of the employment resume which use only the straight narrative or literary approach.

As discussed in Chapter 5, perhaps the greatest secret to brevity and conciseness in resume writing is the technique of starting each statement with an action word or verb. Review of the sample linear resumes at the end of this chapter and in Chapter 8 will show that accomplishment statements have followed this important rule. Thus, each statement is crisp, to-the-point, and conveys a sense of "results orientation" to the resume. The practice of using quantitative descriptions of results achieved is also a powerful technique that will increase the document's impact.

When selecting specific accomplishments for highlighting on your linear resume, care should be taken to list meaningful results achieved. The use of trivial results or citing only job responsibilities (as opposed to accomplishments) can backfire on you should you elect to use the linear resume format. Such choice can serve to highlight mediocrity, and will likely not serve your purpose well at all! Some careful thought about past performance can usually serve to surface at least one or two meaningful accomplishments worth highlighting. If not, however, I strongly suggest that you choose an alternate resume approach rather than employing the linear resume format.

Education

The Education section of the resume has already been described thoroughly in Chapter 5. I suggest that you review the appropriate pages of this chapter prior to constructing the Education section of the linear resume.

Military (Optional)

Review of several hundred linear resumes received by our company suggests that inclusion of a Military section (where appropriate) in the resume is entirely optional. In only a very small percentage of the cases was it shown at all. Should you elect to include it, however, the following format can be followed.

<u>MILITARY</u>

United States Army, 1990–1994
2nd Battalion, Armoured Division
First Lieutenant
Honorable Discharge, 6/2/94

Other (Optional)

As stated earlier in this chapter, there are many variations in titles for and contents of the Other or final section of the linear resume format. Since better than half of the linear resumes do not even bother to include this section and since there is considerable variation in content (when it is used), I will not attempt to provide details on the development of this resume segment. It must be considered optional and thus can be excluded from the resume entirely.

Should you wish to include this section in your own resume, let me suggest that you review the samples provided in Chapter 8 for ideas on how to treat this resume component.

Sample Resume D (Straight Linear Format)

SARRAH B. CARSON
235 Rothchild Boulevard
Barron Heights, IL 18743
Phone: (312) 857-9847

SUMMARY

Senior executive with over 20 years experience in retail manufacturing operations, product development and marketing. Particularly strong skills in marketing and manufacturing, with ability to present well-balanced product mix, prepare and control budgets, motivate and direct people.

PROFESSIONAL EXPERIENCE

STRATHMERE FASHIONS, INC. (New York, NY)   **1996 to Present**

Vice President & Division Manager, Footware

- Report to President of this $320 million retail fashion manufacturing and marketing company.

- Full P&L for $150 million shoe marketing and merchandising operation.

- Directed marketing/merchandising for 23 operating companies, 190 store departments, 1,900 employees.

- Developed and led marketing strategy that increased sales 35% in two years.

- Profitability liquidated obsolete shoe inventory valued at $20 million ($1 million profit).

- Initiated retail sales training program that reduced customer complaints by 92%.

BEAVERTON SHOE COMPANY (Philadelphia, PA)   **1989 to 1996**

Vice President, Retail Division

- Reported to Senior Vice President of this $500 million manufacturer, wholesaler and retailer of men's/women's shoes.

- Directed sales operations and merchandising/marketing for $85 million retail division.

- Initiated and coordinated northeast region co-op advertising program resulting in 20% sales increase.

- Developed successful regional marketing strategy that permitted 10% reduction in number of stores with simultaneous increase in sales of 5% ($6 million savings).

MAXWELL SHOE COMPANY (Hanover, PA)   **1984 to 1989**

Director of Manufacturing (1986 - 1989)

- Reported to Vice President of Operations of this $250 million quality men's shoe manufacturer.

- Full P&L for three plants, 2,200 employees, with annual operating budget of $175 million.

- Reengineered manufacturing operations, consolidating four plants into three, with no loss in production volume and annual cost savings of $25 million.

- Directed installation of SPC-based total quality program with resultant reduction in waste of more than 80%.

General Manager, Dixville Plant (1984 - 1986)

- Reported to Director of Manufacturing.

- Managed 500 employee shoe manufacturing plant with annual operating budget of $52 million.

JORDAN LEATHER & SHOE WORKS (Lancaster, PA)   **1980 to 1984**

Plant Engineer   (1983 - 1984)
Senior Project Engineer   (1981 - 1983)
Project Engineer   (1980 - 1981)

EDUCATION

M.S.,   Penn State University, 1980
Major: Mechanical Engineering
             Farthner Scholarship (2 years)

B.S.,   Bucknell University, 1978
Major: Mechanical Engineering
             Wilson Scholar (4 years)

117

Sample Resume E (Narrative Linear Format)

SARRAH B. CARSON
235 Rothchild Boulevard
Barron Heights, IL 18743
Phone: (312) 857-9847

SUMMARY

Senior executive with over 20 years experience in retail manufacturing operations, product development and marketing. Particularly strong skills in marketing and manufacturing, with ability to present well-balanced product mix, prepare and control budgets, motivate and direct people.

PROFESSIONAL EXPERIENCE

STRATHMERE FASHIONS, INC. (New York, NY)   **1996 to Present**

Vice President & Division Manager, Footware
Report to President with full P&L responsibility for $150 million shoe marketing and merchandising operation consisting of 23 operating companies, 190 shoe departments and 1,900 employees.

- Developed and led marketing strategy that increased sales 35% in two years.

- Profitably liquidated obsolete shoe inventory valued at $20 million ($1 million profit).

- Initiated retail sales training program that reduced customer complaints by 92%.

BEAVERTON SHOE COMPANY (Philadelphia, PA)   **1989 to 1996**

Vice President, Retail Division (1992 - 1996)
Reported to Senior Vice President of this $500 million manufacturer, wholesaler and retailer of men's/women's shoes. Functional responsibility for sales operations and merchandising/marketing of $85 million retail division.

- Successfully repositioned business from low end to better grade footwear resulting in 15% profit increase.

- Implemented automated inventory control system that reduced store inventories by 18% ($2 million savings).

Director of Merchandising, Retail Division (1989 - 1992)
Reported to Vice President, Retail Division with accountability for all merchandising of this $85 million retail division.

- Initiated and coordinated northeast region co-op advertising program resulting in 20% sales increase.

- Developed successful regional marketing strategy that permitted 10% reduction in number of stores with simultaneous increase in sales of 5% ($6 million savings).

118

MAXWELL SHOE COMPANY (Hanover, PA)   **1984 to 1989**

Director of Manufacturing (1986 - 1989)
Reported to Vice President of Operations of this $250 million quality men's shoe
manufacturer. Total P&L responsibility three plant, 2,200 employee shoe manufacturing
operations with annual operating budget of $175 million.

*   Reengineered manufacturing operations, consolidating four plants into three, with no loss
    in production volume and annual cost savings of $25 million.

*   Directed installation of SPC-based total quality program with resultant reduction in waste
    of more than 80%.

General Manager, Dixville Plant (1984 - 1986)
Reported to Director of Manufacturing. Managed 500 employee men's shoe manufacturing
facility with annual budget of $52 million.

JORDAN LEATHER & SHOE WORKS (Lancaster, PA)   **1980 to 1984**

Plant Engineer   (1983 - 1984)
Senior Project Engineer   (1981 - 1983)
Project Engineer   (1980 - 1981)

EDUCATION

M.S.,   Penn State University, 1980
Major: Mechanical Engineering
        Farthner Scholarship (2 years)

B.S.,   Bucknell University, 1978
Major: Mechanical Engineering
        Wilson Scholar (4 years)

PROFESSIONAL AFFILIATION

American Manufacturer's Association:
- President   (1996 - Present)
- Vice President   (1994 - 1996)
- Membership Chairperson   (1992 - 1994)
- Program Chairperson   (1990 - 1992)
- Member   (1988 - 1990)

American Marketing Association   (1989 - Present)
American Society of Mechanical Engineers (1978 - Present)

8

SAMPLE LINEAR
RESUMES

Included in this chapter are a total of 20 sample linear resumes representing 10 different career disciplines. Although all are presented in a linear format, I have intentionally alternated between the narrative linear and the straight linear approach so that you can better make a comparison and choose which of these styles makes the most sense for you. Thus there are 10 samples of the straight linear resume and 10 samples of the narrative linear format for your reference.

If you are looking for sample resumes in a particular career discipline, perhaps the following Resume Locater will prove helpful.

Resume Locator

Experience Level

Field or Discipline	*Senior Person*	*Junior Person*
	(Pages)	(Pages)
Accounting	122	124
Engineering	125	127
Finance	128	130
Human Resources	131	133
Information Services	135	137
Logistics	138	140
Marketing and Sales	142	144
Operations	145	147
Procurement	148	150
Technology	151	153

JOHN R. SMITH
119 South Maynard Road
Willingham, MA 94375
Phone: (216) 552-8879

SUMMARY

Accounting executive with over 14 years experience in increasingly responsible positions. Excellent reputation as creative, innovative and results-oriented senior manager who gets things done. Noted for applying computer systems in streamlining controllership operations. Full range of accounting experience includes: capital and operating budgets, financial statements, accounting policies and procedures, auditing, taxes, general and cost accounting, accounts receivable, accounts payable and credit.

PROFESSIONAL EXPERIENCE

SMITH DAVIDSON CORPORATION (Corporate Offices)   **1995 to Present**

Assistant to Corporate Controller

- Report to Corporate Vice President of Finance for this $320 million manufacturer of computer hardware.

- Manage Corporate Accounting and Brickford Division Accounting functions (32 employees) including consolidation of financial statements for SEC and shareholder reporting.

- Reengineered Coporate Accounting Department workflow design, revamping accounting procedures and practices (annual savings - $1.2 million).

- Directed computerization project to automate standard product cost build-up (annual labor savings - 500 hours).

- Organized, hired and trained Company's first Financial Planning Department.

- Initiated creative lease-back arrangement with foreign corporation on $52 million asset (annual savings - $1.6 million).

ZEBARD METAL CONTAINER CORP. (Corporate Offices)   **1992 to 1995**

Manager of Corporate Accounting (1993 - 1995)

- Reported to Chief Financial Officer of this $150 million manufacturer of overseas shipping containers.

- Managed staff of 14 professionals with responsibility for budget preparation/monitoring ($130 million), monthly and year-end closings, accounting system development/ implementation.

- Computerized consolidation and analysis of monthly and year-end financial statements (annual savings - 800 manhours) and reduced closing turnaround time by 50%.

- Organized and managed task force which provided the first breakout of individualized division P&L statements.

- Raised capital to support $35 million capital expansion program at highly favorable rates and minimal affect on Company credit rating.

Senior Accountant (1992 - 1993)

- Reported to Manager of Corporate Accounting.

- Responsible for consolidation, review and analysis of Company's monthly and year-end closing statements.

BARLEY & JOHNSON, INC. (Richmond, VA)   **1982 to 1992**

Senior Accountant (1987 - 1992)

- Reported to Manager of Cost Accounting and Taxation of this public accounting firm.

- Provided cost and tax accounting consultation and services to clients in the $50 to $150 million range.

Accountant (1982 - 1987)

JORDAN ELECTRONICS, INC. (Woodbury Plant)   **1976 to 1982**

Senior Cost Accountant   (1978 - 1982)
Cost Accountant   (1976 - 1978)

EDUCATION

M.B.A.,   University of Northern Ohio, 1978
Major: Accounting/Finance
          Bettinger Scholarship

B.A.,   Cannon College, 1976
Major: Accounting
          Magna Cum Laude

C.P.A.,   May 1984

DAVID P. BERRINGTON
39 Fowler Place, Apt. 4-C
Syracuse, NY 09872
Phone: (614) 972-4454

SUMMARY

Ambitious, motivated accounting professional with excellent record of growth and accomplishment. Thoroughly trained and ready for first supervisory assignment. Solid professional cost accounting foundation and excellent educational credentials.

PROFESSIONAL EXPERIENCE

MINUTEMAN ELECTRONICS, INC. (Syracuse Plant) **1994 to Present**

Senior Cost Accountant (1996 - Present)
Report to Cost Accounting Manager with full cost accounting responsibility for the Biostar electrical harness (annual manufacturing budget of $45 million). Direct two Cost Accountants in the application of proper cost accounting practices and procedures. Research and develop new cost standards and approaches.

- Developed/implemented computerized cost tracking system for early detection of negative cost trends (annual savings - $1/2 million).

- Breakout of rocker assembly costs allowing better manufacturing control (annual savings - $350,000).

- Improved labor cost estimates for retrofits.

Cost Accountant (1994 - 1996)
Reported to Senior Cost Accountant. Applied established cost accounting standards and procedures in the cost accounting and analysis of sophisticated electrical harness.

- Implemented unique cost tracking system credited with $115,000 annual savings in material costs.

EDUCATION

M.A.,   Cornell University, 1994
Major: Business Administration (Accounting)
       Businessman Fellowship

B.A.,   Syracuse University, 1992
Major: Accounting   G.P.A. 3.45/4.0
Minor: Finance   G.P.A. 3.75/4.0
       Davidson Scholarship (4 years)

Activities: President, Student Government Association
           Captain, Varsity Football and Varsity Track

Sample Linear Resume—Engineering

PETER B. JOHNSON
1835 Linwood Place
Linwood NJ 45973
Phone: (201) 447-2424 (H)
(201) 447-8842 (O)

SUMMARY

Accomplished engineering executive with over 16 years of experience in positions of increasing responsibility with Fortune 200 heating and air conditioning manufacturer. Consistently beat time deadlines and budget targets, resulting in bottom line savings in the millions.

PROFESSIONAL EXPERIENCE

BERRINGTON MANUFACTURING, INC. (Corporate Offices)   **1984 to Present**

Vice President of Engineering (1996 - Present)

- Report to President of this $3.7 billion, Fortune 200 manufacturer of residential and commercial air conditioning and heating systems.

- Direct 250 employee corporate engineering function in the engineering design, installation and start-up of major capital facility projects (annual budget $320 million).

- Directed two year, $850 million expansion program with successful start-up of two complete plants (delivered three months early, and $118 million under budget).

- Reengineered plant engineering functions with consolidation and centralization of most engineering work at Corporate Staff (80% headcount reduction, $120 million annual savings).

- Shifted focus from in-house to contract engineering services, reducing corporate headcount by 10% (annual savings of $8 million in wages and benefits).

Director, Mechanical Engineering (1992 - 1996)

- Reported to Vice President of Engineering with responsibility for direction of 160 employee mechanical project engineering function.

- Provided mechanical engineering support to all corporate capital projects (annual project budget $250 million).

- Directed successful installation and start-up of new, high speed Ram Shear commercial heating equipment manufacturing line (project budget $220 million).

- Engineered and installed $110 million commercial air conditioning line (on time and $1.2 million under budget).

125

<u>Manager, Systems Engineering</u> (1986 - 1992)

- Reported to Director of Systems Engineering.

- Managed department of 20 electrical, instrumentation and control engineers in the engineering of power distribution and computer control systems to support capital projects on corporate-wide basis (annual budget $100 million).

- Successfully managed over 52 capital projects ($575 million) over six year period.

- Brought 65% of projects in under budget (total savings $40 million).

<u>Senior Project Engineer, Heating</u> (1984 - 1986)

- Led project engineering teams in the design, installation and start-up of commercial heating manufacturing lines.

WILCOX ENGINEERING SYSTEMS, INC. (Corporate Engineering))   **1982 to 1984**

<u>Project Engineer</u>

- Designed, installed and started-up commercial heating equipment manufacturing lines.

EDUCATION

M.S.	University of Michigan, 1982
Major:	Mechanical Engineering
	Wainwright Scholarship
B.S.,	University of Michigan, 1980
Major:	Mechanical Engineering
	Magna Cum Laude
	Shearson Scholarship (4 years)
Activities:	President, Tau Beta Psi
	President, Delta Upsilon Fraternity
	Vice President, Greek Council

Sample Linear Resume—Engineering

MARTIN S. SAMPSON
17 Beachwood Lane
Fort Wayne, IN 37655
Phone: (513) 556-7720

SUMMARY

High-energy, results-oriented Senior Project Engineer with five years experience in design, installation and start-up of aluminum manufacturing processes and equipment. Excellent reputation for bringing projects in on time and at or below budget.

PROFESSIONAL EXPERIENCE

ARROW ALUMINUM CO., INC. (Corporate Engineering)   **1984 to Present**

Senior Project Engineer (1996 - Present)
Report to Manager of Mechanical Engineering of this $1.3 billion manufacturer of aluminum. Responsible for design, installation, start-up and debugging of aluminum and magnesium production facilities.

* Successfully managed mechanical design of $20 million furnace complex, including coordination with electrical systems interfaces. (Project on time and 5% under budget.)

* Redesigned refractory lining in flash calciner resulting in 35% reduction in heat loss from existing units and 50% from new units.

* Now designing and installing $12 million furnace. (Project currently on time and under budget.)

Project Engineer (1994 - 1996)
Reported to Senior Project Engineer with responsibility for engineering design, installation and start-up of aluminum manufacturing furnace complexes and material handling systems.

* Assisted in the design and start-up of $18 million furnace complex and associated material handling equipment.

* Purchased and installed $3 million Jet Fire furnace ignition system.

EDUCATION

B.S.,   Drexel University, 1994
Major: Mechanical Engineering   G.P.A. 3.4/4.0
           Cum Laude

Member, Tau Beta Psi
Vice President, American Society of Mechanical Engineers

Sample Linear Resume—Finance

STEPHEN C. TEMPLE
600 Ferrington Road, NW
Chicago, IL 55733
Phone: (513) 772-6464

SUMMARY

Senior financial executive with 13 years experience with $4 billion, Fortune 100 manufacturer of earth moving and excavation equipment. Heavily experienced in all aspects of domestic and international financial planning. Demonstrated ability to meet major capital requirements at exceptionally favorable rates and terms.

PROFESSIONAL EXPERIENCE

TEXTRON INTERNATIONAL CORP. (Corporate Offices)   **1987 to Present**

Vice President and Treasurer (1997 - Present)

- Report to Executive Vice President, Finance and Planning for this $4 billion, Fortune 100 manufacturer of earth moving and excavation equipment

- Direct staff of 48 professionals with responsibility for anticipating/providing the financial resources to fund all domestic and international operations ($400 to $600 million annually).

- Direct the Domestic Finance, International Finance, Money & Banking and Insurance and Pension Funding functions.

- Developed five-year funding strategy to finance $3.1 billion capital expansion plan with interest rates averaging 1% below market.

- Maintained top credit rating status, despite substantial increase in long-term debt load, through aggressive investor relations program with financial community.

- Reorganized and overhauled the Treasury function, recruiting top-flight personnel and substantially upgrading department image.

Director of Corporate Finance (1993 - 1997)

- Reported to Vice President and Treasurer with responsibility for anticipation, planning and execution of financial strategy and plans to meet Company's short and long-term capital needs.

- Directed staff of five Analysts supporting annual financing requirements of $300 million.

- Managed development of five-year financial planning computer model, substantially improving forecasting and planning of capital requirements for international affiliates.

128

- Refinanced $185 million loan for Italian affiliate at considerably improved rates ($24 million savings).

- Created improved credibility and increased demand as a major financial consulting resource to international affiliates.

Senior Analyst, Corporate Finance (1990 - 1993)

- Reported to Director of Corporate Finance.

- Supported top management in five domestic divisions in the development of long-term (five-year) financial planning process.

- Trained management in use of PC-based financial planning models, increasing financial planning proficiency of top management and their respective staffs.

Analyst, Corporate Finance (1987 - 1990)

- Reported to Senior Financial Analyst

- Assisted in the identification, analysis and recommendation of a wide range of business opportunities and evaluation of alternate financing strategies.

EDUCATION

M.B.A., Wharton School, University of Pennsylvania, 1987
Major: Finance
Sun Company Scholar (2 years)

B.A.,   Pennsylvania State University, 1985
Major: Financial Management
Minor: Economics
Magna Cum Laude

JANET N. MORSE
300 Mocking Bird Lane
Newtown Square, PA 19073
Phone: (610) 775-5757

SUMMARY

Accomplished, high-energy Senior Financial Analyst with outstanding educational credentials and six years experience in financial planning with major aerospace contractor. Ability to manage financial planning programs from cost estimate through placement of funding for programs in the $200 to $400 million range.

PROFESSIONAL EXPERIENCE

DELTRON AEROSPACE, INC. (Corporate Offices)   **1992 to Present**

Senior Financial Analyst (1995 - Present)
Report to Manager of Corporate Financial Planning for this $2 billion federal contract supplier of missile guidance systems. Develop manufacturing cost estimates, based on prototype costs, and identify, evaluate and recommend program funding options and sources.

- Developed funding estimates and recommendations for three major development programs in the $200 to $400 million range.

- Recipient of three federal commendations for outstanding service in financial planning work.

Financial Analyst (1992 - 1995)
Reported to Senior Financial Analyst providing assistance in the development of funding requirements and financial strategies to support full-scale manufacture of sophisticated missile guidance systems.

- Played lead role in developing funding requirements for manufacture of two electronic aiming devices (total requirements - $85 million).

SEPTRAM INTERSCIENCE, INC. (Corporate Offices)   **1991 to 1992**

Planning Analyst

EDUCATION

M.B.A.,   Harvard University Business School, 1991
Major: Financial Planning

B.S.,   Cornell University, 1987
Major: Management Science
           Cum Laude
           Torrington Computer Scholarship (4 years)

DAWN M. MARKS
300 Ollinger Avenue
Richmond, Virginia 23375
Phone: (314) 872-4467

SUMMARY

Well-seasoned senior level human resources executive with over 14 years experience in full range of human resource functions. Strong appreciation for the relationship between good human resource management and profitability. Creative leadership skills in organization development and employee productivity improvement.

PROFESSIONAL EXPERIENCE

CARSON MANUFACTURING COMPANY, INC. (Corporate Offices)   **1991 to Present**

Director of Human Resources (1996 - Present)

- Report to Corporate Vice President, Human Resources of this $1.5 billion manufacturer of residential and commercial furniture.

- Direct staff of 14 professionals in providing full range of Human Resource services to the 1,000 employee corporate staff.

- Oversee functional responsibility for Human Resource Planning, Internal/External Staffing, Organization Development and Wage & Salary Administration.

- Directed installation of human resources/payroll information system with estimated annual savings of $1/2 million in labor costs.

- Developed human resource planning computer model for linking human resource planning and business planning.

- Staffed and directed major hiring effort requiring the recruitment of 97 engineers to support capital expansion program (all critical deadlines met).

Manager Corporate Staffing (1993 - 1996)

- Reported to Director of Human Resources with full responsibility for internal/external staffing.

- Managed staff of four professionals and six support personnel with annual staffing budget of $2.1 million (annual recruitment volume 250 employees, 300 internal placements).

- Successfully orchestrated sensitive, high level replacement searches during major top level reorganization.

- Implemented improved recruiting techniques that reduced interview-to-offer ratio by 1/2 with an 80% improvement in the offer-to-hire ratio.

Manager of Administrative Staffing (1991 - 1993)

- Reported to Manager of Corporate Staffing with responsibility for all administrative staffing of corporate headquarters complex.

- Successfully hired 125 employees in two years to staff key positions in Accounting, Finance, Law, Information Services, Logistics, Procurement and Human Resources functions.

- Implemented psychological assessment as a selection tool in the hiring of top management personnel.

- Developed, implemented and trained key hiring management personnel in the use of "focused selection" interview techniques generally credited with substantial improvement and increased reliability of selection process.

BARSOM, CLIFFORD AND JANSEN, INC. (Corporate Offices)   **1983 to 1991**

Senior Consultant (1987 - 1991)

- Reported to Senior Partner of this well-known, international human resources consulting firm.

- Designed, developed and installed new employee evaluation and feedback program at three major client locations.

- Generated $450,000 in new client consulting revenues in slightly over three years.

Consultant (1983 - 1987)

- Performed research in support of development of new employee performance consulting product.

EDUCATION

M.S.,   Michigan State University, 1983
Major: Industrial Psychology
Thesis: The Role of Performance Feedback in the Motivation of
        Professional Employees"

B.A.,   Michigan State University, 1981
Major: Human Resource Management
        Cum Laude

132

DAVID R. JEFFRIES
36 Tartan Road, SW
Birmingham, Alabama 75663
Phone: (314) 872-5533

SUMMARY

Creative Employment Manager with over five years experience at the corporate and division level. Reputation for recruiting the hard-to-find. Thoroughly versed in all aspects of recruiting and employment with excellent track record of achieving results.

PROFESSIONAL EXPERIENCE

COMSTAR MANUFACTURING CO., INC. (Corporate Offices)   **1990 to Present**

Corporate Employment Manager, Operations (1995 - Present)
Report to Director of Corporate Employment of this $2.6 billion manufacturer of electrical products. Manage the staffing support for 25 plant facilities, employing 13,000 employees. Support the hiring of 300 to 500 professionals and managerial personnel annually at a cost of approximately $8 million.

- Successfully planned and managed the staffing of three new plant facilities employing 750 employees over seven-year period.

- Developed/implemented emergency staffing program to recruit 160 experienced engineers in 90 days to staff critical new capital program (all program goals met).

- Managed annual college recruiting program (37 campuses, 64 recruiting schedules) hiring an average of 220 professionals annually.

Employment Manager, Vanstar Division (1992 - 1995)
Reported to Division Director of Human Resources for this 2,500 employee division involved in the precision chemical coating of space vehicle parts. Focused on recruitment of hard-to-find research scientists specializing in the development of exotic chemical coatings for space travel applications.

- Developed creative approaches to identifying rare scientists including patent and computer literature searches.

- Reduced scientific recruitment backlog from 160 to 25 positions in three years.

- Trained over 100 scientists and technical managers in the use of advanced interviewing techniques.

133

Plant Human Resources Manager, Melville Plant (1990 - 1992)
Reported to Plant Manager with responsibility for providing full range of human resources services to this chemical manufacturing plant of 550 employees.

- Successfully thwarted two union drives to maintain union-free manufacturing environment.

- Researched and directed implementation of experimental high performance work system using cutting edge sociotechnical approach.

- Installed new "Safety Alert" program, training all first line supervisors and reducing lost-time injuries by 63%.

JOHNSON AND BARTON, INC. (Westerly Plant)   1989 to 1990

Assistant Human Resources Manager
Reported to Plant Human Resources Manager of this 800 employee clothing manufacturing facility. Assisted manager in providing full range of human resources services to both salaried and hourly employees.

BILTMORE ELECTRONICS, INC. (Westerly Plant)   1986 to 1989

Human Resources Assistant
Entry level human resources position in this 300 employee electronic equipment manufacturing plant. Handled wide range of projects and special studies in human resources field.

EDUCATION

B.A.,   University of Alabama, 1986
Major: Business Administration

JEFFREY A. MORSE
225 Highland Road
Clifton, NJ 18337
Phone: (609) 377-9787

SUMMARY

Information Services executive with over 15 years of experience in all phases of IS work. Currently Director of IS for $2 billion, Fortune 200 corporation. Strong reputation for ability to lead the development and implementation of modern information systems. Known for practicality, utility and cost-effectiveness.

PROFESSIONAL EXPERIENCE

CORBOTT MANUFACTURING CO., INC. (Corporate Offices)   **1988 to Present**

Director of IS   (1997 - Present)

- Report to Executive Vice President of Administration for this $2 billion, Fortune 200 manufacturer of pumps, valves and fittings.

- Direct 50 employee department ($80 million budget) in the corporate-wide development, implementation, maintenance and control of information systems.

- Provide systems support to corporate headquarters, four operating divisions, 16 manufacturing plants in both the United States and Europe.

- Successfully directed completion of $12 million sales forecasting, production scheduling and materials control computer system. (Project completed three months ahead of schedule and $1 million under budget.)

- Reengineered and consolidated field IS operations with 25% headcount reduction and increased efficiency (annual savings - $6 million).

- Installed new matrix management system allowing a 10% reduction in Corporate IS headcount and greater flexibility in assignment of professional personnel (annual savings estimate - $3.2 million).

Corporate Project Manager   (1995 - 1997)

- Reported to Director of IS with management responsibility for five to seven project managers in the design, implementation and start-up of wide range of IS projects ($20 million budget).

- Completed all projects on or before deadline (95% before deadline).

- Completed 87% of projects at or below budgeted target with total capital budget savings of 14% over two years.

- Major systems installed included Human Resources/Payroll, General Ledger Accounting System and Order Entry/Sales Forecasting System.

Manager of Client Planning Services (1991 - 1995)

- Reported to Corporate IS Manager.

- Managed staff of three professionals responsible for planning the future information needs of functional clients.

- Developed long-range information needs plan for five key corporate functions (Controllers, Finance, Operations, Procurement and Human Resources).

Senior Programmer Analyst (1988 - 1991)

- Provided daily direction to two programmer analysts in the development of numerous systems and programs.

MONTGOMERY CORPORATION (Corporate Offices)   **1986 to 1988**

Programmer Analyst

- Developed over 50 programs to support five major systems areas.

EDUCATION

Ph.D., Cornell University, 1986
Major: Computer Science

M.S., Cornell University, 1984
Major: Computer Science
        Data Resources Company Scholarship

B.S., Lawrence University, 1982
Major: Mathematics
        Pennington Scholarship (4 years)

SANDRA D. THOMPSON
32 East March Street
Thornton, Michigan 77599
Phone: (817) 552-9494

SUMMARY

Conscientious, hardworking Technology Programmer Analyst with three years experience providing programming support to Development Engineers in the development of state-of-the-art communications controller. Proficient in the use of data analyzer equipment for conducting studies and troubleshooting network problems.

PROFESSIONAL EXPERIENCE

TRANSCON SYSTEMS LABORATORIES, INC. (Corporate Offices)   **1996 to Present**

Programmer Analyst
Report to Technology Programming Manager with responsibility to provide technical programming support in the development of a state-of-the-art communications controller for major systems engineering firm.

• In-depth knowledge of SNA/ACP/NCP functions of a communications controller in a PEP environment.

• Proficiency with SDLC, various trace facilities, ALC and TSO/WYLBUR/SPF.

• Expert in the use of data analyzer equipment.

• Awarded recognition bonus in appreciation for high level of support to Development Engineering Department.

EDUCATION

M.S., Massachusetts Institute of Technology, 1996
Major: Computer Science
          Ransin Laboratory Fellowship (2 years)

B.S., Massachusetts Institute of Technology, 1994
Major: Computer Science   G.P.A. 3.85/4.0
Minor: Mathematics   G.P.A. 3.78/4.0
          Mattson Foundation Scholarship (4 years)

          Activities: President, Computer Science Society
                        Vice President, Mathematics Honorary

KEVIN P. BURTRAM
32 Worrington Lane, SW
Dallas, TX 33755
Phone: (719) 377-2424

SUMMARY

Senior level logistics executive with demonstrated ability to direct and energize logistics functions that employ state-of-the-art concepts and realize significant contributions to bottom line results. Demonstrated leadership in the application of reengineering, computer and quantitative techniques that streamline operations and add substantial profits.

PROFESSIONAL EXPERIENCE

HERRINGER FOOD PROCESSING. INC. (Corporate Offices)   **1996 to Present**

Director of Logistics

- Report to Senior Vice President - Operations for this $1.4 billion, Fortune 500 food processing corporation.

- Direct development/implementation of strategic and operating plans for corporate-wide Warehousing and Transportation functions (eight plants, 750 employees, $125 million annual budget).

- Directed development/installation of computerized order entry/distribution planning system allowing advance transportation planning (annual freight cost savings - $18 million).

- Directed purchase/installation of computer system controlled palletizer and conveyor system (annual warehouse handling cost savings - $4.7 million).

- Negotiated corporate-wide rail carrier rates with two major carriers (annual savings - $3.9 million).

THE BOSTON BEVERAGE COMPANY (Corporate Offices)   **1987 to 1996**

Logistics Manager (1994 - 1996)

- Reported to Executive Vice President - Operations for this $850 million bottler of carbonated beverages.

- Managed Corporate Distribution Department (250 employees, $85 million budget) with nation-wide distribution network through company-owned and leased warehouses.

138

- Reengineered field warehousing consolidating facilities into five leased regional hub facilities with annual space savings of $10.2 million and freight savings of 18%.

- Managed development/implementation of computer simulated shipping model to determine best shipping point and transportation mode (annual freight savings - $5 million).

Senior Distribution Analyst (1991 - 1994)

- Reported to Distribution Manager with responsibility for conducting several facilities planning and space utilization studies.

- Introduced use of MaxPlan computer simulation space planning software, cutting project planning time by 62%.

Distribution Analyst (1987 - 1991)

- Provided support to Senior Distribution Analyst and Distribution Manager in wide range of studies requiring use of quantitative and computer techniques.

EDUCATION

M.S.,   Georgia Institute of Technology, 1987
Major: Industrial Engineering
            Weller Scholarship (2 years)

B.S.,   Texas A&M, 1985
Major: Industrial Engineering
            Hanson Oil Company Scholarship (4 years)

PETER B. DIRKSON
18 Ocean View Road
Clearview Beach, California 77533
Phone: (714) 377-2525

SUMMARY

Ambitious, results-oriented Logistics Manager with over 12 years experience in all phases of warehousing and transportation. Well-documented track record of ability to translate technical knowledge and leadership into bottom-line results. Fully qualified and eager to run Logistics function for medium-sized company.

PROFESSIONAL EXPERIENCE

ROVER DOG FOOD COMPANY, INC. (Corporate Offices)   **1996 to Present**

Manager of Warehousing
Report to Vice President of Operations for this $300 million manufacturer of pet food. Manage Corporate Warehousing function consisting of corporate warehouse and 12 field warehouse operations (eight leased, four owned). Direct activities of 150 employees (35 salaried, 115 hourly) with annual operating budget of $32 million.

• Implemented palletized railcar loading resulting in $2 million annual savings.

• Directed shipping container redesign allowing shipment of 10% more product per railcar (annual savings $450 thousand).

• Successfully renegotiated warehouse leases at 2% below previous year's rent (annual savings $320 thousand).

HORSHAW FASTENER MANUFACTURING CO. (Fairfield Plant))   **1994 to 1996**

Distribution Center Manager
Reported to Plant Manager with full responsibility for Plant Distribution Center of this $120 million manufacturer of metal fasteners. Directed staff of 65 employees in daily storage and shipment of finished products.

• Installed extendable powered conveyers for truck loading resulting in 10% reduction in labor costs (annual savings $300,000).

• Initiated loading crew training program in improved loading techniques reducing product damage by 75%.

• Redesigned and implemented new storage pattern for warehouse (annual space savings $135,000).

DEITRICK TRUCKING COMPANY (Fairfield Terminal)   **1991 to 1994**

Dispatcher
Accepted and placed orders for truck shipments with full responsibility for allocation and
dispatch of 125 trailers per day.

- Implemented WatchDog PC software package for tracking and scheduling terminal
  equipment (annual labor savings $40,000).

- Improved on-time deliveries from 65% to 98% in two years.

EDUCATION

B.A.,   Anderson College, 1991
Major: Business Administration

MILITARY

United States Marine Corps, 1983 - 1987
Supply Sergeant
Honorable Discharge

SCOTT M. BEATTY
900 Lordon Avenue, SW
Atlanta, Georgia 57994
Phone: (912) 774-3434

SUMMARY

High energy, results-oriented sales and marketing executive with over 14 years of demonstrated achievement in all phases of sales and marketing operations. Known for bold, dynamic and creative leadership that consistently establishes employer as the market leader in most brands.

PROFESSIONAL EXPERIENCE

CORRDIGAN CHEMICALS, INC. (Corporate Offices)   **1997 to Present**

Director of Marketing

- Report to Vice president of Sales and Marketing for this $725 million manufacturer of chemical specialties.

- Direct 25 employee marketing function that includes Market Research, Market Planning, New Market Development, Advertising, Promotion and Field Sales departments.

- Developed dealer network that established Company as the leading marketer of solvents in the European Market and led to a 75% increase in exports ($225 million) in two years.

- Co-developed (with R&D) new low-viscosity resin product which allowed national roll-out in less than 18 months ($150 million new sales in first year).

STANTON CHEMICAL SPECIALTIES, INC. (Corporate Offices)   **1989 - 1997**

Director of Marketing and Sales (1993 - 1997)

- Reported to President of this $525 million specialty chemicals manufacturer with functional responsibility for market research and planning, brand management, advertising and sales.

- Directed 125 employee sales force with responsibility for all domestic and international sales volume.

- Successfully introduced eight new products, in less than four years, increasing total sales by 40% ($210 million).

- Expanded sales force, hiring and training over 60 new sales representatives.

Marketing Brand Manager (1991 - 1993)

- Reported to Director of Marketing and Sales with brand marketing responsibility for *Darcell*.

- Modified brand package and repositioned *Darcell* as low-priced, mid-quality product (through creative advertising) resulting in 225% increase in sales volume in two years. (Improved product ranking from number five to number one in market.)

Associate Brand Manager (1989 - 1991)

- Coordinated all market research and test marketing of Company's *Tetron* brand.

CRISWELL CHEMICALS CORPORATION (District Sales Office)   **1984 - 1989**

Senior Sales Representative   (1988 - 1989)
Sales Representative   (1984 - 1988)

EDUCATION

M.B.A.,	University of Chicago, 1984
Major:	Marketing
B.S.,	Syracuse University, 1982
Major:	Chemistry
Activities:	President, American Chemical Society Chapter
	Vice President, Delta Delta Fraternity
	Captain, Varsity Rowing

ALLAN D. MARKS
100 Cedar Road
Clinton, Michigan 77229
Phone: (713) 559-0085

SUMMARY

Creative sales professional with over six years experience selling complex business systems. Consistent high producer who demonstrates unusual ability to successfully introduce new business machine product lines into complex business and institution applications market.

PROFESSIONAL EXPERIENCE

MICRO GRAPHICS, INC. (Detroit Regional Office)   **1991 to Present**

District Sales Manager (1996 - Present)
Report to National Sales Manager for this $800 million manufacturer of microfilm storage, retrieval and duplicating systems. Manage five-person sales force with territorial responsibility for Michigan, Ohio and Indiana (annual sales of $90 million).

*   Successfully introduced world's first updatable microfilm record keeping system into Midwest Region ($30 million in first year sales).

*   Developed/implemented creative sales strategy that increased regional sales over 300% in last two years. (Sales volume now approaching $100 million.)

Senior Sales Representative (1993 - 1996)
Reported to District Sales Manager with responsibility for working closely with business venture team to introduce new microfilm record keeping system to Midwest market. Focused on developing banking industry applications.

*   Sold, installed and started-up first banking system application in United States.

*   Proved viability of banking industry applications, paving way to $300 million market in just over three years.

Sales Representative (1991 - 1993)
Successfully sold wide range of microfilms and specialty film products through Midwest dealer network.

EDUCATION

B.A.,	University of Michigan, 1991
Major:	Marketing
Activities:	President, Student Government Congress
	President, Kappa Delta Fraternity
	Captain, Varsity Track Team

144

CHRISTOPHER T. BEATTY
106 Summit Avenue
Reading, PA 19330
Phone: (215) 775-0978

SUMMARY

Senior operations executive with 19 years experience in responsible manufacturing management and engineering positions. Excellent record of fast-track growth based upon solid contribution to bottom-line results. Outstanding reputation as organizer and leader who never fails to achieve goals and objectives.

PROFESSIONAL EXPERIENCE

STERLING TUBE CORPORATION (Corporate Offices)   **1989 to Present**

Vice President of Operations (1994 - Present)

- Report to President of this leading producer of copper tubing (annual sales $500 million).

- Full P&L responsibility for two tube manufacturing plants and one copper refinery (2,800 employees, $300 million budget).

- Directed multi-disciplined cost reduction task force which implemented sweeping changes resulting in 20% reduction in manufacturing costs in three years (annual savings - $110 million).

- Installed revolutionary socio-technical work system in two tube manufacturing plants, decreasing supervisory workforce by 50% and increasing worker productivity by 22%.

- Directed installation of new computerized materials management scheduling and controls system which cut raw materials inventories by 28% (annual savings $15 million).

Plant Manager, Norfolk Plant (1989 - 1994)

- Reported to Vice President of Operations with full P&L responsibility for 1,500 employee copper refining and tube manufacturing facility ($375 million operating budget).

- Successfully directed two-year, $125 million plant expansion program, doubling manufacturing capacity. (Project completed three months ahead of schedule and 8% under budget.)

145

- In preparation for start-up, transferred 70% of workers to new jobs over two months with no loss in plant production levels or increase in operating costs.

BRADFORD COPPER COMPANY, INC. (Corporate Offices)   **1979 to 1989**

Manager of Engineering (1984 - 1989)

- Reported to Director of Engineering of this $300 million manufacturer of refrigeration tubing.

- Managed 25 employee Central Engineering Department in the engineering design, installation and start-up of new and expanded tube manufacturing facilities (annual project budget $20 to $30 million).

- Successfully managed $250 million, three-year capital expansion program (largest in Company's history) with all projects completed on time and within budget.

- Managed successful engineering start-up of new state-of-the-art, computer controlled, integrated refinery and tube mill (first of its kind in the United States).

Department Manager, Drawing Operations (1982 - 1984)

- Reported to Plant Manager of the Brackville Plant.

- Managed 100 employee tube drawing operation with annual production value of $85 million.

- Instituted continuous productivity improvement effort resulting in 18% increase in overall department productivity with simultaneous 12% reduction in operating costs.

Project Engineer (1979 - 1982)

- Designed, installed and started-up major capital projects in furnace and drawing operations ($40 - $50 million range).

EDUCATION

M.S.,	Penn State University, 1979
Major:	Mechanical Engineering
	Syracuse Businessman Fellowship
B.S.,	Penn State University, 1977
Major:	Mechanical Engineering
	Tau Beta Psi

MARGARET R. TEMPLE
200 Remmington Drive
Springfield, Ohio 75332
Phone: (315) 772-6767

SUMMARY

Results-oriented manufacturing manager with six years experience in wax and silicone manufacturing. Excellent record of achievement and advancement earned through demonstrated contribution to bottom-line results.

PROFESSIONAL EXPERIENCE

REED MANUFACTURING COMPANY (Linwood Plant)   **1993 - Present**

Assistant Plant Manager (1996 - Present)
Report to Plant Manager of this 1,000 employee manufacturer of silicone based waxes and polishes ($325 million annual sales). Manage the Can Finishing and Warehousing Departments (210 employees, $130 million budget).

- Introduced automated palletizers and palletized railcar loading system, cutting warehouse operating costs by 25% (annual savings $15 million).

- Installed absenteeism control program with resultant 60% reduction in days lost.

- Initiated new "open door" policy that reduced union grievances from 185 to 62 in two years.

Department Manager, Formulations (1993 - 1996)
Reported to Manufacturing Manager with accountability for management of plant formulations and mixing operations. Directed department of 50 employees (5 salaried, 45 hourly) with annual operating budget of $75 million.

- Implemented SPC-based "total quality" effort that identified key process variables and reduced batch rejections by 90% (annual savings $2.1 million).

- Installed JIT materials control program that reduced on-hand raw materials inventories by 27% (annual savings $1.3 million).

CLOVER WAX COMPANY (Radley Plant)   **1991 to 1993**

Supervisor, Formulations

EDUCATION

B.S., Bradley College, 1991
Major: Industrial Technology
Cum Laude

BRUCE B. PARSONS
32 Roam Avenue
Utica, NY 79443
Phone: (319) 447-2242

SUMMARY

Procurement executive with over 13 years demonstrated effectiveness in contributing substantially to bottom line results. Knowledgeable in all facets of modern procurement management including computer applications. Fully qualified to direct procurement function of major corporation.

PROFESSIONAL EXPERIENCE

CARSON MANUFACTURING CO., INC. (Corporate Offices)   **1996 to Present**

Director of Procurement

- Report to Vice President of Operations Services for this $1.2 billion manufacturer of consumer food products.

- Direct staff of eight professionals in the purchase of raw materials, vital supplies and services for corporate staff and eight manufacturing sites (annual budget $580 million).

- Develop, implement and control all procurement policies and strategies including centralized buying programs on consolidated purchases of large volume/big ticket items.

- Implemented modern inventory tracking computer system allowing substantially reduced inventories ($22 million annual savings).

- Consolidated and centralized large volume, raw material purchases, with blanket order releases, permitting sizeable vendor price concessions (annual savings $15 million).

- Convinced company to convert from prime fuel to bio-mass boilers for energy generation, allowing sale of excess capacity to power company (annual savings $12 million).

WILSON BAKING CORPORATION (Corporate Offices)   **1990 to 1996**

Manager of Procurement (1992 - 1996)

- Reported to Vice President of Administration for this $850 commercial baking company.

148

- Managed staff of eight with full centralized purchasing responsibility for five plants (annual purchase volume $325 million).

- Reengineered and centralized procurement function with net headcount reduction of 25% (annual savings $1 million).

- Consolidated and centralized corporate-wide purchase of hundreds of items with first year's savings of $8 million.

Senior Buyer - Vital Supplies (1990 - 1992)

- Reported to Corporate Procurement Manager.

- Directed activities of two buyers and three support staff in the annual purchase of $200 million of vital supplies.

- Installed computer based vital supplies/packaging forecast system permitting JIT delivery approach and substantial reduction of standing inventories. (annual savings $6 million).

JOHNSON FOODS, INC. (CORPORATE OFFICES)   **1986 to 1990**

Manager of Purchasing (1987 - 1990)

- Managed corporate procurement function for this $150 million manufacturer of pretzels and potato chips ($50 million budget, three employees).

Buyer (1986 - 1987)

- Reported to Manager of Purchasing, providing support in the purchase of raw materials and vital supplies inventories.

EDUCATION

B.A.,   Syracuse University, 1986
Major: Business Administration

Activities: President, Student Business Club
             Captain, Varsity Baseball

JAMES R. WINDTHROPE
18 Bay View Place, Apt. 4-D
Briney Beach, California 32775
Phone: (415) 773-4424

SUMMARY

Results-driven procurement professional with over five years of experience in the purchase of vital supplies. Excellent track record of contribution to bottom-line results through finding and implementing major cost-savings opportunities.

PROFESSIONAL EXPERIENCE

HILTON PAPER COMPANY, INC. (Corporate Offices)   **1997 to Present**

Senior Purchasing Agent - Vital Supplies
Report to Manager of Procurement for this $350 million manufacturer of printing and publishing papers. Responsible for purchase of all vital supplies to support manufacturing operations - knock-down cartons, poly wraps, shrink wraps, etc. ($18 million annually).

• Negotiated two-year knock-down carton purchase agreement with new supply source at 20% savings ($1.3 million).

• Studied historical sales forecast vs. actual purchase volume data, formulating mathematical correlation and developing computer simulation model that allows accurate purchase forecasts of within 1% of actual. (Annual savings $1/2 million).

BRANDON PAPER COMPANY (Corporate Offices)   **1994 - 1997**

Vital Supplies Buyer
Reported to Manager of Procurement for this $110 million converter of consumer paper products. Responsible for $4 million annual purchases of vital supplies to support two manufacturing sites.

• Negotiated new poly wrap contract at 10% off previous pricing (annual cost savings of $1/4 million).

• Installed off-the-shelf inventory control computer software package allowing 20% reduction in vital supplies inventories (annual savings of $3/4 million).

EDUCATION

B.A.,   University of Southern California, 1994
Major: Business Administration

CAROLYN B. TABOR
25 Reedsville Road
Sampson, Oregon 77033
Phone: (409) 357-2999 (O)
(409) 357-5673 (H)

SUMMARY

Senior executive with 25 years of dynamic, innovative Technology leadership in Fortune 500 companies. Proven ability to deliver innovative technology that strengthens competitive market position and is the lifeline for profitable new business development. Blend of strong technical and interpersonal skills forms the basis for good management leadership and solid team participation.

PROFESSIONAL EXPERIENCE

OREGON PAPER COMPANY (Corporate Research Center))   **1994 to Present**

Vice President of Technology

- Report to President with responsibility for managing 500 employee corporate research center for this Fortune 100 paper and packaging manufacturer ($4.2 billion annual sales).

- Direct all basic research, product research and process development activities in support of company's strategic objectives (annual budget $32 million).

- Directed development of innovative magnetic fiber forming device providing Company with distinct competitive advantage in the marketing of improved sanitary tissue product (200% improvement in market share).

- Introduced 22 new and/or improved products that have added over $1 billion in new business in seven years.

- Developed proprietary new product expected to add $2 billion of new business over next four years (successful national roll-out now underway).

STRATTON FIBER CORP. (Materials Research Laboratory)   **1977 to 1994**

Research Director, Packaging & Materials (1986 - 1994)

- Reported to Vice President of Research for this $2.9 billion manufacturer of synthetic fiber and film materials.

- Directed 135 professionals and technicians in the research and development of all packaging, nonwoven, plastic packaging and photo-imaging film materials (annual budget $20 million).

- Developed new wet-lay nonwoven manufacturing process expected to create high demand for Stratton's Syntex fibers (annual sales potential $80 million in two years).

151

- Developed new high technology frozen food packaging material that prolongs thaw time by 300%, reducing food processing spoilage by 30% (substantial competitive advantage).

- Directed development of TEP electronic scanning photo-imaging technology that allows pictures to be taken with electronic cameras providing clear resolution superiority over conventional photographic film.

Research Manager, Synthetic Fibers (1981 - 1986)

- Reported to Research Director with responsibility to manage 38 professionals in the development and application of novel synthetic fibers to packaging and consumer paper webs.

Senior Research Scientist, Polymer Research (1977 - 1981)

- Pioneered and accelerated development of proprietary polymer materials through experimental and theoretical studies using experimental design and computer modeling and simulations.

VELSTAR ELECTRONICS & SPACE LABORATORY (Corporate Laboratories) **1976 to 1977**

Research Specialist

- Developed exotic coated materials for Velstar communications satellite heat shield. Performed re-entry simulation testing and designed predictive models using computer techniques.

EDUCATION

Ph.D.,	University of Michigan, 1976
Major:	Chemical Engineering
	Pennington Scholar
M.S.,	Rochester Institute of Technology, 1974
Major:	Materials Engineering
B.S.,	Rochester Institute of Technology, 1972
Major:	Chemical Engineering
	Magna Cum Laude
	Barlow Scholarship (4 years)

PATENTS AND PUBLICATIONS

22 U.S. Patents (four pending)
45 professional publications and papers

J. WALTER LOFTEN, Jr.
315 Post Road, South
Benton Harbor, Michigan 45776
Phone: (917) 472-3927

SUMMARY

Highly innovative Ph.D. polymer engineer with demonstrated track record in achieving excellent product and process development results. Holder of ten U.S. patents and inventor of revolutionary new polymeric material allowing successful entry into several new markets.

PROFESSIONAL EXPERIENCE

NORWOOD CHEMICAL SPECIALTIES, INC. (Corporate Technology) **1993 to Present**

Senior Research Engineer, Polymers (1995 - Present)
Report to Manager of Polymer Research for this $1.2 billion chemical manufacturer. Provide technical leadership to research team in the development of novel polymer-based materials for use in boat hulls.

- Developed Sampson TMM, a revolutionary new polymeric material having twice the strength of fiberglass at half the cost (projected annual sales of $1 billion).

- Awarded three key patents and generally recognized as the principal contributor to the above product development effort.

- Recipient of Norwood "Inventor of the Year" award.

Research Engineer, Polymers (1993 - 1995)
Professional accountability similar to that described above for Senior Research Engineer. Emphasis more on process rather than product development.

- Developed process for efficient manufacture of new synthetic fabric having unique finishing characteristics.

- Successfully transferred new technology from bench to full-scale production in record time.

- Awarded four patents and received special recognition bonus award for "exceptional contributions" to the commercialization effort.

HAWTHORNE CHEMICAL COMPANY (Central Research) **1991 to 1993**

Polymer Chemist
Developed high temperature resistant molding polymers and inherent fire retardant plastics.

EDUCATION

Ph.D.,   Massachusetts Institute of Technology, 1991
Major: Polymer Engineering

M.S.,   Rochester Institute of Technology, 1989
Major: Chemical Engineering

B.S.,   Massachusetts Institute of Technology, 1987
Major: Polymer Science

9

THE
FUNCTIONAL
RESUME

No book on the subject of resume writing would be complete without a chapter on the functional resume. Although, as a seasoned employment professional, I must admit to not being a strong advocate of this style of resume, I will quickly add, however, that it does occasionally have its place in the employment process. As an indication of this fact, I would estimate that approximately 5 to 10 percent of all resumes received by corporations make use of the functional format. This makes the functional format the second most popular resume style (second only to the chronological format which is estimated to account for 90 to 95 percent of all resumes). The chronological resume format, as you will recall from our discussion in Chapter 7 also includes the now highly popular narrative resume, which has grown enormously in its usage.

ADVANTAGES OF FUNCTIONAL RESUME

Advocates of the functional resume are quick to point out that it makes use of an excellent marketing strategy. This resume format is designed to capture the interest of the resume reader right from the beginning. This is accomplished by positioning the candidates's most salable strengths at the beginning of the resume in the form of some brief statements that capsulize the candidate's major accomplishments and most salable professional experience.

The marketing premise upon which this resume design is based is that most employment professionals are not thorough in their reading of employment resumes. Further, advocates of this style of resume would tell you that many employment professionals in fact read only the first paragraph or two of a resume. If these initial paragraphs do not capture their interest, the reader simply discards the resume and moves on to the next.

Although there may be some employment professionals who are not particularly thorough and conscientious in their resume reading. My experience suggests that this is certainly not the case with most. In my opinion, the majority of employment professionals discover early in their professional career that thorough resume reading is a must. In having read thousands of resumes as an employment manager, I have found that the specific experience and/or skills sought by my employer were sometimes not described until the second or third page of the applicant's resume. This experience has conditioned me to read resumes with a fair degree of thoroughness. Most professional employment managers are likewise sufficiently concerned with finding well-qualified employees for their organizations that they are equally thorough in their resume-reading approach.

This is not to say that there are not those who are less diligent in their reading. To the contrary, I am sure there are some who are much less thorough. Such individuals may be superficially impressed with these opening paragraphs and may elect to invite the candidate in for an employment interview with a less than a complete screening of the candidate's qualifications. In the better companies, however, this superficial approach to resume screening will quickly attract attention and the employment professional will soon be exposed as a nonprofessional. Poor resume screening will assuredly result in unnecessary interviews, wasting the valuable time of line managers and costing the company unnecessary money in the form of candidate travel reimbursement. Such inefficiencies will not long be tolerated, and careless employment managers may well find themselves in the unemployment line.

Of course there are well-qualified candidates who without professional guidance sometimes elect to use the functional employment resume. It is up to the employment manager, therefore, to thoroughly read the *entire* resume to determine whether or not the candidate possesses the prerequisite skills and qualifications sought by his or her company.

SOME CAUTIONS

Perhaps the biggest drawback of the functional resume is that it seems to be the format most frequently chosen by individuals who wish to disguise some flaw in their credentials. In fact, as an employment professional who has read several thousand resumes, I would estimate that in seven out of every ten cases functional resumes have intentionally been chosen by the employment candidate to camouflage such problems. Awareness of this history of deception causes most employment professionals to become suspicious when this particular format is used. The tendency is thus to read these resumes as if one were on a witch hunt. Energy and focus are directed toward finding out what is wrong with the candidate instead of being directed toward whether the candidate possesses the desired qualifications.

I have discussed my feelings concerning the functional resume with several other personnel executives and have frequently found that their feelings are generally similar to my own. In general, the consensus appears to be that if an employment candidate uses the functional resume format, he or she is probably attempting to hide one or more of the following facts:

1. *Job Hopper.* The applicant has worked for an abnormally high number of employers in a relatively short period of time and would therefore be a high employment risk.

2. *Older Worker.* The applicant is older and is attempting to hide this fact.

3. *Employment Gap.* There is an undesirable or unexplained gap or break in the candidate's employment history. Since this gap is frequently unexplained, it leads the employment executive to conjure up all kinds of undesirable explanations (for example: major illness, marital problems, alcoholism). Most of these spell high risk in the minds of the employment professional.

4. *Educational Deficit.* The applicant lacks the requisite educational credentials normally required for the position for which he or she is applying.

5. *Minimal Experience.* The candidate has little if any meaningful experience related to his or her job objective.

CHOOSING WHICH RESUME FORMAT TO USE

The rule of thumb for choosing between the chronological (both classical and linear) and the functional resume is fairly simple. If you have good credentials and a solid work history, I strongly recommend that you use a form of the chronological resume. Why cast unnecessary doubt on otherwise excellent credentials?

The reciprocal of the above statement is also true. If you have some good experience and major credentials, but also have one or more of the aforementioned problems, you may well want to seriously consider use of the functional resume format.

Resume Format Test

If you are still in doubt, perhaps the following practical test may be of assistance to you in deciding whether to use the functional resume format.

Answer each of the following questions with a yes or no.

1. Have you worked for four or more employers in the last 10 years? Yes _____ No_____

2. If employed for more than 10 years, have you averaged less than three years of service per employer? Yes_____ No_____

3. Have you been employed with more than seven companies during your professional career? Yes_____ No_____

4. Are you age 50 or older? Yes_____ No_____

5. Have you been unemployed (or substantially underemployed) for a period of more than one year in the last 10 years? Yes_____ No_____

6. Have you been unemployed (three months or longer) more than once in the last five years? Yes_____ No_____

7. Do you have the necessary educational qualifications normally required by most employers for your occupation? Yes_____ No_____

8. Do you lack the experience normally required by most employers for your profession? Yes_____ No_____

If you answered yes to one or more of the first three questions, by most standards you would be considered a job hopper. Use of the chronological resume would highlight this problem early in the resume and, in many cases, would result in your being screened out. Use of the functional resume under these circumstances is to your distinct advantage.

Although illegal, the screening out of candidates because of age continues. Some inroads have been made in this area and it appears that most employers are now paying less attention to age than they are to the qualifications of the individual. Unfortunately, however, age 50 appears to be a bench mark of sorts for many employers. Rightly or wrongly, many employers assume that a candidate who is age 50 or older lacks the necessary energy and vitality to be a productive worker. This fact suggests that candidates who are in this age group should attempt, where possible, to conceal this fact. The functional resume format can be particularly effective in accomplishing this objective.

Questions 5 and 6 have to do with gaps in the employment history. Should you have such a gap or should you have been substantially underemployed for a period of time, you may wish to employ the functional resume to focus on your strengths and accomplishments and to draw attention away from this employment gap.

If you answered no to question 7, chances are that use of the chronological resume may cause you to be screened out on the basis of educational credentials. The functional resume, on the other hand, gives you the opportunity to highlight your strengths and accomplishments early in the resume and may generate interest sufficient to cause the prospective employer to disregard your educational deficiency.

If question 8 was answered yes, you will probably do better in adopting the functional resume. Here again the reader's attention will be focused on what you consider your strengths and accomplishments rather than on your lack of specific job experience.

Having satisfied yourself that you are a candidate for use of the functional resume, you should continue on with the rest of this chapter. If as a result of the above test, however, you have concluded that you are not a candidate for this type resume, I would suggest that you use either the classical chronological or narrative chronological resume formats described in Chapters 5 and 7.

FUNCTIONAL RESUME COMPONENTS

Although there are several different styles or versions of the functional resume, the most frequently used format is comprised of the following components:

1. Heading
2. Qualification summary
3. Major accomplishments
4. Work history
5. Education

The order in which these components are presented on the resume can vary, but the sequence represented above is the most commonly used, accepted, and recommended format. The most frequent deviation from this recommended sequence, however, is the positioning of the education and work experience components. Note that the sample resume at the end of this chapter has been positioned such that education follows work experience, while other resumes in the chapter containing sample functional resumes (Chapter 10) have education positioned before work history.

The general rule for deciding whether to position education before or after work experience on the functional resume is this: Always position education after work history unless it will clearly serve to enhance your marketability to do otherwise.

In cases where the candidate has exceptionally strong educational credentials and this would be clearly recognized as the case by prospective employers, it would be in the candidate's best interest to position education prior to work history on the resume. Conversely, a candidate whose work history is extensive but whose educational credentials would be considered somewhat light by most employers' standards should definitely position education following the presentation of work history.

Additionally, it is recommended that younger candidates with good educational credentials and little work experience list education first. By contrast, older workers with considerable experience and persons who do not have strong educational credentials are generally best served by placing education after work experience.

For the older worker, placing education first in the resume can often draw attention to his or her age—something that should be avoided. This makes it easy for those employers who are in defiance of federal law, still practicing age discrimination, to weed you out. If you are successful in getting such employers to review your work experience and major accomplishments first, and thereby convince them that you have something of value to contribute to their organization, perhaps less attention will be paid to your age.

You are now ready to begin the step-by-step process of preparing the functional resume. The approach that we follow examines each resume component in some detail and provides some practical exercises that will assist you in developing each of these components. This is the same "kit" approach that was used earlier in this book in the preparation of the chronological resume. As with any kit, if you follow the step-by-step directions provided, you will conclude this chapter having prepared a logical, professional resume that will effectively portray and market your qualifications to prospective employers.

Heading

The resume heading consists of three parts: your full name, complete address, and home telephone number. Some sample resume headings follow:

DAVID C. JOHNSON
18 Smith Road
Richmond, Ohio 19870
Phone: (815) 852-4310

CAROLYN A. CRISWELL
401 East 7th Street
Knoxville, Tennessee 19760
Phone: Home (315) 769-6588
Office (315) 766-4233

Your name should be typed in capital letters and in bold type so that it stands out from the rest of the heading. Your address and telephone number, on the other hand, are typed in lower case. It is advisable to exclude your office telephone number from your resume unless you are in a position to accept employment-related telephone calls at your office. Should you be on a confidential voice mail system where you are the only one who can access your messages, this is likely not a problem. Listing your office telephone number on your resume, however, sometimes raises suspicion on the part of a prospective employer that you are "on the skids" with your current employer and that your current employer is cooperating with you in your job search. It is therefore advisable to avoid listing your office telephone number on your employment resume unless by excluding it you would be making it difficult for prospective employers to reach you.

Most employment managers do not mind placing telephone calls in the evening to prospective candidates. These managers can be encouraged to do so by inclusion of a simple request to call you at home in the evenings. Such a request can easily be inserted into your cover letter. For example, you might include a statement similar to the following in the cover letter that accompanies your resume.

> *I can usually be reached at my home telephone number during the evening hours after 8:00 P.M. In the event that you find this inconvenient and wish to contact me during business hours, my husband, George, will be pleased to relay your message. George can be reached at (315) 972-8051.*

Using the instructions provided above, try your hand at developing your own heading.

Summary

The purpose of the Summary section of the functional resume is twofold. First, it is intended to convey the breadth and scope of your experience as a professional. Second, it is intended to provide you with the opportunity to sell your key strengths. The overall intent is to hook the resume reader so that he or she will be encouraged to read further.

Let's now examine a few summary statements.

1. *Summary.* Marketing executive with over 20 years of experience in sales and marketing management. Excellent reputation as a creative, innovative manager capable of revitalizing old product lines and introducing new ones. Full range of marketing and sales experience to include: market research, market planning and analysis, advertising and promotion, sales, and sales management.

2. *Summary.* Accomplished human resources professional with over 25 years experience in all phases of human resources management. Excellent reputation as an individual who truly understands the relationship between human resource utilization and profitability. Full range of human resources experience includes: human resource planning, internal and external staffing, organization design and development, compensation and benefits, employee and labor relations, and public affairs.

3. *Summary.* Creative design engineer with 15 years experience in innovative design of high speed electromechanical devices. Well known for innovative, practical, and cost-effective designs that work. A real contributor to bottom-line results.

In reviewing these summary statements, you will note certain similarities. First, the initial sentence of each summary statement gives the writer's career/professional area and indicates the number of years of experience. The second sentence is used to market particular strengths possessed by the writer. The third sentence, as in the case of the marketing executive and human resources professional, can be used to further communicate the breadth of the writer's experience. As an option to this, as shown in the designer's summary statement, the resume writer can use this third sentence to further market some unique skill or fact that would likely prove valuable to the prospective employer.

Another similarity between these summary statements is that they are fairly concise. In preparing your summary statement, you should avoid lengthy, rambling paragraphs that will only serve to dilute your message to the prospective employer. The key to this section is to be concise while stating sufficient positive information to entice the reader to continue. Additionally, your summary statement should convince the prospective employer that you have something of value to contribute to their organization.

Note that these sample summary statements are not written in complete sentences. These statements are simply descriptive phrases that are intended to convey strong meaning in as few words as possible. They are short "bullets" much the same as you would find in magazine or newspaper advertising. As with such advertising copy, each is intended to convey value and to compel the reader to respond favorably.

Review of the sample summary statements will also reveal the lack of the articles "a" and "the." Each sentence begins with an adjective followed by a noun. Following this type of format will force you to write concise, brisk statements that have considerably more marketing impact than the normal sentence.

Now try your hand at writing your own sample summary statements. Try writing this statement three times with the idea of bringing about quantum improvement with each successive writing.

Major Accomplishments

The Major Accomplishments section is intended to point out specific accomplishments that you have realized during your professional career and to highlight these accomplishments in discrete, functional areas. The functional areas under which these accomplishments are highlighted are normally major subfunctions or subactivities of your profession. Some examples of these functional areas would be as follows:

Marketing Executive

1. Market research
2. Advertising and promotion
3. Marketing and sales management

Human Resources Executive

1. Human resource management
2. Labor negotiations
3. Employment
4. Compensation and benefits

Research Engineer

1. Conceptual design
2. Prototype development
3. Prototype testing
4. Redesign
5. Reduction to practice

In preparation for this section of your resume, make a detailed listing of all of the subfunctions relating to your career specialty. Think in terms of the major components of your present and past positions—the key functional areas for which you were accountable in each of your past positions. Having done this, you are now ready to develop a listing of your major accomplishments for each of the corresponding functional areas that you have listed.

A good exercise for stimulating your memory is to list each of your past employers in reverse chronological order, including each of the respective positions you have held. Starting with the most recent employer, make a list of the most significant results that you have realized—the most significant contributions you have made to each employer. As you list each of these major accomplishments, be sure to include, wherever possible, some kind of quantitative measurement that will serve to convey to the reader the significance of this result to your past employer. Think in terms of the savings in time and money that your accomplishments provided. Additionally, think in terms of other ways you have positively affected the profitability of your employer. In this regard, actions that you have taken to increase employee productivity, sales volume, and so on should certainly be included in the category of major accomplishments.

Although the procedure described may seem laborious, it will prove to be extremely worthwhile to you as you begin the job-hunting process. In addition to providing you with an excellent basis for the construction of your functional resume, this personal analysis of major accomplishments will provide you with the information and confidence necessary to perform well during the interview phase of your employment campaign. Take time therefore to carefully develop this inventory of major accomplishments.

After you have listed your major accomplishments by functional area, you are ready to begin to rework these for inclusion in the final draft of your functional resume. Before doing this, however, review the major accomplishments section of the sample resume contained at the end of this chapter. You will note that this area of the resume is comprised of only three functional areas: market research, advertising and promotion, and marketing and sales management. It is important that your resume contain no more than three or four functional areas which you plan to highlight. Listing more than four areas will serve to dilute the impact that is intended when using the functional resume. This intent is to highlight and market your major areas of strength. Listing more than four functional areas with accompanying major accomplishments may serve to give the resume reader the impression that you are a jack of all trades but master of none. The reader will begin to question the credibility of your accomplishments rather than being impressed with a carefully chosen few.

A careful review of your list of past employers and positions held will highlight your major accomplishments and contributions. Scanning these accomplishments will show that several are similar in nature and can fit nicely under the key functions that you have chosen to feature on the resume. Picking what appear to be the most prominent three or four subfunctions, put each of these subfunctions as a heading on a separate piece of paper. Then systematically go back over your employment history, extract each major accomplishment and add it to the page containing the functional heading under which it fits. In following this procedure you will soon see the major accomplishments section of your functional resume taking shape.

Your next step is to decide in what order these key functions should be listed in the major accomplishments section of your resume. There are two schools of thought relative to the order in which these functions should be listed. The first school of thought focuses on the old adage "lead from strength." This adage suggests that you should list that function in which you have made the greatest contributions and have realized the most significant accomplishments. This approach reasons that your most marketable or salient qualifications should be listed first since they are your areas of greatest strength and therefore are those areas that will be of greatest value to any prospective employer. The second school would argue that you should position that function first that most closely parallels your job-hunting objective. For example, if you are a human resources professional and are seeking a position as director of labor relations, you would obviously wish to cite your accomplishments in the area of labor relations first. Prospective employers looking for a director of labor relations are probably less concerned about your expertise in the area of compensation and benefits.

Both of the above schools of thought have their point. This may leave you a bit confused as to which function to list first. As a general rule of thumb, I would suggest listing first that function that most closely relates to your current career objective. However, should your accomplishments in this area be less than stellar, I would suggest listing your area of strongest accomplishment first without respect to job-hunting objective. The remaining functional areas should be listed in a priority sequence based upon the significance of the accomplishments in each of these respective functions.

In this section of your resume, writing style can be extremely important if you wish to have maximum impact on the reader. I have extracted two functions from the major accomplishments section of the resume contained at the end of this chapter for your review. The first is market research:

—Investigated and analyzed European market for U.S. lumber export with resultant successful market entry.

—Worked closely with R&D in development of consumer mini pocket calculator. Careful design of test market and resultant market feedback assured successful product development and subsequent market entry ($5 million sales in 2 years).

—Developed market research computer model to forecast 10-year market projection for microwave ovens.

The second function is advertising and promotion:

—Coordinated company efforts with major New York City consumer advertising agency to develop effective campaign to revitalize failing product line (fishing reels). Campaign expenditure ($2 million) yielded annual increase in sales of $4.1 million in 1 year.

—Developed creative special value coupon and supporting advertising campaign that increased annual sales volume for photographic film product line by 35% over 2-year period.

In reviewing these accomplishments you will note that each statement begins with a verb or action word. By starting most of your statements with a verb or action word, you will be forced to be brief, concise, and to the point in your statements. Additionally, you will be forced to state specific results and accomplishments that you contributed.

To assist you in getting started with this effective resume-writing technique, a list of key verbs or action words has been provided at the end of this chapter. You are encouraged to refer to this list and to make use of these verbs while developing this section of your functional employment resume.

Another effective technique to employ in developing the Major Accomplishments section of your resume is to use quantitative descriptions, where these serve to highlight your specific accomplishments and contributions. For example, consider the following:

Wrong   Increased sales significantly in first year.

Right   Increased sales by 50% from $100 to $150 million in first year alone.

Wrong   Developed new equipment design that saved the company a lot of money.

Right   Developed new plastic extrusion equipment design resulting in $1 million company savings in 1995 alone.

Wrong   Developed and installed computerized brand costing system resulting in substantial payroll savings.

Right   Developed and installed computerized brand costing system resulting in elimination of 12 positions and annual payroll savings of $385,000.

You are now ready to develop the Major Accomplishments section of your resume. Use the format illustrated here to carefully develop each of the functions you wish to highlight with specific accomplishments. Remember to begin each of your statements with an action word and to use quantitative descriptions wherever possible. Although you will wish to highlight only three or four functional areas, rewrite each functional area at least twice. Experiment by attempting to upgrade your second writing of each function by being more concise and choosing words that have greater impact.

Functional Area: _____

Accomplishments: _____

1. _____

   _____

2. _____

   _____

3. _____

   _____

4. _____

   _____

Functional area:_____

Accomplishments:_____

1. _____

_____

2. _____

_____

3. _____

_____

4. _____

_____

Work History

The Work History section of the resume should be organized in reverse chronological order. Shown first should be your most recent employer, second, your second most recent employer, and so forth back to your original employer. Shown on the left should be dates of your employment, when you began and when you left. Adjacent to these dates should be the name of the employer followed by the position or positions held. The following work history section has been extracted from the sample functional resume at the end of the chapter.

WORK HISTORY:

1997 to Present   **U.S. Paper & Wood Products**
Manager of Corporate Marketing

1995 to 1997   **Photo Films International**
National Sales Manager

1993 to 1995	**Self-Employed**
	Marketing Consultant

1992 to 1993	**Microwave Ovens, Inc.**
	Manager of Market Research

1991 to 1992	**Self-Employed**
	Marketing Consultant

1977 to 1991	**National Calculators, Inc.**	
	Director of Marketing	(1989–1991)
	National Sales Manager	(1985–1989)
	Regional Sales Manager	(1982–1985)
	Salesperson	(1977–1982)

There is nothing sacred about the order of position held and employer in this section of the resume. When the candidate has been employed by major corporations and highlighting this fact could prove to the candidate's advantage from a marketing standpoint, Company Name should be listed first with job title to follow on the next line. The answer to sequence is really marketability. List first, either job title or employer, whichever you feel consistently gives you the greatest advantage from a marketability standpoint.

Listing position first followed by employer will work well as long as you have held only one position with each employer. In those cases where you have held multiple positions with a single employer, however, you will need to list employer first, followed by the positions held. (Note the National Calculators, Inc. section of the above sample Work History.) You will note that National Calculators, Inc. is listed first, with the positions held listed following the company name. You will also note that the dates of the positions held at National Calculator are shown in brackets following each of the job titles of the positions held.

The Work History section of the resume is intended to be simple. No additional information other than company name and job title should be included in this section. Space is provided below for you to develop the Work History section of your own functional resume.

From: _____ To: _____   Employer: _____

_____

Job Title: _____

_____

From: _____ To: _____   Employer: _____

_____

Job Title: _____

_____

From: _____ To: _____   Employer: _____

_____

Job Title: _____

_____

From: _____ To: _____   Employer: _____

_____

Job Title: _____

_____

From: _____ To: _____   Employer: _____

_____

Job Title: _____

_____

From: _____ To: _____   Employer: _____

_____

Job Title: _____

_____

Education

The Education section of a functional resume should include the following items:

1. Degree awarded
2. School attended
3. Year of graduation
4. Major field of concentration
5. Grade point average (G.P.A.) (List only if good and education is recent)
6. Honoraries

Some sample education statements have been provided below for your reference.

1. <u>Education:</u> Ph.D., Massachusetts Institute of
   Technology, 1997
   Major: Chemical Engineering

   M.S., Rochester Institute of Technology, 1995
   Major: Chemical Engineering
   G.P.A. 3.85/4.0

   B.S., Rochester Institute of Technology, 1993
   Major: Chemical Engineering
   G.P.A. 3.75/4.0

2. <u>Education:</u> M.S., University of Pennsylvania, 1996
   Major: Statistics
   G.P.A. 3.5/4.0
   Dixon Mathematics Scholarship

   B.S., Drexel University, 1994
   Major: Mathematics
   G.P.A. 3.6/4.0
   Kettering Award (Mathematics Honorary Award)

3. <u>Education:</u> M.S., University of Michigan, 1996
   Major: Mechanical Engineering

G.P.A. 3.4/4.0
Sloan Engineering Scholarships

B.S., University of Maryland, 1995
Major: Mechanical Engineering
G.P.A. 3.4/4.0
Tau Beta Pi (Engineering Honorary)

4. <u>Education:</u>   B.A., North Carolina State University, 1996
Major: Business Administration

Generally, unless you are a recent college graduate, you should leave little space for the Education section of your employment resume. The general rule to be followed in developing this section of the resume is "The further along you are in your professional career, the less important are your educational credentials and the more important are your work experience and specific accomplishments." Additionally, since you have chosen the functional resume for the purpose of highlighting your experience and accomplishments, it stands to reason that the Education section of the resume will be de-emphasized.

You now can develop the Education portion of your resume using the instructions provided.

Miscellaneous

In almost all cases, extracurricular activities and hobbies should be completely excluded from the resume unless they are directly related to your qualifications for the position you seek. On occasion, however, there may be some advantage to listing a specific extracurricular activity or hobby, that is, if it further enhances your marketability to a specific employer. For example, if you are applying for a position with a sporting goods manufacturer, your athletic interests may be to your advantage. Likewise, if you are applying to a company that places a lot of stress on providing leadership in your local community, you may want to include such information as (1) President, Parent Teachers Organization, (2) Chairperson, March of Dimes Campaign,

(3) President, School Board. The above are carefully chosen exceptions to the rule. In general, however, hobbies and extracurricular activities are specifically excluded from the modern resume.

In the case of technical professionals, such things as publications, papers, and patents can be important. This is particularly true for items that are directly related to the professional's employment qualifications. These may help to increase the candidate's marketability to prospective employers. List only those items that are truly important and meaningful, however, and do not list minor or insignificant publications.

BRUCE B. CHAMBERS
813 Locust Lane
Lake City, Texas 09413
Phone: (217) 855-3939

SUMMARY

Marketing executive with over 20 years experience in sales and marketing management. Excellent reputation as a creative, innovative manager capable of successfully revitalizing old product lines and introducing new. Full range of marketing and sales experience to include: market research, market planning & analysis, advertising & promotion, sales, and sales management.

MAJOR ACCOMPLISHMENTS

Market Research
* Investigated and analyzed European market for U.S. lumber export with resultant successful market entry.
* Worked closely with R&D in development of consumer mini-pocket calculator. Careful design of test market and resultant market feedback assured successful product development and subsequent market entry ($5 million sales in two years).
* Developed market research computer model to forecast ten-year market projection for microwave ovens.

Advertising & Promotion
* Coordinated company efforts with major New York City consumer advertising agency to develop effective campaign to revitalize failing product line (fishing reels). Campaign expenditure ($2 million) yielded annual increase in sales of $4.1 million in one year.
* Developed creative special value coupon and supportive advertising campaign that increased annual sales volume for photographic film product line by 35% over two-year period.

Marketing & Sales Management
* Managed national sales organization of 95 employees (ten regional managers and 75 salespersons) in the sale of consumer photographic film to wholesale and retail trade.
* Directed Corporate Marketing Staff (25 employees) in the development of all marketing plans and strategies for manufacturer of consumer hardware (annual sales volume $500 million).
* Successfully organized, trained and motivated new national sales organization of 45 employees for manufacture of consumer calculators. Sales reached $20 million in four years.

WORK HISTORY

U.S. PAPER & WOOD PRODUCTS Manager of Corporate Marketing	**1997 to Present**
PHOTO FILMS INTERNATIONAL National Sales Manager	**1995 to 1997**
SELF EMPLOYED Marketing Consultant	**1993 to 1995**
MICRO OVENS, INC. Manager of Market Research	**1992 to 1993**
SELF EMPLOYED Marketing Consultant	**1991 to 1992**

NATIONAL CALCULATORS, INC.   **1977 to 1991**
Director of Marketing   (1989 - 1991)
National Sales Manager   (1985 - 1989)
Regional Sales Manager   (1982 - 1985)
Salesperson   (1977 - 1982)

EDUCATION

B.A.,   Utah State University, 1977
Major: Business Administration

10

SAMPLE FUNCTIONAL RESUMES

This chapter contains a total of 20 sample functional resumes for your review and reference. You will note in reviewing these samples that there are 10 separate business disciplines or functions represented. These 10 disciplines represent a logical functional breakdown of a typical manufacturing company and thus provide an excellent cross section of business functions. For each of these 10 functions you will find two sample resumes. The first is the resume of a fairly experienced, senior individual, with the second resume representing a less experienced, junior person.

The following Resume Locator should be helpful in locating those sample resumes that are of greater interest to you.

Resume Locator

	Experience Level	
	---	---
Field or Discipline	*Senior Person*	*Junior Person*
	(Pages)	(Pages)
Accounting	181	183
Engineering	184	186
Finance	188	190
Human Resources	191	193
Information Services	195	197
Logistics	198	200
Marketing and Sales	201	203
Operations	204	206
Procurement	207	209
Technology	210	212

Sample Functional Resume—Accounting

JOHN R. SMITH
119 South Maynard Road
Willingham, MA 94375
Phone: (216) 552-8879

SUMMARY

Accounting executive with over 21 years experience in increasingly responsible positions. Excellent reputation as creative, innovative and results-oriented senior manager who gets things done. Full rage of accounting experience includes: capital and operating budgets, financial statements, accounting policies and procedures, auditing, taxes, general and cost accounting, accounts receivable, accounts payable and credit. Noted for ability to apply computer technology in streamlining controllership operations.

MAJOR ACCOMPLISHMENTS

General Accounting
- Reviewed and revamped accounting procedures of Corporate Accounting Department with resultant annual savings of $1.2 million.
- Computerized consolidation and analysis of monthly and year-end financial statements saving 8,000 manhours annually and reducing turnaround time on closings by 50%.
- Managed a five-person task force which provided the first breakout of individual division P&L statements for a $320 million corporation.

Cost Accounting
- Developed/implemented computerized materials cost tracking system which resulted in increased raw material turnover with annual savings estimated at $500,000.
- Organized and managed cost accounting procedures task force which conducted in-depth review of cost accounting procedures and developed standard procedures manual for use by all manufacturing plants in four months.
- Developed computer model for effectively estimating material costs for new electronic circuit brands (proven accuracy of + or - 1%).

Finance
- Initiated creative lease-back arrangements with foreign corporation with resultant $500,000 annual savings.
- Raised necessary capital to support major capital expansion program ($35 million) at unusually favorable rates.
- Organized, hired and trained company's first Financial Planning Department.

WORK HISTORY

SMITH DAVIDSON CORPORATION (Corporate Offices)   **1996 to Present**
Assistant to Corporate Controller

ZEBARD METAL CONTAINER CORPORATION (Corporate Offices)   **1993 to 1996**
Manager of Corporate Accounting   (1994 - 1996)
Senior Accountant   (1993 - 1994)

BARLEY & JOHNSON, INC. (Richmond, VA)   **1983 to 1993**
Senior Accountant   (1989 - 1993)
Accountant   (1983 - 1989)

JORDAN ELECTRONICS, INC. (Woodbury Plant)   **1979 to 1983**
Senior Cost Accountant   (1981 - 1983)
Cost Accountant   (1979 - 1981)

EDUCATION

M.B.A., University of Northern Ohio, 1979
Major: Accounting/Finance
         Bettinger Scholarship

B.A.,   Business Administration, Cannon College, 1977
Major: Accounting
         Magna Cum Laude

CPA.,   May 1980

Sample Functional Resume—Accounting

DAVID P. BERRINGTON
39 Fowler Place, Apt. 4-C
Syracuse, New York 09872
Phone: (814) 972-4454

SUMMARY

Highly-motivated accounting professional with excellent record of growth and accomplishment. Thoroughly trained and ready for first supervisory assignment. Solid professional cost accounting foundation and excellent educational credentials.

MAJOR ACCOMPLISHMENTS

Material Costs
- Developed procedure for material cost breakout of sophisticated electronic Rocker Assembly worth savings of $50,000 annually.
- Developed computerized cost accounting and analysis system for tracking material consumption during manufacture of electrical harnesses with $115,000 annual savings in reduced materials inventory.

Labor Costs
- Initiated major projects to identify labor costs for discrete manufacturing operation. Worked with Industrial Engineering to effect labor savings of $85,000 annually.
- Thoroughly experienced in all aspects of labor cost analysis.

Management
- Successfully trained and directed the daily work activity of two new Cost Accountants.

WORK HISTORY

MINUTEMAN ELECTRONICS (Syracuse Plant)   **1994 to Present**
Senior Cost Accountant   (1996 - Present)
Cost Accountant   (1994 - 1996)

EDUCATION

M.A.,	Business, Luster University, 1994
Major:	Accounting
	Syracuse Businessman Fellowship
B.A.,	Business Administration, Syracuse University, 1992
Major:	Accounting G.P.A. 3.45/4.0
Minor:	Finance G.P.A. 3.75/4.0
	Davidson Scholarship (4 years)
Activities:	President, Accounting Honorary Society
	President, Student Government Association

PETER B. JOHNSON
1835 Linwood Place
Linwood NJ 45973
Phone: (201) 447-2424 (H)
(201) 447-8842 (O)

SUMMARY

Engineering executive with over 16 years of experience in positions of increasing responsibility in major facility engineering for Fortune 200 manufacturer of residential and commercial heating and air conditioning equipment. Reputation for consistently beating time deadlines and budgets on major projects resulting in bottom line savings in the millions.

MAJOR ACCOMPLISHMENTS

Engineering Management

- Managed two-year, $850 million expansion program including successful installation and start-up of two complete residential air conditioning manufacturing plants.
- Managed 120 employee Corporate Engineering Department for Fortune 200 manufacturer of heating and air conditioning equipment ($450 million annual budget).
- Directed 80 employee Mechanical Engineering Section with annual budget of $250 million.
- Managed 20 employee Instrumentation and Control Engineering Department with responsibility for installation and start-up of computer control systems.

Project Savings
- Brought largest expansion program in Company's history ($850 million) in three months early and $110 million under budget.
- Completed $245 million commercial heating manufacturing equipment installation project two months early with savings estimated at $12.5 million.
- Completed all project assignments ahead of schedule and under budget.

Technologies
- Fabrication and assembly of commercial and residential air conditioning equipment.
- Fabrication and assembly of commercial and residential heating equipment.
- Engineering application of instrumentation and control systems (including minicomputers and microprocessors) to equipment fabrication and assembly lines.
- Engineering of large scale bio-mass boiler power generation systems.

WORK HISTORY

BERRINGTON MANUFACTURING, INC. (Corporate Engineering)   **1985 to Present**
Vice President of Engineering   (1997 - Present)
Director, Mechanical Engineering   (1993 - 1997)
Manager, Instrumentation & Control Engineering   (1987 - 1993)
Senior Project Engineer, Heating   (1985 - 1987)

WILCOX ENGINEERING SYSTEMS, INC. (Corporate Engineering)   **1983 to 1985**
Project Engineer

EDUCATION

M.S.   University of Michigan, 1983
Major: Mechanical Engineering
              Wainwright Scholarship

B.S.,   University of Michigan, 1981
Major: Mechanical Engineering
              Magna Cum Laude
              Shearson Scholarship (4 years)

              Activities: President, Tau Beta Psi

Sample Functional Resume—Engineering

MARTIN S. SAMPSON
17 Beachwood Lane
Fort Wayne, IN 37655
Phone: (513) 556-7720

SUMMARY

High-energy, results-oriented Senior Project Engineer with five years experience in design, installation, start-up and debugging of aluminum manufacturing processes and equipment. Excellent reputation for consistently bringing projects in on time and below budget.

MAJOR ACCOMPLISHMENTS

Facility Design
- Managed mechanical design of $20 million aluminum furnace complex. Project completed on time and 10% under budget.
- Managed mechanical design of $12 million furnace and associated material handling equipment. Project is on time and under budget.
- Designed power and free conveyor material handling equipment systems for several plant locations.

Facility Improvements
- Redesigned refractory lining in a flash calciner process to reduce heat loss by 30% in existing units and 50% in new units.
- Designed innovative material handling system which allows 50% reduction in time to convert process from one product to another.
- Installed waste heat boilers on two furnaces resulting in annual steam production valued at $400,000 annually.

Design Innovations
- Initiated use of computer assisted design to draw standard furnace designs with estimated savings of 40% in design engineering phase.
- Developed innovative furnace design projected to decrease process energy requirements by 10% annually.

WORK HISTORY

ARROW ALUMINUM CO., INC. (Corporate Engineering)   **1994 to Present**
Senior Project Engineer   (1996 - Present)
Project Engineer   (1994 - 1996)

EDUCATION

B.S.,   Drexel University, 1994
Major: Mechanical Engineering   G.P.A. 3.4/4.0
             Cum Laude Graduate

             Member, Tau Beta Psi
             Vice President, Amer. Society of Mechanical Engineers

AFFILIATIONS

American Society of mechanical Engineers
Association of Aluminum Manufacturing Engineers

STEPHEN C. TEMPLE
600 Ferrington Road, NW
Chicago, IL 55733
Phone: (513) 772-6464

SUMMARY

Senior financial executive with 13 years experience with $4 billion, Fortune 100 manufacturer of earth moving and excavation equipment. Heavily experienced in all aspects of both domestic and international financial planning. Demonstrated capability to meet major capital requirements at exceptionally favorable rates and terms.

MAJOR ACCOMPLISHMENTS

Capital Acquisition
- Developed five-year funding strategy to finance $3.1 billion capital expansion program. Capital acquired on average of 2% below market rate. Financial rating maintained despite substantial increase in long-term debt.
- Successfully manage annual capital requirements of $400 to $600 million at very favorable rates and terms.
- Secured $185 million loan for Italian affiliate at exceptionally favorable rate and term.

Financial Planning
- Developed financial strategy to support $3.1 billion, five-year expansion program.
- Provide leadership in the development of planning strategy to support annual capital requirements of $400 to $600 million.
- Developed and implemented computer model to assist five domestic divisions in forecasting and planning financial requirements as part of five-year plan.

Investor Relations
- Cultivated many key financial contacts in a wide range of financial institutions in both the domestic and international markets.
- Excellent rapport with key outside analysts with resultant maintenance of top financial ratings despite substantially increased long-term debt.

WORK HISTORY

TEXTRON INTERNATIONAL CORPORATION (Corporate Offices)   **1987 to Present**
Vice President and Treasurer   (1997 - Present)
Director of Corporate Finance   (1993 - 1997)
Senior Analyst, Corporate Finance   (1990 - 1993)
Analyst, Corporate Finance   (1987 - 1990)

EDUCATION

M.B.A.,   Wharton School, University of Pennsylvania, 1987
Major: Finance

B.A.,   Pennsylvania State University, 1985
Major: Financial Management
Minor: Economics
              Magna Cum Laude

Sample Functional Resume—Finance

JANET N. MORSE
300 Mocking Bird Lane
Newtown Square, PA 19073
Phone: (610) 775-5757

SUMMARY

Accomplished, energetic Senior Financial Analyst with outstanding educational credentials and six years experience in financial planning with major aerospace contractor. Ability to manage financial planning projects from cost estimate to placement of funding for programs in the $200 to $400 million range.

MAJOR ACCOMPLISHMENTS

Capital Planning
* Developed manufacturing cost estimates and funding requirements for sophisticated missile guidance systems ($200 to $400 million range).
* Developed computer model to automate process for performing manufacturing cost estimates reducing manual effort by 80%.
* Developed several computer models to support long-range financial planning process.

Capital Acquisition
* Provided capital funding for $1.5 billion of expansion programs over five-year period.
* Received six government commendations for outstanding work in financial planning.

WORK HISTORY

DELTRON AEROSPACE, INC. (Corporate Offices)   **1992 to Present**
Senior Financial Analyst   (1995 - Present)
Financial Analyst   (1993 - 1995)
Analyst   (1992 - 1993)

SEPTRAM INTERSCIENCE, INC. (Corporate Offices)   **1991 to 1992**
Planning Analyst

EDUCATION

M.B.A.,   Harvard University Business School, 1991
Major: Financial Planning

B.S.,   Cornell University, 1989
Major: Management Science
           Laude
           Torrington Computer Scholarship (4 years)

DAWN M. MARKS
300 Ollinger Avenue
Richmond, Virginia 23375
Phone: (314) 872-4467

SUMMARY

Senior level human resources executive with over 14 years experience in full range of human resources functions. Strong appreciation for the relationship between good human resource management and profitability. Enjoy excellent reputation for innovative programs designed to maximize human productivity and overall organization effectiveness.

MAJOR ACCOMPLISHMENTS

Human Resource Planning
- Designed and installed company's first human resource information system resulting in estimated annual savings of $500,000 in time and productivity.
- Designed and implemented human resources computer model providing first-time link between human resources planning and business planning.

Employee Productivity
- Developed and implemented bold new management incentive system credited with significant morale improvement and substantially increased management productivity.
- Designed and installed professional exempt employee internal posting system recognized as a key factor in improving the overall morale and productivity of professional employees.

Employee Staffing
- Successfully directed major hiring campaign resulting in the employment of 90 engineers in five months to meet stringent deadline in support of major capital expansion programs.
- Saved $750,000 per year in recruiting costs through the implementation of effective prescreening and recruiting techniques.
- Implemented unique candidate assessment process credited with substantial improvement in the quality of employee assessment and selection.

Management
- Managed Corporate Human Resources Department of 52 employees with annual budget of $3.2 million.
- Managed Corporate Staffing Department of eight employees and annual budget of $2.1 million.

WORK HISTORY

CARSON MANUFACTURING CO., INC. (Corporate Offices)   **1991 to Present**
Director of Human Resources   (1996 - Present)
Manager Corporate Staffing   (1993 - 1996)
Manager of Administrative Staffing   (1991 - 1993)

BARSOM, CLIFFORD AND JANSEN, INC. (Corporate Offices)   **1983 to 1991**
Senior Consultant   (1987 - 1991)
Consultant   (1983 - 1987)

EDUCATION

M.B.A.,   Michigan State University, 1983
Major: Human Resource Management
Thesis: "The Role of Performance Feedback in the
               Motivation of Professional Employees"

B.A.,   Michigan State University, 1981
Major: Human Resource Management
               Cum Laude
               Salem Scholarship (4 years)

DAVID R. JEFFRIES
36 Tartan Road, SW
Birmingham, Alabama 75663
Phone: (314) 872-5533

SUMMARY

Creative employment manager with over five years experience at the corporate and division levels. Reputation for recruiting the hard-to-find. Thoroughly versed in all aspects of recruiting and employment with excellent track record for achieving results.

MAJOR ACCOMPLISHMENTS

College Recruiting
- Developed and successfully directed first corporate-wide college recruiting effort covering six divisions and 14 manufacturing plants.
- Prepared and distributed the "College Recruiters Guide" - a complete "how to" guide for the new recruiter.
- Conducted corporate-wide recruiter training program designed to improve the interviewing and selection skills of campus recruiters.
- Developed company's first integrated college relations program including all divisions. Highly effective programs begun at 18 colleges and universities in first year alone.

Technical Recruiting
- Developed novel, creative approaches to locating hard-to-find technical scientists and engineers making use of computerized patent database.
- Used direct mail for first time in the recruitment of technical personnel. Bought computer printed mailing lists and initiated letter campaign that resulted in 30 engineering hires in two months at a total cost of $3,000.

Recruiting Costs
- Reduced the average cost per hire from $4,000 to $2,000 in three years -- a 50% decrease!
- Reduced candidate travel expense by 35% through more extensive use of telephone prescreening.
- Reduced the offer-to-hire ratio to an acceptance rate of 80%.

WORK HISTORY

COMSTAR MANUFACTURING CO., INC. (Corporate Offices)   **1990 to Present**
Corporate Employment Manager - Operations Employment (1995 - Present)
Manager of Employment Services   (1992 - 1995)
Plant Human Resources Manager   (1990 - 1992)

JOHNSON AND BARTON, INC. (Westerly Plant)   **1989 to 1990**
Assistant Personnel Manager

BILTMORE ELECTRONICS, INC. (Westerly Plant)   **1986 to 1989**
Human Resources Assistant

EDUCATION

B.A.,   University of Alabama, 1986
Major: Business Administration

JEFFREY A. MORSE
225 Highland Road
Clifton, NJ 18337
Phone: (609) 377-9787

SUMMARY

Information services executive with over 15 years experience in all phases of IS work. Currently Director of IS for $2 billion, Fortune 200 corporation. Strong strategic and leadership skills in planning and implementing information systems that contribute to company profitability.

MAJOR ACCOMPLISHMENTS

Planning
- Developed and implemented first five-year corporate information systems strategic plan for Fortune 200 manufacturer.
- Developed long-range information requirements plans for five key business functions. including: Manufacturing, Human Resources, Controllers, Finance and Procurement.

Project Implementation
- Successfully directed development and start-up of $7 million system for control of the sales forecasting, production scheduling and materials management functions with estimated annual savings of $6 million. Project completed three months early and 20% under budget.
- Delivered numerous systems ahead of schedule and under budget including the following major projects: Human Resource Information System, Payroll System, Production Scheduling System, Finished Goods Inventory Control System and Raw Materials & Vital Supplies Control System.

Management
- Directed 60 employee ($8 million budget) Corporate IS function for Fortune 200 corporation.
- Managed eight to 12 project managers and an annual budget of $5 million in corporate-wide implementation of information systems projects.
- Managed six professionals in development of long range information systems plans for functional clients.

WORK HISTORY

__CORBOTT MANUFACTURING CO., INC.__ (Corporate Offices)   __1988 to Present__
Director of Information Management Services·   (1997 - Present)
Corporate Project Manager   (1995 - 1997)
Manager of Client Planning Services   (1991 - 1995)
Senior Programmer Analyst   (1988 - 1991)

__MONTGOMERY CORPORATION__ (Corporate Offices)   __1986 to 1988__
Programmer Analyst

EDUCATION

Ph.D., Cornell University, 1986
Major: Computer Science

M.S.,   Cornell University, 1984
Major: Computer Science
        Data Resources Scholarship (2 years)

B.S.,   Lawrence University, 1982
Major: Mathematics
        Pennington Scholarship (4 years)

Sample Functional Resume—Information Services

SANDRA D. THOMPSON
32 East March Street
Thornton, Michigan 77599
Phone: (817) 552-9494

SUMMARY

Research and development programmer analyst with three years experience in providing programming support to development engineers in the development of state-of-the-art communications controller. Proficient in the use of data analyzer type equipment for studies and troubleshooting network problems.

TECHNICAL HIGHLIGHTS

- In-depth knowledge of the SNA/ACP/NCP functions of a communications controller in a PEP environment.

- Proficiency in SNA/ACP/NCP internals.

- Proficiency with SDLC, various trace facilities, ALC and TSO/WYLBUR/SPF.

- Expert in use of data analyzer equipment

WORK HISTORY

TRANSCON SYSTEMS LABORATORIES, INC. (Corporate R&D)   **1996 to Present**
Programmer Analyst

EDUCATION

M.S.,   Massachusetts Institute of Technology, 1996
Major: Computer Science
            Ransin Laboratory Fellowship (2 years)

B.S.,   Massachusetts Institute of Technology, 1994
Major: Computer Science   G.P.A. 3.85/4.0
Minor: Mathematics   G.P.A. 3.78/4.0
            Mattson Foundation Scholarship (4 years)

            Activities: President, Computer Science Society
                           Vice President, Mathematics Honorary

KEVIN P. BURTRAM
32 Worrington Lane, SW
Dallas, TX 33755
Phone: (719) 377-2424

SUMMARY

Senior level logistics executive with demonstrated ability to effectively organize and lead logistics function that employs state-of-the-art concepts and realizes significant contribution to bottom line results. Leadership in the application of computer and quantitative techniques that streamline operations and add substantial profits.

MAJOR ACCOMPLISHMENTS

Management
- Director of Logistics for Fortune 500, $1.4 billion corporation. Manage eight warehouses, 750 employees and annual budget of $125 million.
- Managed Corporate Distribution function for $850 million beverage bottler -- 250 employees, budget $85 million.
- Functions managed include both Warehousing and Transportation.

Cost Savings
- $18 million per year through computerization of order entry and distribution planning system.
- $10.2 million per year through regional consolidation of leased warehouse facilities.
- $5 million per year through development of computer model for use in determining best carrier and routing.
- $4.7 million per year through installation of automatic palletizers and computer controlled conveyor system.
- $3.9 million per year through corporate-wide negotiation of rail carrier rates.

Information Systems Applications
- Designed corporate order entry and distribution planning system.
- Installed computer controlled conveyor system and automatic palletizers.
- Implemented use of computer model for determination of best shipping point for best delivery and cost by order received.

WORK HISTORY

HERRINGER FOOD PROCESSING. INC. (Corporate Offices)   **1996 to Present**
Director of Logistics

THE BOSTON BEVERAGE COMPANY (Corporate Offices)   **1987 to 1996**
Distribution Manager   (1994 - 1996)
Senior Distribution Analyst   (1991 - 1994)
Distribution Analyst   (1987 - 1991)

EDUCATION

M.S.,   Georgia Institute of Technology, 1987
Major: Industrial Engineering
             Weller Scholarship (2 years)

B.S.,   Texas A&M, 1985
Major: Industrial Engineering
             Hanson Oil Company Scholarship (4 years)

PETER B. DIRKSON
18 Ocean View Road
Clearview Beach, California 77533
Phone: (714) 377-2525

SUMMARY

Ambitious, results-oriented logistics manager with over 12 years experience in all phases of warehousing and transportation. Demonstrated track record of translating technical knowledge and leadership into bottom line results. Fully qualified and eager to run logistics function of medium-sized company.

MAJOR ACCOMPLISHMENTS

Management
- Managed Corporate Warehousing function for $300 million manufacturer of dog food (150 employees, 12 warehouses, $32 million budget).
- Managed Corporate Distribution Center for $120 million manufacturer of metal fasteners (65 employees, $12 million trucking company, 85 trucks).

Cost Savings
- $2.1 million per year in shipping costs for truck shipments through greater use of "gypsy" carriers.
- $450,000 per year through packaging redesign allowing 10% more product to be shipped per railcar.
- $320,000 through renegotiation of warehouse leases.
- $300,000 per year through installation of extendable power conveyors for truck loading.
- $135,000 per year through redesign of warehouse storage pattern.
- $115,000 per year in reduced product damage through product handling training for warehouse crews.

WORK HISTORY

ROVER DOG FOOD COMPANY, INC. (Corporate Offices)   **1996 to Present**
Manager of Warehousing

HORSHAW FASTENER MANUFACTURING CO. (Fairfield Plant)   **1989 to 1996**
Distribution Center Manager   (1994 - 1996)
Shipping Manager   (1989 - 1994)

DEITRICK TRUCKING COMPANY (Fairfield Terminal)   **1986 to 1989**
Dispatcher

EDUCATION

B.A.,   Anderson College, 1986
Major: Business Administration

Sample Functional Resume—Marketing & Sales

SCOTT M. BEATTY
900 Lordon Avenue, SW
Atlanta, Georgia 57994
Phone: (912) 774-3434

SUMMARY

High-energy, results-oriented sales and marketing executive with over 14 years of demonstrated achievement in all phases of marketing and sales. Excellent track record of bottom line results. Noted for innovative ideas that dramatically increase sales volume and establish brand leadership in the marketplace.

MAJOR ACCOMPLISHMENTS

Marketing
- Established unique network of dealerships which catapulted company to number one in European sales in specialty resins. Export sales increased 75% to $225 million in two years.
- Led national roll-out of new low-viscosity resin product accounting for $150 million new sales in first year.
- Introduced eight major new products accounting for increase in total sales of 40% ($210 million) in less than four years.
- Realized a 225% increase in sales volume of old product in two years through repositioning of product in market and creative advertising program.
- Conducted market research resulting in successful recommendation to increase price of major product by 20% with no loss in sales volume.

Management
- Directed 115 employee marketing and sales organization for major chemical specialties manufacturer (annual sales $725 million).
- Managed 95 employee marketing and sales function for $525 million manufacturer of chemical specialties.
- Managed five-employee brand management function.

Sales
- Increased sales by 15% in one year while selling chemical specialties to pharmaceutical industry in four-state area.
- Received national sales award for greatest sales volume increase for years 1986, 1987 and 1988.

WORK HISTORY

CORRDIGAN CHEMICALS, INC. (Corporate Offices)   **1997 to Present**
Director of Marketing

STANTON CHEMICAL SPECIALTIES, INC. (Corporate Offices)   **1989 to 1997**
Director of Marketing and Sales   (1993 - 1997)
Marketing Brand Manager   (1991 - 1993)
Associate Brand Manager   (1989 - 1991)

CRISWELL CHEMICALS CORPORATION (District Sales Office)   **1984 to 1989**
Senior Sales Representative   (1988 - 1989)
Sales Representative   (1984 - 1988)

EDUCATION

M.B.A.,   University of Chicago, 1984
Major: Marketing

B.S.,   Syracuse University, 1982
Major: Chemistry

Activities: President of Chemical Society

ALLAN D. MARKS
100 Cedar Road
Clinton, Michigan 77229
Phone: (713) 559-0085

SUMMARY

Creative sales professional with over six years of experience in selling complex business systems requiring exceptional application sales skills. Demonstrated ability to successfully introduce new business machine product lines involving complex business and institutional applications.

MAJOR ACCOMPLISHMENTS

New Product Introduction
- Successfully launched and marketed world's first updatable microfilm record keeping and retrieval system with sales now approaching $100 million.
- Sold and developed first banking industry application for new microfilm storage system. Annual sales now $300 million.

Equipment Sales
- Increased sales of new microfilm systems by 300% in last two years.
- Developed and trained dealership network increasing sales of microfilm and other specialty photo-imaging films from $1.8 million to $5.2 million in two years. -- a 189% increase!

Marketing
- Worked as part of venture team in the test marketing of new updatable microfilm record keeping system. Work resulted in highly successful marketing strategy.

WORK HISTORY

MICRO GRAPHICS, INC. (Detroit Regional Office)   **1991 to Present**
District Sales Manager   (1996 - Present)
Senior Sales Representative (1993 - 1996)
Sales Representative   (1991 - 1993)

EDUCATION

B.A.,   University of Michigan, 1991
Major: Marketing

Activities: President, Student Government
                  President, Delta Upsilon Fraternity
                  Captain, Varsity Track Team

CHRISTOPHER T. BEATTIE
106 Summit Avenue
Reading, Pennsylvania 19330
Phone: (215) 775-0978

SUMMARY

Senior operations executive with 19 years experience in responsible operations management and engineering positions. Excellent record of fast-track growth based upon solid contribution to bottom line results. Outstanding reputation as organizer and leader who never fails to achieve goals and objectives.

MAJOR ACCOMPLISHMENTS

Manufacturing
- Directed successful $125 million, two-year capital expansion program doubling plant manufacturing capacity. (Completed three months ahead of schedule and 10% under budget.)
- Directed cost reduction task force resulting in overall reduction of manufacturing costs by 20% ($110 million) in three years.
- Cut raw material inventories by 30% ($15 million) through implementation of computerized production scheduling and inventory control system.
- Moved 75% of hourly employees to new jobs in less than two months with no loss in plant output.

Engineering
- Managed company's largest capital expansion program ($250 million, two years) with start-up four months ahead of schedule and project under budget.
- Engineered numerous projects in the $40-$50 million range with all projects completed ahead of schedule and within budget.

Management
- Directed all manufacturing activity for 5,300 employee manufacturer of copper tubing (sales $500 million).
- Managed $2,700 employee copper refinery and tube manufacturing facility ($375 million budget).
- Managed 150 employee Central Engineering Department for major manufacturer of refrigeration tubing.

WORK HISTORY

STERLING TUBE CORPORATION (Corporate Offices)   **1989 to Present**
Vice President of Operations   (1994 - Present)
Plant Manager (Norfolk Plant)   (1989 - 1994)

BRADFORD COPPER COMPANY, INC. (Corporate Offices)   **1979 to 1989**
Manager of Engineering   (1984 - 1989)
Department Manager, Drawing Operations (Bradford Plant)   (1982 - 1984)
Project Engineer   (1979 - 1982)

EDUCATION

M.S.,   Pennsylvania State University, 1979
Major: Mechanical Engineering

B.S.,   Pennsylvania State University, 1977
Major: Mechanical Engineering
           Tau Beta Psi

MARGARET R. TEMPLE
200 Remmington Drive
Springfield, Ohio 75332
Phone: (315) 772-6767

SUMMARY

Results-oriented manufacturing manager with six years experience in wax and silicone manufacturing. Excellent record of achievement and advancement earned through demonstrated contribution to bottom-line results.

MAJOR ACCOMPLISHMENTS

Manufacturing
*   Introduced automatic product palletizing and palletized railcar loading, cutting warehouse operating costs by 25% ($15 million annual savings).
*   Organized and coached hourly employee cost reduction task force accounting for implementation of several cost savings projects with $7.5 million savings in one year.
*   Increased department productivity by 18% in two years through employee job rotation and enrichment program.

Management
*   Managed 210 employee, two-department manufacturing operation in the manufacture of silicone-based waxes and polishes (annual budget $130 million).
*   Managed wax Formulations Department of 50 employees and annual budget of $75 million.

Employee Relations
*   Initiated absenteeism control program reducing absenteeism from 11% to less than 4% in one year.
*   Reduced union grievances from 185 to 62 in two years through effective employee relations practices.
*   Awarded best department safety award in both 1991 and 1992.

WORK HISTORY

REED MANUFACTURING COMPANY (Linwood Plant)   **1993 to Present**
Assistant to Plant Manager   (1996 - Present)
Department Manager, Formulations   (1993 - 1996)

CLOVER WAX COMPANY (Radley Plant)   **1991 to 1993**
Supervisor, Formulations

EDUCATION

B.S.,   Bradley College, 1991
Major: Industrial Technology
          Cum Laude

BRUCE B. PARSONS
32 Roam Avenue
Utica, NY 79443
Phone: (319) 447-2242

SUMMARY

Procurement executive with over 13 years demonstrated effectiveness in contributing substantially to bottom-line results. Knowledgeable in all facets of modern procurement management including computer applications. Fully qualified to direct procurement function of major corporation.

MAJOR ACCOMPLISHMENTS

Management
- Direct procurement function for $1.2 billion manufacturer of consumer food products (eight plants). Direct staff of 15 professionals and $580 million budget.
- Managed corporate procurement function of $850 million baking company with professional staff of eight and annual budget of $325 million.
- Managed department of four with annual budget of $200 million in the purchase of all vital supplies.
- Managed department of three and annual budget of $50 million with corporate-wide procurement responsibility for $150 million manufacturer of pretzels and potato chips.

Cost Savings
- Saved $36 million per year through computerization of raw materials tracking and forecasting.
- Saved $22 million through corporate-wide consolidation of all packing supply purchases.
- Realized $18 million annual savings through conversion to biomass fuels with long-term purchase contract.
- Centralized procurement function realizing $16.5 million annual savings through corporate-wide consolidation of all purchasing.
- Saved $3.2 million per year through installation of computer systems for vital supplies and packaging materials forecasting and inventory control.
- Negotiated two-year shipping carton purchase contract worth savings of $1.3 million annually.

WORK HISTORY

CARSON MANUFACTURING COMPANY, INC. (Corporate Offices)   **1996 to Present**
Director of Procurement

WILSON BAKING CORPORATION (Corporate Offices)   **1990 to 1996**
Manager of Procurement   (1992 - 1996)
Senior Buyer - Vital Supplies   (1990 - 1992)

JOHNSON FOODS, INC. (Corporate Offices)   **1986 to 1990**
Manager of Purchasing   (1987 - 1990)
Buyer   (1986 - 1987)

EDUCATION

B.A.,   Syracuse University, 1986
Major: Business Administration

Activities: President of Business Club
             Captain, Varsity Baseball

JAMES R. WINDTHROPE
18 Bay View Place, Apt. 4-D
Briney Beach, California 32775
Phone: (415) 773-4424

SUMMARY

Results-driven procurement professional with over four years of experience in procurement of vital supplies. Excellent track record of contribution to bottom-line results through finding and implementing major cost savings opportunities.

MAJOR ACCOMPLISHMENTS

Cost Savings
- Saved $1.3 million through negotiation of two-year contract to purchase knockdowns at 20% below current price.
- Realized annual savings of $575 through inventory reductions resulting from tighter control through computer forecasting.
- Saved $200,000 annually through renegotiation of poly wrap contract at 10% reduction in purchase price.
- Saved $125,000 annually through use of computer forecasting of vital supply requirements and subsequent inventory reductions.

Information Systems
- Developed and implemented computer system for accurate long-range forecasting of vital supply requirements permitting reduced supply inventories.
- Computerized vital supplies delivery schedule with all deliveries made to manufacturing on time and with no shortages.

WORK HISTORY

HILTON PAPER COMPANY, INC. (Corporate Offices)   **1997 to Present**
Senior Purchasing Agent - Vital Supplies

BRANDON PAPER COMPANY (Corporate Offices)   **1994 to 1997**
Vital Supplies Buyer

EDUCATION

B.A.,   University of Southern California, 1994
Major: Business Administration
          Cum Laude

          President, Delta Upsilon Fraternity
          President, Student Government Association
          Janzen Scholarship (4 years)

CAROLYN B. TABOR
25 Reedsville Road
Sampson, Oregon 77033
Phone: (409) 357-2999 (O)
(409) 357-5673 (H)

SUMMARY

Over 20 years of dynamic, innovative technology management leadership in Fortune 500 companies. Demonstrated capability in achieving business goals through innovative technology. Broad range of technical expertise coupled with highly effective communications skills.

MAJOR ACCOMPLISHMENTS

Managerial Leadership
- Managed 500 employee corporate research center for Fortune 100 paper company ($32 million annual research budget).
- Directed packaging & materials laboratory of 135 professionals for leading fiber corporation ($12 million budget).
- Managed 38 professional employee synthetic fiber research department ($1.2 million budget).

Technical Leadership
- Realized $300 million in annual savings through invention of unique forming device permitting 30% reduction in product raw material fiber.
- Allowed entry into $125 million new market through development of unique paper-like synthetic material.
- Increased sales by 15% in two years through development and introduction of five major new consumer products.
- Pioneered development of revolutionary new freezer wrap prolonging room temperature thaw time by 300% and reducing frozen food spoilage by 30%.

Innovation
- Invented unique and highly successful magnetic forming device for high speed sheet formation of non-woven materials.
- Pioneered new innovative process permitting the forming of a synthetic fiber web on high speed wet lay technology paper machine.
- Developed thermal mechanical pulping process allowing 5% reduction in TMP energy requirements.

WORK HISTORY

OREGON PAPER COMPANY (Corporate Research Center)   **1994 to Present**
Vice President of Technology

STRATTON FIBER CORPORATION (Packaging & Materials Laboratory)   **1986 to 1994**
Research Director, Packaging & Materials

BARTON INTERNATIONAL FIBER, INC. (Corporate Research)   **1977 to 1986**
Research Manager, Synthetic Fibers   (1980 - 1986)
Senior Research Scientist, Polymer Research   (1977 - 1980)

VELSTAR ELECTRONICS & SPACE LABORATORY   **1976 to 1977**
Research Specialist

EDUCATION

Ph.D.,   University of Michigan, 1976
Major: Chemical Engineering
                Pennington Fellowship

M.S.,   Rochester Institute of Technology, 1974
Major: Materials Engineering

B.S.,   Rochester Institute of Technology, 1972
Major: Chemical Engineering
                Magna Cum Laude
                Barlow Scholarship (4 years)

                President, Chemical Engineering Society

PUBLICATIONS

45 professional publications and papers (1976 - 1994)

AFFILIATIONS

American Society of Chemical Engineers
American Chemical Society
American Physical Society
Technical Association of Pulp & Paper Industry
American Management Association

J. WALTER LOFTEN, Jr.
315 Post Road, South
Benton Harbor, Michigan 45776
Phone: (917) 472-3927

SUMMARY

Highly innovative Ph.D. polymer engineer with demonstrated track record in achieving excellent product and process development results. Hold ten U.S. Patents and am credited with development of major new polymeric materials allowing successful entry into several new markets.

MAJOR ACCOMPLISHMENTS

Creativity, Innovation
- Invented fiberglass substitute with twice the strength and half the cost, allowing successful entry to $300 million new market.
- Pioneered new synthetic wool-like fiber from product development stage through successful pilot plant testing.
- Recipient of Norwood Chemical "Inventor of the Year" award.
- Holder of ten U.S. Patents.

Bottom Line Contributions
- Developed polymer material for manufacture of boat hulls with estimated annual market potential of $300 million.
- Developed synthetic wool substitute allowing successful entry into market valued at $150 million annually.
- Invented five new polymer-based products, four of which have led to new market entry and one of which is now in test market (estimated annual sales of $350 million to date).

WORK HISTORY

NORWOOD CHEMICAL SPECIALTIES, INC. (Corporate Technology)   **1993 to Present**
Senior Research Engineer, Polymers   (1995 - Present)
Research Engineer, Polymers   (1993 - 1995)

HAWTHORNE CHEMICAL COMPANY (Central Research)   **1991 to 1993**
Polymer Chemist

EDUCATION

Ph.D.,   Massachusetts Institute of Technology, 1991
Major: Polymer Engineering
Thesis: "Copolymerization of Diamond Polymers"
          Hawthorne Fellowship

M.S.,   Rochester Institute of Technology, 1989
Major: Chemical Engineering
             Ludwig Scholarship

B.S.,   Massachusetts Institute of Technology, 1987
Major: Chemical Engineering
             Stanton Scholarship (3 years)

             President, Polymeric Society
             Magna Cum Laude

PATENTS

Awarded ten U.S. Patents since 1991

AFFILIATIONS

American Society of Polymer Scientists
American Society of Chemical Engineers
National Institute for Polymer Research

11

PROBLEM
RESUMES

C hances are fairly high that, if you have elected to read
this particular chapter, you anticipate having some
difficulty with your resume that could prove detrimental to
your employment candidacy. Knowing how to treat this
problem in the employment resume is imperative if you are
to be successful in competing with the thousands of other
resumes that find their way into the employment manager's
mail folder. Failure to handle this problem in an appropriate
manner could result in the screening out of your resume,
with little or no consideration given to your qualifications
for employment.

Since there are probably tens if not hundreds of reasons
why a resume may be a "problem resume," it is not my intent
to attempt to deal with the unusual or rare problem. Thorough coverage of such a broad topic would require a book in
itself. Instead, this chapter will focus on the seven most common reasons for classifying a resume as a problem. These
seven reasons are believed to account for approximately 80

percent (or better) of all problem resumes. The seven most common resume problems can be classified as follows:

1. *Age.* The applicant is over age 40 and may experience age discrimination.
2. *Job Hopper.* The candidate has worked for a number of employers in a fairly short period of time.
3. *Employment Gap.* The applicant has had one or more periods of lengthy unemployment (or substantial underemployment).
4. *Educational Deficit.* The applicant lacks a formal degree or generally lacks the requisite educational qualifications necessary to attain his or her employment objective.
5. *Experience Deficit.* The candidate has insufficient experience or lacks the appropriate type of experience normally required for the position sought.
6. *Chronic Handicap.* The applicant suffers from a physical or mental handicap that might be thought by some employers to impede performance.
7. *Changing Careers.* The candidate wishes to enter a new field in which he or she has little or no experience.

We will examine each of these problems in some detail, and I will share some practical and effective ways to deal with these problems in the employment resume. Here again, as in other chapters of this book, this advice is based on firsthand observation as a former Fortune 200 human resources executive who has played a very active role in his company's employment process. Hopefully my practical experience will help you over what otherwise might prove a difficult obstacle to your development of an effective employment resume.

AGE

When is age an obstacle to employment? This question is becoming more and more difficult to answer for two basic reasons. First, there is the matter of demographics. Second, there is the factor of civil rights legislation. Let's take a moment or two to consider the effect of these two items on the employment process and therefore the employment resume.

Most of you are familiar from reading about the previous financial plight of Social Security, U.S. census data, and other similar articles and reports dealing with the changing age demographics in the United States, that the age mix of the population is moving from younger to older. As this population ages, older persons are becoming an increasingly larger percentage of the total, with younger individuals becoming a proportionately smaller percentage of the population. Along with this shift in demographics there is a corresponding change of attitude toward age in the employment process. With fewer younger workers and an increasing number of older workers now constituting the labor market, employers have been forced to give stronger consideration to older workers than in the past. Thus age is becoming less and less of an employment barrier with the passage of time. Depending upon circumstances, however, age may still be a very real barrier to employment—all things being equal.

An important civil rights law, the Age Discrimination in Employment Act of 1967, made it illegal for employers to discriminate against individuals on the basis of age when making employment decisions. This law, coupled with highly publicized age discrimination lawsuits, has served to direct the focus of the employment professional's attention away from age as the basis for screening out employment candidates. It has forced employment managers to refrain from using age alone to screen out employment candidates who are otherwise qualified for a given employment opening. Thus the average age of candidates employed by enlightened companies has gradually risen over the years. However, this does not mean that such discrimination has been eliminated. It simply means that blatant cases have all but disappeared, and employment managers have become more sophisticated and creative in practicing this form of discrimination.

Both the changing demographics and the age discrimination legislation have served to make companies more flexible in hiring older workers. The question of age, however, still remains a relative factor. When faced with otherwise equal qualifications, many employers would still prefer to hire the younger worker. Since the law forbids this, however, the employment professional may scrutinize the qualifications of the older candidate more thoroughly in an effort to eliminate this candidate on the basis of some job-related qualification.

For many employment managers, the question of age is a relative one—usually relative to the level of the position sought. Thus an individual who is 45 or 50 years of age may not be thought of as too old for a position as vice president. It would take 25 to 30 years to accumulate sufficient experience to qualify for such a position. Likewise, candidates who are 35 to 45 years of age may be acceptable candidates for a director-level position for similar reasons. By contrast, however, a 25-year-old person may well be preferable to a 45-year-old individual for a position as a project engineer, a position that may require only three or four years of experience. Many firms might question the motivation and drive of a 45-year-old engineer who had only attained the level of project engineer after 24 years of experience.

You can see from this discussion that age still plays a role in the employment process. Therefore, if you are an older worker and have not reached a reasonable level or position for your peer group, you should attempt to disguise your age on the employment resume. Should you still have some questions on whether age represents an obstacle to your employment, let me suggest the following guidelines:

1. Age 30—Junior-level professional position
2. Age 35—Senior-level professional position
3. Age 35—Lower-level managerial position
4. Age 40—Mid-level managerial position
5. Age 45—Director-level position
6. Age 50—Vice president-level position

These are not hard and fast rules but merely guidelines based on my discussions with numerous human resources and employment professionals. The supply-to-demand ratio for a given field (computer programming, for example) may dictate that age cannot be a factor when considering the qualifications of such a scarce resource in a high-demand market. Likewise, firms with compensation packages (wages and benefits) that are considered substandard for their industry may be considerably more flexible on the age issue. Nonetheless, you would be well advised to keep the above guidelines in mind when considering whether to reflect age on your resume.

To disguise your age on the employment resume, simply apply the following basic rules:

1. Do not list your age or birthdate on your resume.
2. Do not list the year you graduated in the Education section of the resume.
3. Do not list all of the positions that you have held or all the employers for whom you have worked since the beginning of your career. Simply list your most recent positions and employers, going back in time only as far as is necessary to convince the prospective employer that you have sufficient experience to handle the position for which you are applying.
4. When listing patents, professional publications, and so forth on your resume, omit issue and publication dates.
5. Carefully review your resume for any dates that may give a prospective employer a clue regarding your age and remove the date (or item) from your resume.

You shouldn't feel guilty in applying these rules for disguising your age since it is illegal for employers to discriminate against you on the basis of age. Additionally, you could well be better qualified than your younger counterparts but never have the opportunity to establish this through a personal interview if you provide prospective employers with the chance to screen you out on the basis of your age.

There is no written law or rule that says the employment resume *must* include *all* employers or past positions held. The purpose of the resume is simply to provide the prospective employer with a synopsis of your employment credentials. It does not purport to reflect all qualifications. On the other hand, the employment application form normally requires that the applicant list all past employers and positions. Should you have a potential age problem, therefore, it is recommended that you skillfully avoid completion of a formal application form until after you have had the benefit of an employment interview. By all means avoid indication (or giving clues) of your age on the resume when doing so could cause you to be screened out. If you are otherwise qualified for the position in question, you deserve the benefit of a personal employment interview. Don't deny yourself this opportunity!

JOB HOPPER

As with the subject of age, it is difficult to establish set rules or guidelines for the job hopper. Simply put, the job hopper is one who is considered to have held too many jobs with too many employers in too short a period of time. As with age, the frequency of changing employers can vary considerably between industries. What may constitute an acceptable level of job hopping in one industry may well be totally unacceptable in another.

For example, engineers who work for a contract firm or "job shop" are subject to frequent layoffs throughout their careers compared to professionals in many other fields. As large contracts wind down these firms simply don't have a need for as many engineers, and if no new contracts are on the horizon, they are forced to lay off many of their professional workforce. These firms are economy dependent. When the economy is healthy and expanding, many companies are engaged in vigorous capital-expansion programs requiring the services of engineering contract firms in the engineering and construction of new facilities. During such periods the contract firms undergo substantial hiring programs and expand their professional ranks. Conversely, when things get tough and the economy is contracting, most companies forego expansion plans and the demand for contract engineering support drops off. The result of this decreased demand is the layoff of engineers.

For the most part, experienced employment professionals are very much aware of those industries in which high employee turnover is a normal fact of life. When reviewing the resumes of professionals working in such industries, therefore, the employment manager will not be alarmed to see a large number of employers in a fairly short period of time. The knowledgeable employment professional is fully aware that this unusually high job turnover probably has little to do with the candidate's ability or performance and is simply a reflection of the normal turnover pattern within that particular industry. Thus a contract engineer who has averaged a new employer every two or three years does not raise any unusual concern.

Where the pattern of job turnover is considered high for a particular industry, however, the employment professional becomes most reluctant to give serious consideration to the employment applicant. High job turnover conjures up a wide range of negative assumptions in the mind of employment managers. The single word used to categorize individuals with high job turnover is "unstable." The causative factors underlying this pattern of instability could be poor performance, incompetence, incompatibility with management or fellow workers, absenteeism, alcoholism, marital problems, and so on. The list of possibilities is almost endless.

Bear in mind that the resume review process is essentially a negative screening process. The employment manager's objective is to screen out those candidates who are either unqualified on the basis of technical skills and experience or who are considered undesirable on the basis of some other factor that suggests that the candidate is a high risk. Thus if the applicant's past has been one of high job turnover, why would this pattern be any different in the future? Why should the employment manager risk hiring this individual when other candidates are available who have demonstrated a history of low job turnover and great stability in the past? The answer to these questions is simple: They won't!

Consider for a moment the risks associated with hiring an individual who has had a poor history of job stability. The financial implications of a poor employment decision are fairly dramatic. First, there is the employment agency fee.

Assuming an annual salary of $70,000 and a fee of 30 percent, the agency fee amounts to $21,000. Second, there is the matter of reimbursement of moving expenses. Most companies with a fairly comprehensive moving-expense reimbursement policy estimate moving expenses at approximately 1½ times annual salary (for a homeowner with a family). In our example, therefore, moving expenses are estimated at approximately $105,000. Thus direct replacement costs (agency fee and moving expenses) alone total $126,000. This does not even begin to take into consideration such indirect replacement costs as dual training costs (the cost of having trained the departed employee plus the cost of training the replacement) and the loss of productivity while both the past and present incumbents were in training.

Considering the substantial costs associated with making a poor employment decision, it can be readily understood why employment managers are reluctant to give much consideration to job hoppers. This is especially true when other candidates with more favorable employment histories are available. Additionally, the costs associated with bringing a candidate in for interviews can also mount up in a hurry. First, there is plane fare (say $800 round trip). Next, there is the cost of meals and lodging (estimate one day at $175). Third, there are the salaries of those managers and professionals who participate in the interview process (estimate four at one hour each at $50 per hour). Thus the typical costs associated with interviewing just one employment candidate can quickly add up to hundreds of dollars for the employer. The employment manager is responsible for keeping these expenses to a minimum by inviting in for interviews only those candidates who have a reasonable probability of being made an employment offer.

Being classified as a job hopper will place you at a decided disadvantage when compared to others of equal qualifications but whose employment history is considerably more stable. This is not to say that you are not a good candidate or that you don't have good reasons for having changed employers with some frequency. This may well be true. I am in no way passing judgment on your qualifications and abilities. What I am doing is attempting to be realistic with you—sharing with you the truth of how your resume will be perceived by the typical employment professional as he or she reviews your overall qualifications relative to other candidates with whom you may be competing. If you believe that you might be classified as a job hopper, there are some steps that you can take to at least minimize the overall effect of your employment history. The following recommendations should prove helpful.

Use of the functional resume format (see Chapter 9) can be fairly effective in reducing the potentially negative impact of a high frequency of past job turnover. The organization of this format is to list major areas of experience and accomplishment on the resume first, followed by a listing of past employment history (dates, employers, and positions held). If you have made substantial contributions to past employers, citing these early in the resume may create sufficiently positive impact on the reader to overcome concerns regarding your past employment record. This is especially true when the employer has had a particular problem where it is felt that your major contributions of the past are directly related to these areas of need. In such a case the employer may well feel that the value of solving this particular problem far outweighs the risk of turnover. In any event, use of the functional resume format is strongly recommended where there has been a history of high job turnover but where significant past contributions and accomplishments can be cited.

Although this technique is *not* recommended for those who have had a solid record of employment stability, it is one that can prove helpful to the individual whose resume must reflect a poor employment history from a turnover standpoint. Where appropriate, consider offering an explanation for leaving past employers. This should be shown in the Work History section of the functional resume format as follows:

1996 to 1997   Manager of Contract Sales
                Smith Collison Corporation
                Reason for Leaving: Change in marketing
                strategy—company went to cash sales
                only—position eliminated.

1995 to 1996   Controller
                Johnson and Parker
                Reason for Leaving: Replaced by owner's
                son.

1994 to 1995   Corporate Vice President,
                Manufacturing
                Hollingsworth Company
                Reason for Leaving: Company purchased by
                Karlson Reed Corporation—all top
                management replaced by Karlson Reed
                personnel.

If using the chronological resume format, a reason for leaving should be positioned following description of position and accomplishments. It should not follow either name of employer or title of position held. To do so could distract the reader from giving full attention to the description of the position held and accomplishments. This is not the case with the functional format, however, where major accomplishments have already been described at the beginning of the resume.

In the general parlance of most employment professionals, certain reasons for having left past employers are considered to fall into the "acceptable" category. Perhaps the following categories may serve to give you some ideas as to the parameters of acceptability from the employment manager's standpoint.

1. *Job Elimination.* Elimination of position, department, or function (especially if your previous duties have not been absorbed by others).

2. *Acquisition.* Acquisition of your employer by another company (especially where the new parent company has replaced the management of the acquired company with its own personnel).

3. *Nepotism.* Where the candidate has been replaced by a relative of the owner (especially where there has

been a past pattern of this type of practice within the company).

4. *Contraction.* Where there has been significant contraction of the company with reduction in future advancement opportunity.

5. *Deemphasis of Function.* Where there has been significant deemphasis on the candidate's functional specialty (for example: Research and Development budget reduced by 50%).

6. *Lack of Advancement Opportunity.* Where it can be demonstrated there has been little or no opportunity for professional growth. (Care should be exercised in using this as a reason since it is frequently used by individuals to disguise other forms of discontent with past employers.)

7. *Health.* Where the candidate is allergic to certain chemicals or other items used in the manufacturing process, or when a family member has a health problem requiring relocation to a different climate. (Care should be used in citing health reasons if the effect is to create the impression that you are not a healthy individual or could be prone to excessive absenteeism.)

On the other hand, the following reasons for separation from past employers are considered unacceptable by most employment professionals:

1. *Poor Performance.* Where the candidate has been discharged from a past employer on the basis of poor performance.

2. *Incompatibility.* Where the candidate has either been discharged or has left a past employer voluntarily for reasons of incompatibility with management or fellow workers.

3. *Absenteeism.* Where the individual has been discharged by a past employer for absenteeism or chronic lateness.

4. *Dishonesty.* Where the candidate has been discharged by a past employer for lying, cheating, or stealing.

5. *Quit.* Where the individual has quit without providing the past employer with reasonable advance notification (normally at least two weeks).

If your past employment history could potentially classify you as a job hopper, you can readily see why it may be important to state your reasons for leaving past employers, especially where such reasons would be considered acceptable. If no reason is cited, the employment manager is left to assume the worst, that is, poor performance, incompatibility, dishonesty, and so on. It is strongly recommended, therefore, that you list the reasons for leaving past employers on your employment resume.

If your reasons for departure from past employers are deemed acceptable in most cases, and you elect to show these on your resume, it is not necessary to list reason for departure in the case of all past employers. In those cases where your reason for leaving would be considered unacceptable, simply do not show a reason or, where appropriate, indicate "personal—will discuss during interview." When in doubt as to whether a specific reason for leaving a past employer is acceptable, the general rule to be followed is "Don't show a reason." Why show information that could provide the basis for the reader to screen you out?

EMPLOYMENT GAP

Another topic of major concern to the novice resume writer can be how to handle employment gaps, that is, periods of unemployment or substantial underemployment. By the term "underemployment" I mean being employed for a period of time in a position that is substantially below your obvious experience level or professional capability. Either of these events can sometimes cast a shadow of doubt on what otherwise may be excellent credentials. The obvious question that is raised in the mind of the employment manager when encountering such employment gaps is: "How could a person with otherwise good credentials possibly be unemployed or underemployed? Something is wrong. What is it?" As with the case of the job hopper, periods of unexplained

unemployment or underemployment represent a high risk
to the employment professional and must be dealt with effectively if you are going to be successful in landing an employment interview.

One rule to follow when dealing with periods of unemployment or underemployment of less than one year is "Simply don't show it." Thus, if you were unemployed for the
period from January 21, 1995 until August 1, 1995, your
resume would show the following:

WORK EXPERIENCE

1995 to Present	Senior Project Engineer Deltoid Corporation
1980 to 1995	Project Engineer Syntaf Corporation

There is no written rule that says the employment resume
must list all periods of employment and unemployment. To
the contrary, the resume is intended to be a brief sketch or
synopsis of one's employment credentials. Why then list information that is not relevant to one's professional qualifications and which may have an adverse effect on one's
employment candidacy? In my opinion, to list this information is utter foolishness.

This is not to say that I believe in dishonesty. To the contrary, I believe that there is a time and place to disclose this
information to the prospective employer. For example, if at
the time of the employment interview you are asked to complete a formal employment application that requires that you
account for all time spent, by all means don't try to hide this
period of unemployment. Additionally, at an appropriate time
in the interview process (preferably after you have had
an opportunity to interest the prospective employer in your
qualifications), you should volunteer this information to the
interviewer (I suggest the employment or human resources
manager) along with an appropriate explanation. In fact, if
you don't share this information with the company and
should they accidentally discover this information during a
subsequent background investigation or reference check,

such action might result in the decision not to make you an employment offer. At best it would cause feelings of distrust and uneasiness about your integrity. Therefore, should you elect not to show this information on the resume itself, be sure to voluntarily disclose it at an appropriate point in the interview process.

If the period of unemployment or underemployment extends to a year or longer, there are two suggested ways of dealing with this problem period on the resume. Assume that the period in question is December 12, 1994 until January 3, 1996. Here are the two ways:

Example 1:

1996 to Present	Senior Project Engineer Delray Corporation
1994 to 1996	Personal (will discuss during interview)
1992 to 1994	Project Engineer Johnson & Lipford Corporation

Example 2:

1996 to Present	Senior Project Engineer Delray Corporation
1992 to 1994	Project Engineer Johnson & Lipford Corporation

In Example 1 there is no attempt to hide an unexplained time gap on the resume. The designation as "personal," although raising some questions in the mind of the employment professional, leaves a somewhat neutral feeling. There is simply not sufficient information provided for the employment manager to make a decision one way or another. Chances are if you were unemployed or underemployed, you will at least have an opportunity to discuss this with the employment manager and offer a reasonable explanation. Otherwise, had you shown this information on the resume, you might well have been screened out without the opportunity to explain the circumstances.

Example 2 simply omits this information from the resume entirely, including dates. Here again the argument that could be used to defend this intentional omission is that the resume is intended to summarize the highlights of one's employment credentials only. It is not intended to provide complete information as in the case of the formal employment application form, which requires that complete information be furnished.

EDUCATIONAL DEFICIT

For purposes of this discussion, the term "educational deficit" means lacking the requisite educational qualifications normally required by employers in filling the type of professional position that you are seeking. There are still many employers who get hung up when the applicant does not have a college degree, does not have the appropriate degree level (B.S., M.S., Ph.D.), or does not have a degree in the appropriate field. This is one of those employment facts of life that must be dealt with, however, if you expect to have the opportunity to interview and discuss your qualifications in person.

The first step in dealing with this particular resume problem is to determine the magnitude of your problem. If most employers require a B.S. degree in Mechanical Engineering and you have no degree at all, your educational deficit represents a fairly major stumbling block. If, on the other hand, most employers prefer a B.S. degree in Mechanical Engineering and your degree is a B.S. in Electro/Mechanical Engineering, you do not have a major problem. In fact, in the latter example, you probably have no problem at all.

Another type of educational deficit problem is having an unusual degree with which most employers are unfamiliar. An example of this would be a B.S. degree in Pulp and Paper Technology. The term "technology" suggests that it is a science degree, but where is the emphasis? Is it heavily chemistry oriented, biology oriented, or more oriented toward engineering? Another example is a B.S. degree in Engineering Technology. Here again several questions are raised in the mind of the resume reader. Is this a heavy applications-oriented degree light on engineering theory? Which of the traditional engineering educations does this degree most resemble—chemical engineering, mechanical engineering, electrical engineering, or civil engineering?

Each of these educational deficits is slightly different and requires, therefore, a slightly different solution. Let's examine these situations one at a time and arrive at some possible answers.

The first basic premise to keep in mind is that most employment professionals are primarily interested in whether the individual can perform the position in question. Stated differently, does the candidate have the necessary understanding of the technical principles necessary to solve the more complex problems he or she will be called upon to address? Is there reasonable evidence, based upon past experience and accomplishments, that the candidate has the technical qualifications to perform the job at a reasonably high level and make important contributions to the business? Questions of this type are paramount in the mind of the employment manager when attempting to gauge the technical competence of an individual employment applicant. Believe it or not, in most cases educational qualifications are secondary to experience and accomplishment. This is especially true in markets where certain skills are in great demand and the supply of qualified candidates is limited. Unfortunately, it is less true where there are many candidates but few openings. In the latter case, the probabilities are high that proper educational credentials will play a much greater role and will become a primary factor in the resume screening process.

Not having a degree, having the wrong degree, or not having the right level of degree in most cases is far from fatal to your employment candidacy assuming you have the right experience and can cite demonstrated accomplishments. If you can impress the prospective employer sufficiently with your actual experience and accomplishments in the field in question, the fact that you have an educational deficit may be overlooked or at least substantially discounted as a factor in determining whether you should be invited in for an interview.

The key to dealing with this type of educational deficit is to cite your experience and accomplishments near the beginning of the resume with your educational credentials shown later. Both the chronological resume format (see Chapters 5 and 7) and the functional resume format (see Chapter 9) provide for such positioning of your educational credentials. If your resume is to be successful in overcoming this educational handicap, however, the experience and accomplishments sections of your resume must be well developed. You are counting on these portions of your resume to convince a prospective employer that you are well worth interviewing even though you do not possess the educational credentials required. Chapters 5, 7, and 9 will provide you with a great deal of help in developing the experience and accomplishments sections of your resume and should help to maximize your resume's effectiveness.

Possession of an unusual degree, with which many prospective employers will be unfamiliar, requires a slightly different tactic. In this case, educational credentials should also be positioned later in the resume (following description of experience and accomplishments); however, some reasonable description of the degree will also be needed to provide the resume reader with a better understanding of the degree. Where possible, and without stretching the truth, some correlation should be cited with more commonly known degrees and academic disciplines. For example, if a B.S. degree in Pulp and Paper Technology has a strong chemical engineering concentration, it might be shown on the resume as:

B.S. Pulp and Paper Technology (heavy emphasis in Chemical Engineering)

or

B.S. Pulp and Paper Technology (approximates B.S. ChE)

Handling the degree description in this fashion helps the resume reader to associate the degree with a more traditional and commonly understood academic curriculum, usually making the reader feel more comfortable.

In extreme cases of educational deficit, you may not want to list education on the resume at all. For example, let's assume that following high school you took some trade school courses in mechanical drafting. Let's assume further that you are bright and have read several engineering textbooks on your own. Further, you have 25 years of experience, starting as a draftsman and advancing into the professional engineering ranks. Your current job title is Senior Project Engineer, and you are handling relatively sophisticated engineering projects related to the design, installation, and start-up of multimillion-dollar steel-rolling equipment. Even though you are heavily experienced and exceptionally well qualified, showing that you lack a formal degree in mechanical engineering could prove to place you in a disadvantaged position and cause you to be screened out automatically with no opportunity to demonstrate your capability through a personal interview. In such cases I strongly recommend that you exclude the education section of the resume entirely.

Here again, I am not proposing that you be dishonest or devious in your approach. On the contrary, you should volunteer the fact that you do not have a formal degree during the course of the employment interviews when people will have the opportunity to explore your technical knowledge and competence and to satisfy themselves that you have what it takes to perform the job. At least you will have the benefit of these discussions rather than being arbitrarily screened out on the basis of having no degree.

EXPERIENCE DEFICIT

In this discussion the term "experience deficit" means that the individual lacks either sufficient experience or the appropriate type of experience normally required by employers in filling the position that the candidate is seeking. By sufficient experience I mean the required number of years of experience. We will explore both of these experience deficits in some detail, and I will provide you with some helpful advice in effectively dealing with them.

The experience deficit is perhaps one of the most difficult resume problems to handle. Most employers put considerably more weight on experience than any other factors when judging a candidate's qualifications for employment. The professional employment community has long subscribed to the belief that the best single predictor of future success is past experience coupled with past success. Thus it is felt that there is considerably less risk involved in hiring someone who has actually performed the work in question than in hiring someone who has never performed this type of work before.

The problem with this thinking is that it does not take into consideration the individual's desire to do the work or the level of motivation required to do the work at an exceptionally high level of quality and/or volume. In other words this philosophy ignores the potential for individual productivity. It ignores the fact that some individuals, who have minimal or no experience but have sufficient technical knowledge and training, may well have the motivation and desire to far outproduce their experienced counterparts! Although most employment professionals are willing to concede this possibility, they are still faced with the dilemma of somehow distinguishing such individuals from the large population of applicants. Second, there is the problem of convincing the line manager to whom the potential employee would be reporting that he or she should consider interviewing someone who clearly does not have the experience called for in the candidate specification. These are two very difficult hurdles to overcome and, if there are sufficient experienced candidates from which to choose, most employment professionals will not even try. In such cases, it is simply not an efficient use of their time.

The truth of the matter is that the employment resume itself can do little to overcome this particular problem. Attempting to establish personal contact through a mutual acquaintance with the individual having the opening is the best-known method for overcoming this barrier. Second, the cover letter that accompanies the employment resume provides some limited opportunity to convince the prospective employer that you are "short on experience but long on motivation and desire." From the resume standpoint, however, there are some things that you can do to at least improve your chances. Here are some basic ideas.

In this case the functional resume format (see Chapter 9) is clearly your best bet. The following minor modifications to this format, however, are in order:

1. Eliminate the Summary section at the beginning of the resume. If you do not have appropriate experience, there is no point drawing attention to this fact at the beginning of the resume.

2. In the place of the summary statement, substitute an objective statement setting forth your job-hunting objective. Care should be taken that this objective is not too narrowly stated. This could serve to screen you out from other related opportunities that could be of interest to you. See Chapter 5 for specific instructions on how to prepare an effective objective statement.

3. Instead of the heading Major Accomplishments, use the heading Key Qualifications. (Instructions for preparing this section of the resume follow.)

Some thoughtful analysis at this point can make a considerable difference in the effectiveness of your resume. Therefore, make a careful list of the probable qualifications that an employer will be looking for in a good candidate. Since it is already a foregone conclusion that your experience is inadequate, you should focus your analysis on other factors. In order to get started, try answering the following questions:

1. *Technical Knowledge:*

What specific technical knowledge is required to perform this job? Describe in the space provided below:

_____

_____

_____

_____

Are you proficient in any of these areas of required knowledge? If so, which areas? List below:

_____

_____

_____

_____

_____

How did you obtain this proficiency (education, hobbies, other)? Describe below:

_____

_____

_____

_____

_____

2. *Technical Skills:*

What specific technical skills are required to perform this type job successfully? (for example: mathematical, statistical, analytical, instrumental analysis, oral communications, written communications.) Which are the most critical skills? List below:

_____

_____

_____

_____

_____

Are you proficient in any of these critical technical skills? If so, which ones? List below:

_____

_____

_____

_____

_____

How did you acquire these skills? What have you done to attain this level of proficiency? Describe below:

_____

_____

_____

_____

_____

Now that you have completed this exercise, go back and review your answers. Try to place yourself in the role of an employment manager. Which of these areas of knowledge and/or skill are the most impressive and convincing? Which might tempt you to give serious consideration to the candidate even though he or she lacks the specific experience required?

Returning to the functional resume format (see Chapter 9), substitute these key technical knowledge and skills as headings in place of the functional headings normally used on the functional resume format. A typical key qualifications section might read as follows:

Key Qualifications:

Instrumental Techniques—Proficient in a wide range of instrumental techniques including gas chromatography, ultrasonic scanning, electron microscopy. Over 60 credit hours in Physical Chemistry and Physics dealing with the use of instruments and instrumental techniques.

Biological Science—Thoroughly schooled in the field of Biological Science with over 30 credit hours in Zoology. Worked as laboratory assistant to Dr. Charles Von Zeit, world renowned in the area of DNA genetic research.

Written Communications—Excellent written communications ability. Have written several technical articles for *Biological Science Magazine* summarizing Dr. Von Zeit's experimental findings in the field of genetic research. Served as editor of college newspaper.

With this style of organization the reader's attention is drawn away from the fact that you lack specific work experience and is instead focused on those areas of job-related knowledge and skills critical to the successful performance of the position in question. This should be sufficient to carry you through to the interview stage.

CHRONIC HANDICAP

For purposes of this discussion, the term "chronic handicap" means a physical impairment that interferes with the performance of a normal life function: that is, seeing, hearing, walking, using arms or hands, exercising muscular control, and so on. This terminology also applies to diseases or medical disorders of life-threatening proportion (cancer, heart disease, M.S., etc.) as well as those that are temporarily disabling (asthma, migraine headache, chronic allergy, etc.).

The subject of chronic handicap is a difficult one to deal with from a resume perspective since these handicaps are individually unique and manifest themselves in symptoms dependent upon the individual case in question. Due to this variance in severity it is difficult to generalize about any one particular type of physical handicap. I therefore attempt to deal with the question of severity rather than to simply lump similar conditions into a single category.

Federal law prohibits employers from discriminating against the employment of individuals on the basis of physical handicap. Even when such a handicap may impair the individual's ability to perform the job at normal productivity, employers are prohibited from using the handicap as an excuse not to hire. In such cases, under the law, the employer is required to provide "reasonable accommodation" to allow the handicapped individual to perform the job. The term "reasonable accommodation" is interpreted to include minor modification and adaptation of the work environment to allow the handicapped person to function in a normal manner. Thus adaptations such as special desks, chairs, ramps, and modified rest room facilities are today commonplace.

From a resume standpoint, the biggest issue confronting the handicapped person is whether to disclose the fact that he or she is physically handicapped in the resume. This is not an easy question to answer.

There is little doubt in my mind that discrimination on the basis of physical handicap is still practiced today. People who are severely handicapped can readily attest to this statement if they have tried time and time again to find meaningful employment. I am convinced, however, that such discrimination is rooted in productivity issues rather than in disdain or discomfort with the handicap itself. There is genuine concern on the part of the employer, or more specifically the hiring manager, that the individual may not be able to perform the job and that as a result department productivity will fall. Since the department manager's performance evaluation and salary increases are based on the overall productivity of the department, it is important that the most productive workers available are hired. Thus the issue is principally one of productivity. Managers would much prefer to hire a highly motivated and productive handicapped person than hire a nonhandicapped individual who is poorly motivated and nonproductive!

In my opinion, a good deal of discrimination based upon physical handicaps stems from general ignorance of the disease and/or condition. The idea of cancer or heart attack, for example, conjures thoughts of fatality in the mind of the employer. It also brings to mind the thought of lost productivity and long periods of absence from work. Although there may be reasonably high probabilities for both of these in the most chronic of cases, there are substantially increasing numbers of individuals with these diseases who can expect to live a fairly normal existence thanks to numerous advances in medical technology. From the employment standpoint, however, unless specific information is provided concerning future prognosis, employers will tend to think the worst, and many will avoid the issue entirely by moving on to the next resume.

I have a recommendation regarding how to handle your physical handicap from a resume standpoint. The answer is a fairly simple one. It is principally related to your level of comfort with handling your handicap in an interview situation. If you feel fairly comfortable with your handicap and are not easily embarrassed by someone else's (namely, the interviewer's) surprise or feelings of awkwardness, *by all means do not list your physical handicap on your resume!* If, however, you are severely handicapped and feel compelled to advise the employer of this in advance, then do so, *but not in the resume!* Instead, make use of the cover letter to accomplish this objective. Be sure, however, to offer a fairly detailed and accurate description of your physical limitations and how these relate to your ability to perform the job. If you must disclose your handicap to employers, then don't leave them guessing concerning your ability to perform the job. If you do, they'll assume the worst!

If you elect to make use of the cover letter to disclose your physical handicap, make sure that you don't overdo it. Remember, the employer is really interested in your qualifications for the job. It is important, therefore, that you start the letter by very convincingly summarizing your qualifications for the position so that you create interest on the part of the reader in your employment candidacy. Introduce the subject of your handicap along with a frank description of your limitations and some convincing evidence of how this condition will not prohibit your performance of the job for which you have applied.

CHANGING CAREERS

Changing careers or fields is one of the more difficult problem areas from the standpoint of resume preparation. The degree of difficulty, however, is related to how far along the individual is in their current career and their overall qualifications for the new field of endeavor. For those who are early in the occupational life cycle, say a year or two, changing fields can be a fairly simple matter (assuming reasonable qualifications). Conversely, for someone who has invested several years in a particular occupational endeavor and who then elects to make a switch, the barriers can be substantial.

Here again it is difficult to generalize since there are several variables that affect one's ability to make an occupational change. Perhaps the single greatest factor is the law of supply and demand. When an individual elects to move into a new field that is categorized by high demand and a limited number of qualified applicants (computer programming, for example), the transition can be fairly easy, provided he or she has the appropriate technical qualifications. By contrast, transition to a field of little demand and an oversupply of qualified candidates (for example, forestry) can be extremely difficult unless the applicant has some unique credentials or has personal contacts in the field.

In addition to supply and demand, the relative qualifications of the individual wishing to make a career change are extremely important to success probability. By "relative" I mean the individual's credentials as compared to the employment qualifications of the other candidates with whom he or she must compete. Obviously, for individuals with strong qualifications the transition can be fairly smooth one. In such cases, however, the individual does not have a resume problem to address.

The obvious drawback to changing careers from a resume standpoint is lack of specific experience in the new field. Although educationally you may be well qualified, the fact is that you will probably be competing with individuals who have equivalent educational credentials and also have the added advantage of direct experience in the field. In such a case you are obviously at a competitive disadvantage.

There is an added dimension to making a career switch that you must also take into consideration. The fact that you elected to pursue a different career path initially may cause some understandable concern on the part of prospective employers. They are going to wonder why you have elected to make this change. Unless properly addressed, there may be a lot of negative concern surrounding your decision. Some of these feelings center on the following notions:

1. *Judgment.* There will be concerns about your judgment. The decision to change directions implies that you did not think through your initial decision properly. Will this be indicative of the judgment you exercise on the job?

2. *Patience.* Employers may question why you didn't stick it out. Some may deduce from your decision to make a change that you are a person who is unable to exercise patience, constraint, or self-control—that you may have a tendency to abandon things when the going gets tough.

3. *Maturity.* Some employers may interpret your actions as a sign of immaturity. They may be concerned that you are somewhat impulsive and don't think things through before acting.

These feelings must be addressed in a positive manner if you expect your resume to be effective in leading to the interview stage of the employment process. Some logical, rational explanation of your decision must be offered.

As with a chronic handicap, the most logical place to present your reason for making a job change is the cover letter that accompanies your employment resume. A brief, logical explanation of your rationale for making this change should be provided at the beginning of the letter. Be sure not to dwell on all the negative reasons that caused you to make this transition. Pick only one or two and then quickly change the focus of the letter to the positive reasons that have attracted you to the new field as well as your qualifications for entry. The following is a brief example:

Having watched the rapid decline of the steel industry and realizing the long-range implications from a career stand-point, I have elected to pursue opportunities elsewhere.

I have observed, with great interest, the rapid expansion and growth of the pharmaceutical industry in recent years. Your company, Stanford Pharmaceutical, in particular, has made great strides in the development and introduction of several new drugs used in the treatment of malignant melanomas. I find this area of research interesting and exciting since I was a research assistant to Dr. James R. Dwight, a renowned cancer researcher, while a graduate student at the University of Pennsylvania.

As you can see in this example, the explanation offered to the prospective employer for making a career change is brief, to-the-point, and very plausible. You will also note how quickly the transition is made to the new area of career interest and the tie-in with the applicant's qualifications for the new job objective. You are encouraged to be equally brief and to-the-point—don't waste time before quickly moving the reader's attention to your job objective and employment qualifications.

In most cases, the single biggest problem in making a career change is the lack of specific experience in the new field or occupational specialty. This was referred to earlier in this chapter as "experience deficit." Although as the saying goes, "there is no substitute for experience," there are some steps that you can take to address this problem and to improve the overall effectiveness of your resume. Rather than repeat these recommendations here, however, I suggest you refer to the section entitled Experience Deficit earlier in this chapter.

12

THE
ELECTRONIC
RESUME

R eengineering of work processes, and the resultant rush
by businesses to electronically automate much of their
repetitive, nonvalue-adding work, has not escaped the employment functions of most corporations. Many human resources functions, hard hit by corporate downsizing, are
now being forced to look at computer automation as an answer to the growing demand on their functions to do more
work with reduced staffs and fewer resources.

For instance, in her book, *Electronic Resume Revolution*
(2nd ed., John Wiley & Sons, 1995), noted syndicated career
columnist and author, Joyce Lain Kennedy, cites sources
showing that almost 55 percent of all larger employers (i.e.,
those with over 5,000 employees) today make use of computer systems in the identification and selection of people
for positions in their firms. These include both applicant
tracking systems as well as computerized employee skill

inventories. Further, Ms. Kennedy quotes James Lemke of Resumix (the leader in the field of resume tracking systems) as saying that he believes that within the next five years an estimated 80 percent of all medium-sized and large companies will process incoming resumes using electronic scanners and computers.

Clearly there is an enormous explosion taking place in the ever-growing use of computers as a replacement for people in the reading, storage, and retrieval of employment resumes. This fact alone provides compelling reason for the job seeker to become rapidly knowledgeable of the guidelines for producing resumes that can be efficiently read, stored, and retrieved by modern resume tracking systems.

HOW RESUME TRACKING SYSTEMS WORK

When received by an employment department that is using modern resume tracking technology, the resume is first read through an electronic scanner. The electronic resume image created by the scanner is then transferred to a computer using OCR (optical character recognition) software, which converts the resume text into a universal computer language known as ASCII. Stored as ASCII text, this allows other computers that are tied into the same resume database system to electronically access, search, retrieve, and print out the resume text of qualified candidates.

The process used by employers to identify the resumes of qualified candidates in the computerized resume tracking system is known as *key word search.* By inputting a combination of key words (e.g., project engineer, paper machines, towel, tissue, design, installation, start-up, forming devices, transpiration dryers, mechanical engineering, B.S.M.E.), the computer searches out those resumes having the prescribed combination of key words contained in them. These key words are most often the same words as contained in the candidate specification being used by the employer to conduct the employment search.

When using the system to conduct a search, the employer can either expand or contract this list of key words to yield a different size population of qualified candidates.

244 THE ELECTRONIC RESUME

For example, if the number of resumes initially identified is too voluminous, by expanding the list of key words to include additional "qualifiers," the number of resumes matching the key word criteria can be reduced to a more manageable number. Conversely, by decreasing the list of key words being used to conduct the resume search, the employer can expand the number of qualified candidates identified by the system.

THE IMPORTANCE OF KEY WORDS

Having your resume contain the right key words is absolutely critical to the computer's identification and selection of your resume for the type of job you are seeking. To assure success, prepare your resume by being sure that those key words, most likely used by employers to identify candidates for this type of work, are incorporated into your resume document right from the start.

Most resume tracking systems, when conducting a key word search of resumes stored in their database, tend to "key in" primarily on nouns. Thus, it is important, when constructing your resume, to be sure that the resume document is well stocked with specific, concrete nouns that describe the areas in which you have experience and expertise.

THINKING LIKE THE EMPLOYER

To be sure that your resume fully captures the key words that are required for your resume to be selected as part of a computerized key word search, it is important for you to think like the employer. Pretend you are the employer, and that you are conducting a key word search of a resume database to fill the target position you are seeking. What key words would you input into the computer to identify candidates having the basic qualifications for this position?

Here are some guideline questions that might prove helpful in determining what key words should be included:

1. What is the industry(ies) you have targeted for purposes of your job search? (Examples: steel, chemical processing, pharmaceutical, paper.)

2. By what alternate names is this industry known (if any)? (Example: The paper industry is sometimes referred to as the "pulp and paper industry" or the "forest products industry.")

3. What is the business function in which you would be working (e.g., accounting, finance, manufacturing, human resources)?

4. What synonyms might be used by employers as alternative titles for these business functions? For example:

   (a) Human resources could also be called "personnel" or "employee relations."

   (b) Manufacturing is also known as "operations."

   (c) Distribution might also be called "logistics."

   (d) Purchasing is often referred to as "procurement."

   (e) Product development and "process development" are often used interchangeably.

5. What are the major areas of accountability (or subfunctions) for which you would be accountable in your target position (and for which employers may be looking in their key word search)?

   For example:

   (a) Human resources can include subfunctions or principal accountability areas such as internal staffing, external staffing (or employment), training, development, management development, organization design, compensation, benefits, labor relations, safety, security, employee wellness.

   (b) Subfunctions of finance might be international finance, domestic finance, money and banking, financial planning, financial analysis, investor relations.

   (c) Subfunctions of technology might encompass areas such as basic research, product development, process development, analytical testing, technology transfer.

(d) Accounting subfunctions could include auditing, cost accounting, taxes, payroll, accounts payable, accounts receivable.

6. What specific skill or knowledge areas are normally required by a successful candidate to perform this type of job? Examples might be:

(a) Statistical process control

(b) Design of experiments

(c) Behavioral interviewing techniques

(d) Reengineering

(e) Total quality

(f) Wet lay technology

(g) Transpiration drying equipment

(h) Computer modeling

(i) Knowledge of WordPerfect 5.2

7. For a management position, what words best describe the organizational environment and management style sought? (Assume an employer is seeking someone who has managed in a participative, team environment.) Examples are:

(a) Key words describing organizational environment:

(1) Participative management

(2) Team environment

(3) High-performance work team

(4) Sociotechnical systems

(b) Key words describing management style:

(1) Coach

(2) Teacher

(3) Facilitator

(4) Enabler of others

Thus, if you were an employer seeking a mechanical project engineer with five or more years experience in the design, installation, and start-up of a tissue paper machine utilizing transpiration drying technology, key words would likely include: B.S.M.E., mechanical, project engineer, design, installation, start-up, tissue, paper machine, transpiration drying.

Each of these key words is critical to your selection by the resume tracking system. If any key words are missing from your resume, but are all contained in the resume of a competitor job applicant, you are likely to be passed over in favor of the other candidate, despite the fact that you may well be the better qualified person.

The computer is totally impersonal and impartial, making no exceptions when doing a key word search. A key word is either there or it is not. If the key word is present, your resume will be selected. If the key word is missing, the computer will simply pass your resume by in search of resumes containing the key word it has been programmed to select.

The lesson for the job seeker is simple. Make sure you carefully think through the list of key words most likely to be chosen by employers using word search to find someone with your qualifications, and make sure that these key words are in your resume!

KEY WORDS SUMMARY

One approach to capturing these important key words in the resume is the growing use of the "key words summary." Such a summary might be positioned at the beginning of the resume, perhaps immediately following the statement of the job search objective. Alternatively, it could be positioned later in the resume immediately following work experience or education. Titles for use with this section vary, but might include: Qualifications Summary, Key Skills, Functional Expertise, Technical Skills. The specific heading probably matters less than the key words contained in the summary itself. It is, after all, these key words that the computer will be seeking.

Using the project engineering position previously described as our example, the following might be incorporated into the resume in the form of a key word summary.

Technical Expertise

Have technical expertise in the following areas:

- paper machines
- transpiration dryers
- Yankee dryers
- control systems
- wet lay technology
- tissue machines
- after dryers
- Beloit machines
- twin wire formers
- wet end formation
- sheet formation
- Black Clawson machines

Another example of how such a key word summary might be incorporated into a resume is illustrated next. This resume section, for example, might routinely be placed in an administrative assistant's resume, where it is commonly known that such positions frequently require extensive computer software skills.

Computer Software Proficiency

- WordPerfect 5.2
- Excel
- Lotus 1-2-3
- DOS 6
- PowerPoint
- Works
- One-Write Plus
- Harvard Graphics

When considering the possible creation of a key word summary on the resume, a good rule to follow is first to utilize the conventional resume formats as described earlier in this book to write your resume. Then, once written, carefully scan the resume to determine whether or not you were able to incorporate all of your key words naturally as part of this conventional resume design. In most cases, if the resume has been well written, you will find that you have been able to do so.

When this is not the case, however, think of an appropriate resume section heading that might be used to incorporate those key words missed in the original resume design. Perhaps a good catch-all might be "Additional Skill Areas," for example:

Additional Skill Areas

Additional areas of expertise include the following:

- Design of experiments
- MRP 2
- Reengineering
- Statistical process control

- SAP
- Total quality
- Just-in-time
- ISO 9000
- Dry forming

OTHER TIPS

Using relatively sophisticated word search software, most modern resume tracking systems today have the ability to extract key qualifications and skills from many different resume styles. Because of their common usage, however, both the chronological (narrative and linear forms) and functional resumes, as described earlier in this book, are formats that lend themselves particularly well to these electronic resume systems. The developers of these systems have paid particular attention to creating systems that would be particularly adept at handling these style resumes due to their wide usage.

Beyond the standard formatting of chronological and functional style resumes, however, there are some additional tips that you will want to heed in assuring that your resume will serve you well in the new world of cyberspace and computer-based applicant tracking, including:

- Use standard 8½" × 11" white or off-white paper (avoid other darker or off-colors).
- Use common typefaces such as Times, Courier, Helvetica, Palatino (avoid out-of-the-ordinary fonts).
- Provide original copy using high-quality printing that is crisp and neat (preferably a laser printed or typewritten original—high quality photocopy, although not preferred, is acceptable).
- Use 12 point font size, although 10 and 14 point are normally acceptable.

- Minimize use of bold highlighting and underlining; avoid unusual effects such as shadows, reverse typeset (i.e., white type on dark background), etc.
- Keep it simple—sticking to text only and avoiding use of graphics, tables, charts, and the like.
- Follow standard resume formats employing common resume section headings (as already described in detail earlier in this book).
- Describe your qualifications and skills in specific, concrete terms (avoiding vague or broad-sweeping statements).
- Use standard terminology when describing your field, specialty, type of work performed, and skills.
- Scan your resume carefully to be sure you have made effective use of key words that will most likely be used to identify candidates for the type of position you are seeking.

Once you are satisfied that you have prepared a resume that will serve you well in the new electronic age, you may want to further explore the many new job search options now available to you using electronic means. Knowing how to get your resume out onto the Internet, for example, may expose your qualifications to the thousands of employers now just beginning to use on-line systems to identify employment candidates.

If this topic interests you, I whole-heartedly recommend that you take time to stop by your local bookstore and pick up Joyce Lain Kennedy and Thomas J. Morrow's book, *The Electronic Job Search Revolution*, 2nd ed. (John Wiley & Sons, Inc., 1995).

This book is recognized as the most authoritative work on this subject available today. It will thoroughly educate you on the many job-hunting possibilities now open to you through the world of cyberspace.

13

PHYSICAL APPEARANCE OF THE RESUME

The physical appearance of the resume is an extremely important factor, since the resume almost always represents the first contact with a prospective employer. It is imperative, therefore, that it create a favorable impression.

A well-organized, concise, neat resume will go a long way toward achieving that important favorable first impression: The candidate is neat, well-organized, and concise. Conversely, a resume with ragged margins, misspelled words, and coffee stains will leave a very different impression.

Review the sample resumes included in Chapters 6, 8, and 10. Note the neatness, organization, concise layout, and overall readability. Copy is well-spaced, margins are even, and key areas are thoughtfully highlighted with capital letters and effective underlining.

Once the final draft of your employment resume has been completed and is ready for typing, seek out a professional typist and have the job done right. Remember, you will be counting solely on your resume to create a sufficiently favorable impression to lead to an employment interview. It is well worth the extra money to achieve this important objective.

If you do not know a professional typist, check the *Yellow Pages* of your telephone directory. Such services are normally listed under the headings of "Word Processing Services," "Secretarial Services" or "Typing Services." Do some competitive shopping by phone; you will find that fees can vary substantially. You may also wish to use the same typing service for typing cover letters later in your job-hunting campaign. Take care to select a good one with reasonable fees.

Be sure that resume typing is done on a top-quality word processor (using a laser or other comparable quality printer). Select neat, clean, conventional type and have the resume typed on a high-quality, white bond paper. Your professional typist can usually advise you on the best style of type to use and the proper grade and color of paper for reproduction purposes.

Before trotting off to the printer or your local copy service, be sure to carefully proofread your resume. Make sure that the original is neat, well-spaced, uncluttered, and easy to read. Check carefully for proper punctuation and spelling. If you do not have a high level of confidence in your own punctuation and spelling skills, it may be a good idea to have a friend who is proficient in these skills give your resume the once-over prior to going to print.

Printing should be done by a professional using quality photo-offset printing equipment. In many quarters, high-quality Xerox copies or copies printed on a high-quality laser printer will be just as acceptable. Printing should be done on quality bond paper that is off-white or white in color.

14

THE
COVER
LETTER

Quite a bit has been written on the subject of cover letters and their importance to the employment process. Much has been said about the supposed power and mystique of these letters as they relate to an effective job-hunting campaign. Some claim that the cover letter is more important than the resume itself. Proponents of this viewpoint argue that the resume alone is nothing more than a sterile document and that the cover letter is the instrument that compels the reader to act. It is sometimes argued that without the cover letter many resumes would, in fact, go unread. I do not support this contention.

The *truth* of the matter is that most employment professionals pay little initial attention to the cover letter. In the course of a year the professional employment manager may frequently read in excess of 20,000 resumes along with accompanying cover letters. Considerable experience in reading these letters has led most employment professionals to realize that most cover letters add little meaningful new information. Most are of the "broadcast" variety and are redundant to the actual resume. Faced with thousands of applications, therefore, valuable time would be lost if the employment manager were to read each and every cover letter thoroughly. From the employment manager's standpoint, it is much more important to proceed with the reading of the resume, since this is the document that details the specifics of the candidate's background and qualifications, and as such, is used for comparing these qualifications with the candidate specification of the position that the employment manager is attempting to fill.

When first glancing at a cover letter the employment manager is usually looking to see whether the letter is a mass mailed "broadcast" form letter, or whether it contains something of a more personal and specific nature. Care is taken to ferret out those letters that indicate a firsthand association with the company, that is, friends of employees and executives, shareholders, local community leaders, and so forth. Each of the aforementioned categories usually requires a more personalized response. Care is thus taken to read such cover letters with greater diligence so that an inappropriate form response is not sent. Letters of a less personal type such as general broadcast letters, however, receive very little attention from the employment professional.

Admittedly there are some cases when a cover letter has been particularly cleverly written and may heighten the interest of the reader. Such letters are extremely rare, however, and the reader's interest is normally increased only because of the relationship between the candidate's qualifications and the position that the employer is attempting to fill. Additionally, when the resume has been sent to someone other than the employment manager (for example: the director of marketing, research and development manager, personnel director, or some other executive), the cover letter may serve to increase interest in the applicant's employment candidacy.

In general, the cover letter serves as a business letter used for transmitting one's resume to a prospective employer. The purpose of the cover letter is to create sufficient interest on the part of the reader to warrant further reading of the employment resume. If written particularly well, it can also convey a sense of value to the employer. This is particularly true if the writer emphasizes his or her ability to contribute something of importance or value to the prospective employer.

TYPES OF COVER LETTERS

There are essentially four types of cover letters used for transmittal of the employment resume. They are as follows:

1. Broadcast letters—to employers
2. Broadcast letters—to executive search firms
3. Employment advertising responses
4. Personal referral letters

Although there are some similarities between these various types of cover letters, there are also some differences. You should be aware of these differences and should tailor your cover letter appropriately. Please take a few minutes to review the sample cover letters contained in Chapter 15 of this book. You will note that there are five sample letters for each of the four cover-letter categories. We now examine each of these different letters in greater detail and provide you with the necessary instructions for the development of interesting and effective cover letters.

The Broadcast Letter—To Employers

The broadcast letter is the transmittal letter used by the job applicant to mass mail his or her resume to a number of prospective employers. Although the technique of mass mailing one's resume is frequently used by many if not most job seekers, it is also known for not being a particularly effective technique. Experts generally agree that a favorable response of 2 to 5 percent is considered an excellent response rate. I have personally been involved in several outplacement programs and have observed the results of mass-mailing campaigns on a firsthand basis. This 2 to 5 percent return rate is borne out by my own experience.

Thus in a broadcast campaign, where the individual mails his or her resume to 500 companies, he or she can expect to elicit favorable response from only 10 to 25 employers. After the initial phone screen by the employer, however, these numbers may be quickly reduced to three or four actual employment interviews. This would appear to be a tremendous amount of effort for a minimal result. However, if such a campaign results in an interview for the "perfect" position, this effort will have paid off handsomely.

Design of an effective cover letter for a broadcast campaign need not be a cumbersome task. Essentially, the letter is comprised of the following components:

1. Return address
2. Employer's address
3. Salutation
4. Introductory paragraph
5. Statement of purpose
6. Brief summary of qualifications
7. Reason for making change (optional)
8. Salary requirements (optional)
9. Geographical preferences/restrictions (optional)
10. Request for response

Wherever possible, it is preferable to mail letters of this type to a specific individual within the corporation. This individual should be at a reasonably high level in the corporation and should be within the discipline or business function most closely related to the position for which you are applying. Thus if you are an Engineering professional, you should mail your letter to the manager or director of Engineering. Similarly, if you are a human resources professional seeking a managerial position, you should be writing to the director of human resources. An individual who is already at the director level, however, should be writing to the company president or chief operating officer.

Notice that I have not recommended that you send your resume to the human resources department or to the attention of the employment manager. The reason for this is simple.

Since I have been a corporate human resources executive, I most certainly am not suggesting that you circumvent the human resources function, but the human resources manager or the employment manager may have knowledge of only those positions that are *currently* open. He or she may not be aware of the positions that the director, chief operating officer, or other line manager is thinking about filling. A good resume, appropriately timed, may actually trigger the line manager to advise the human resources manager of the opening and, at the same time, deliver your resume along with a request that you be scheduled for an employment interview. Even if the line manager does not take the time to read your resume, chances are it will be forwarded to the employment department for a response. In any event, directing your resume to the top functional officer in your discipline gives your campaign an added dimension and increases the likelihood of a favorable response.

If your employment search is intentionally limited to a specific industry, one key source for executive names is the trade directory for that industry. Although some industries do not have directories, many, in fact, do. If your industry does have a trade association, a simple phone call in many cases is all that is necessary to obtain a trade directory. Additionally, if you are currently employed, chances are that your research or marketing libraries will already have a copy of the trade directory that you can use. Also, if your funds are limited, and you do not wish to pay the cost of such directories, you could try your local or county library.

In addition to industry trade directories, professional associations frequently publish membership rosters. These rosters contain the names, addresses, and titles of various members. Such membership rosters can be extremely helpful in obtaining the names and titles that you need, adding a personal dimension to your cover letter.

Another approach that can be used to develop a mailing list to include specific names, titles, and addresses is personal contact. Make a thorough list of every professional acquaintance who you know or have met. Call them and ask for the names, titles, and addresses of the appropriate functional manager from their own company. In addition, ask them for contacts at additional companies as well. Although from the same industry, these contacts need not be from the same professional specialty. They, in turn, can be used as contacts to find out the names, titles, and addresses of the appropriate individuals within their own companies. Although this is a time-consuming task, it is far better than simply mailing your resume to a title or to the human resources department. Additionally, it is possible that these contacts will be aware of specific openings and provide you with some direct leads!

You will note in reviewing the five sample broadcast letters to employers in Chapter 15 that although the exact same format is used in showing return address, employer's address, and salutation, the introductory paragraphs are all different. There is no standard or uniform way to introduce the subject of the letter to the reader. This fact stresses the individuality of letter writing. All are quite effective introductory paragraphs, however, and any one would serve its purpose effectively.

One fairly uniform component of each of these five sample letters is a brief summary of qualifications. The emphasis is on the word "brief." You don't want to bore the reader or insult his or her intelligence by repeating a lot of the information already contained in the resume. Whenever possible, try to provide some additional information beyond that reflected in the employment resume. Additionally, whenever possible, cite some specific results or accomplishments you feel will be of particular interest to the prospective employer.

Early in the letter, it is important to make the prospective employer aware that you are seeking employment. In most cases it is appropriate to list a generic job title (corporate credit manager, research scientist, director of engineering, and so on) to communicate effectively the level and type of position you seek. This is particularly true if you are absolutely firm on the type and level of position that is acceptable. Otherwise, be fairly general about your objective or state no job objective at all. Remember, if too narrow a position objective is stated, however, it could have the effect of screening you out from job opportunities in which you might be very interested.

In some cases, you will want to include an explanation of your reason for making a job change. This is particularly true in cases of massive layoffs, shutdown of facilities, severely limited future advancement opportunity, and so forth. If you elect to include this information, be sure your explanation is reasonable, plausible, and understandable. Where this information is fairly positive in nature, it can help remove some of the suspicion in the mind of the reader and satisfy his or her curiosity.

If, on the other hand, your reason for leaving your current employer could be construed to be negative, do not volunteer this information in either the cover letter or the resume itself. Thus, if you were or are being terminated involuntarily for reasons of poor performance, absenteeism, negligence, misconduct, or anything similar, do not provide this information. There is no rule that requires you to voluntarily furnish this information in the cover letter or on the resume. It is best left off both. Inclusion is sure to result in your being eliminated from further consideration.

The issue of salary requirements is also a subject of great debate when it comes to cover letters and resumes. Some argue that it should be included, others that it should be excluded. Those that favor exclusion argue that to state either current salary or salary requirements in the cover letter could serve to automatically screen you out from career opportunities in which you would have been quite interested.

I personally feel that this type of argument is a lot of nonsense! Employers are usually dealing with a salary range and frequently have some flexibility in what they are able to pay. If they see somebody who looks particularly good and whose salary requirements are a little high, there is usually some way of addressing this issue. In some cases, it may mean upgrading the current job, and in others it may mean an increase for the person to whom the position is reporting. Either way, there is normally some way around this problem if the interest is strong enough. If on the other hand your salary requirements are totally out of range for the prospective employer, why not know in advance? A lot of valuable time can be saved by you and the prospective employer if this information is known at the onset!

I would argue in favor of the inclusion of salary require-ments in the cover letter. This is provided you are firm on what you are willing to accept as fair compensation for your skills and ability. Certain situations, however, may warrant an exception to this general rule. Essentially, this is related to two factors: (1) how high you are now paid and (2) how desperate you are for employment. If you are working for the highest-paying employer in your industry and you know that your salary is already usually high, you may want to moder-ate your salary requirements or simply not state them in the cover letter. Also, if you have been unemployed for several months and future prospects look glum, you may likewise wish to exclude salary requirements from the cover letter.

With the preceding exceptions in mind, I generally recom-mend inclusion of salary requirements in the cover letter. It is recommended, however, that appropriate wording be used to allow for some flexibility. As with statement of job objec-tive, too narrow a statement of salary requirement could also have the effect of screening you out from what other-wise would have been a very interesting opportunity. Note how salary requirements are worded in the sample cover let-ters in Chapter 15.

A statement of geographical preference or restriction is an-other optional requirement of the cover letter. Here again, care should be taken not to automatically screen yourself from an excellent opportunity by statement of a restriction. For example, if the employer is located in upper New York State, but most division and plant locations are in the South, a geographical restriction to the Northeast may screen you from consideration for a home-office opportunity. The em-ployer may realize that future advancement would require relocation to an area in the South and automatically elimi-nate you from further consideration.

The rule of thumb to be followed when deciding whether or not to include a statement of geographic restriction in the cover letter is "don't include it unless it is an absolute re-quirement." You can always decide at a future point whether the opportunity is truly worth the exception. Stating a geo-graphical preference is not nearly so final. It will not auto-matically screen you from further consideration.

The final component of the letter is the request for response. Let the employer know that you expect to hear something regarding your employment candidacy. Request that you be advised of the outcome of your employment inquiry. Obligating the employer to respond to your application may force him or her to be a little more thorough in reviewing your credentials.

The Broadcast Letter—To Executive Search Firms

Before reading this section, it is suggested that you carefully review the five sample broadcast letters to executive search firms in Chapter 15. This will give you a better understanding and appreciation for the recommendations and ideas contained in this section of the chapter. It will also serve to familiarize you with those letters that most appropriately fit your particular circumstances.

This particular type of letter is very similar to the broadcast letter to employers. In addition to executive search firms, this letter will suffice for use with employment agencies as well. Components of this type of letter are:

1. Return address
2. Search firm or employment agency address
3. Salutation
4. Introductory paragraph or statement
5. Statement of job objective
6. Brief summary of qualifications
7. Reason for making change (optional)
8. Salary requirements (optional)
9. Geographical preferences/restrictions (optional)
10. Statement of willingness to provide additional information
11. Contact instructions for reaching you
12. Thank you

When contrasted with the letters to employers, there are only a few minor differences. First, there should be an acknowledgment that the firm is an executive search firm and that you realize that they do search work for client companies. Don't make the mistake of asking them to help you to find a job. This would imply that you are somewhat naive in business-related matters and would reflect poorly on your general awareness and employment candidacy. This is not the case, however, with the employment agency. Employment agencies work both sides of the fence. They act as agents on behalf of the employment candidate by helping him or her to find employment. Likewise, they may also represent client companies by helping them to locate and recruit candidates to fill their personnel requirements. For purposes of the cover letter, however, I would use the same approach with the employment agencies. Some will feel complimented that you do not make this distinction and are aware that they represent client companies as well.

Most of the comments and qualifications made earlier in this chapter regarding letters to employers apply to letters to executive search firms as well. This is particularly true in the areas of statement of job objective, summary of qualifications, salary requirements, geographical preferences/restrictions, and reason for making the change. I won't repeat the same information.

When writing to the search firm or employment agency, it is important to volunteer to provide additional information should they require it. Additionally, you may wish to include contact instructions in the cover letter to make it easy and convenient to reach you. Don't forget to thank them for their consideration of your credentials and tell them that you look forward to the possibility of hearing from them.

Rest assured, if you have appropriate qualifications to fill one of their current client searches, you will be hearing from the search firm quickly. Chances are, if they do not have a compatible current search and you have reasonably good credentials, they will file your resume and cover letter for future reference. Many now use computers and may scan your information into their computer resume data base as well.

Cover Letter—Response to Advertisement

Review of the sample cover letters headed "response to advertisement" in Chapter 15 of this book will reveal the presence of the letter components below. These components are in addition to the normal return address, employer's address, and salutation.

1. Reference to advertisement
2. Expression of interest in position
3. Comparison of position requirements with own qualifications
4. Statement of additional reasons for serious consideration (optional)
5. Statement of salary requirements (optional)
6. Statement of geographical preference (optional)
7. Contact information
8. Request for response or interview
9. Thank you for consideration

Careful review of the sample letters will reveal that not all of these components are included in each of the letters. With the exception of additional reasons for serious consideration, other components designated as optional can be included or excluded dependent upon whether each adds or detracts from your overall employment candidacy. Again, these components have been thoroughly discussed earlier in this chapter, but I will spend some time exploring the more standard letter components in some detail.

In each of the five sample letters, the introductory paragraph makes specific mention of the position advertisement. Included in this reference are the name of the publication in which the ad appeared, the date of publication, and the position title. It is important that all three of these components be included so that the employer can readily identify the position for which you are applying. It is possible that the employer may be running more than one recruitment ad (sometimes 30 or 40 if a large company) at a time, and, without this specific reference, there may be some confusion concerning your interests.

Also, in all five letters there is a specific statement of interest in the position being advertised. In addition to merely stating your interest in this position, it is important to convey some sense of enthusiasm. This adds a note of positive energy, which does not go unnoticed and suggests to the reader that he or she might have a special need to read your cover letter and resume with a little greater care. Your interest and enthusiasm suggest that you feel that you have some fairly good credentials for the position in question. This serves to heighten interest in your candidacy.

Another commonality between these sample cover letters, and by far the most important, is the comparison of position requirements with your own qualifications. You will note the line-by-line comparison of qualifications with the candidate specification as set forth in the ad. This approach is extremely powerful! It has the effect of leading the reader to one simple conclusion—you *are* qualified (if not well qualified) for the position.

In reviewing the sample letters in Chapter 15, it should be absolutely clear to you that your cover letter must go far beyond simply stating that you are qualified. You must offer direct proof of this fact by offering the reader a point-by-point comparison of your qualifications and the job requirements. To maximize the effectiveness of this technique requires more than a cursory stab at providing a general description of your qualifications. Instead, it will require a much more systematic and analytical approach on your part. The following section will help you to more effectively employ this technique.

The first step in organizing your comparison is to do a careful analysis of the advertisement itself. In doing so, here are the questions that you need to ask. (I suggest that in order to make this exercise more meaningful, you perform an analysis on an actual employment advertisement, especially if you can find one that is close to your career objective.)

1. What are the educational requirements (degree level and major) of the position? Describe below:

_____

_____

2. What is your educational background (degree level and major)? Describe below:

_____

_____

3. Beyond the formal educational degree, is any special skill training required or preferred? If so, describe below:

_____

_____

4. Have you had this special skill training? If so, describe the skill and nature of training you received.

_____

_____

5. What technical or scientific knowledge does the job require (for example: polymer chemistry, Hay job evaluation,

contract negotiation, Occupational Safety & Health Act, and so on)? List below:

_____

_____

_____

_____

_____

6. In which of these areas are you knowledgeable? What is your level of knowledge or proficiency? What have you done that demonstrates this level of proficiency?

_____

_____

_____

_____

_____

7. If a managerial position, what is the scope of experience required (for example: functional areas managed, number of people and levels, budgets, and so on)? Describe:

_____

_____

_____

_____

_____

_____

8. Which of the above managerial experience requirements do you meet? Describe below:

_____

_____

_____

_____

_____

9. How many years of experience are sought and at what
level? (By "level" I mean professional vs. managerial level.)
Describe:

_____

_____

_____

10. How many years of experience do you have at these
levels? Show below:

_____

_____

_____

Having completed this analysis, you are in excellent
shape to make a direct comparison between your own qualifications and the qualifications required by the position.
Review of the five sample form letters in Chapter 15, however, will reveal that there are two ways in which this comparison can be made. Which one should you use for greatest
effect?

The first approach is a point-by-point delineation of qualifications preceded by a statement of your belief that you are

well-qualified for the position. In this approach, there is no specific mention of the qualifications required in the ad, only a general reference to these "specs." The second is a more literary approach, in which each key qualification stated in the ad is mentioned followed by a brief description of the candidate's qualifications as related to this requirement. For ease of discussion, I will refer to the first approach as the "linear" approach and the second approach as the "literary" approach.

In general, of the two approaches, I recommend using the linear approach. This is particularly true when the candidate has most or all of the qualifications called for in the ad. This line-by-line description of qualifications is easily read. Also, the reader may find this a little less offensive since it does not repeat what is contained in the advertisement. Although such cases are few, there are instances where the reader might be offended by this repetition of ad content. It may imply to some that you feel they are incapable of recalling the qualifications of the position as stated in the ad.

Where only some of the qualifications are met, however, do *not* use the linear approach. This approach tends to make it easy for the reader to check off those qualifications that you have. The drawback, however, is that it also tends to highlight those qualifications that you are missing. In a nutshell, it makes it too easy for the reader to make this direct comparison. In this case, I recommend use of the literary approach.

There is one more additional point to be made if you are going to get the most out of this comparison approach. This has to do with the focus of the ad. Most ads are slanted to emphasize the need for particular strength in a given area. Reread the ad to see if you can discover the slant or focus. What is it?

Here are a few clues to help you identify the slant or focus of the ad. Look for the following key words or phrases:

must be

must have

required

must be capable of

ability to _____ is highly desirable

must have strength in

must be thoroughly knowledgeable of/versed in

Additionally, look for thoughts or qualifications that are repeated more than once in the ad. The statement may not be identical, but the thought or theme might be repeated in a slightly different way. Such repetition usually signals that the author of the ad wanted to make sure that the point was well covered. It will usually tell you that the writer was preoccupied with this particular need as a key requirement.

Where you are able to discover this slant or focus in the ad, be sure to take full advantage of it. If you have strong qualifications in this area, include in your cover letter a brief, separate paragraph that highlights your qualifications in this key area of need. Such a paragraph can often prove to be the clincher that gets you an interview.

The balance of the components of the cover letter that is a response to an advertisement are pretty straightforward. They have been well addressed earlier in this chapter, so I will not repeat them here. Let's now move on to the final type of cover letter, the personal referral.

Cover Letter—To Personal Referral

As suggested earlier, I would recommend that you take a few minutes to review the five sample cover letters of this type shown toward the end of Chapter 15. This will enable you to better understand the recommendations and thoughts represented in this section.

Review of these sample, personal-referral cover letters reveals that they can be divided into two categories: direct and indirect. The direct letter is one in which the applicant makes the addressee aware that he or she knows of a specific opening in their company. This type of letter is represented by the sample letters addressed to B. David Carter and J. Perrington Russel (see Chapter 15). By contrast, the indirect letter (sometimes called the networking letter) professes no specific knowledge of an opening and simply solicits the assistance of the addressee in helping the applicant in his or her job search. The indirect approach is typified by the sample letters addressed to Mr. Marcus, Mr. Davis, and Ms. Harrison.

Careful analysis of these letters reveals the following common components. Although not *all* of these components appear in every sample letter, *most* are used in each letter.

1. Personal opening
   (a) Name of person making referral
   (b) Relationship to applicant
   (c) Something of a personal nature
2. How referral came about
3. Reason for job change
4. Direct reference to existing opening (where known opening exists)
5. Indirect approach (where no known opening exists)
6. Reference to enclosed resume
7. Action to initiate personal meeting
8. Thank you

If carefully written, the personal referral or networking cover letter can be a very effective tool. If a good job is done in establishing a sense of close personal relationship with the individual making the referral, a strong sense of personal obligation is created, and the addressee feels compelled to respond.

After all, friends don't let friends down. When there is a need, they respond and offer to help. This is a somewhat sacred relationship, however, and one should not abuse it.

The personal tie-in is usually established in the first paragraph of the letter. Note the first paragraphs of the sample letters. They include the name of the person making the referral, the relationship of the referror to the applicant, and usually some special story or other experience of a personal nature.

Although not always included in the first paragraph, the writer usually tells the addressee how the referral came about. Care should be taken in how one goes about describing the events that led up to the referral. If made to sound too casual, it may give the addressee the idea that the referral was made on a courtesy or polite obligation basis, as opposed to a strong, meaningful referral. This lessens the sense of obligation on the part of the addressee. Be careful, on the other hand, not to overdo it. It will surely turn the addressee off if you take advantage of the relationship and claim a stronger referral than the referror intended.

Unlike other kinds of cover letters, the personal referral letter almost always offers an explanation as to why the writer/applicant wishes to make a job change. In a more personal relationship, such as that represented in the personal-referral cover letter, there is a stronger sense of needing to share this information with the addressee. There is an almost unwritten obligation to do so. If the reason could be construed to be fairly negative (poor performance, misconduct, or so forth), however, I would question the wisdom of volunteering this information prematurely. Once again, I would recommend excluding this information from the cover letter. It is better to discuss it during the personal interview. If you value your friendship, however, you had better think long and hard about not sharing this information with the addressee during your personal meeting. At least you will have the opportunity to explain any extenuating circumstances that led to this decision. If you have a reasonable explanation, chances are he or she will give you the benefit of the doubt.

In the sample letters addressed to Mr. Carter and Mr. Russel (see Chapter 15), there is a direct reference to a specific opening. In fact, in the Carter letter the applicant indicates that the referror, John Bristol, has given him permission to use him as a reference. This type of direct approach is quite acceptable. This is one of the special things about friendship—you can sometimes go a little further than you might with a complete stranger. You must be careful, however, to walk a fairly narrow line but not cross over and give the impression that you are acting in poor taste or are abusing this special relationship. The sample letters provided in Chapter 15 are in good taste and professional in their approach. By tailoring your personal referral letters with these as your guide, you should be right on target.

You will note that those personal referral letters using the indirect style use a much more subtle approach than the direct letters. In these cases the applicant does not know whether the addressee is aware of an appropriate opening with his or her company. In such cases the applicant should avoid putting the addressee on the spot. Instead, as shown in the sample letters, the applicant takes a more casual approach indicating that he or she realizes that "it is unlikely" that an appropriate opening exists, and then goes on to solicit the addressee's counsel and assistance in helping to make contacts with others who may be aware of appropriate job opportunities.

Review of the sample letters in Chapter 15 will also reveal that in every case the applicant has initiated action to arrange a personal meeting with the addressee. This is a very important part of the process. This action creates a greater sense of obligation on the part of the addressee to help in some way. Chances are, therefore, that he or she will make a greater effort to develop a more meaningful list of contacts, check openings of the current employer, and so on. Thus taking action to initiate such meetings is important to the overall effectiveness of the referral process. In those cases where geography makes such meetings impractical, indicating that you will be phoning to discuss the matter can be almost as productive as the personal meeting.

Manners are always an important part of any friendship. Although it may sound trite, don't forget a "thank you" near the close of the letter. Little things like this are important. It at least acknowledges your appreciation for any effort that the addressee may make on your behalf.

15

SAMPLE COVER LETTERS

This chapter contains a total of 20 sample cover letters. They represent a variety of approaches and styles, and you should be able to find samples that will help you with most of your letter-writing requirements. They, of course, follow the basic letter-writing principles and guidelines as outlined in Chapter 14. As with Chapter 14, these sample cover letters are organized into four basic categories. For each category there are five sample letters. Each uses a slightly different approach from the others. I have also attempted to provide a fairly good cross section of career disciplines and fields. You should find these helpful as guidelines in designing your own cover letters. The samples are of professional quality and should enable you to write effective and professional quality cover letters of your own.

2222 Strenton Drive
Sharon Hills
Utica, NY 82289
August 3, 1996

Dr. Richard P. Stevenson
Director Research & Development
Kriston Laboratories, Inc.
1435 Claymont Way
Wawa, OR 57338

Dear Dr. Stevenson:

As you are undoubtedly aware, Keystone Chemical Corporation has made a decision to close its entire Research Center in Utica, New York effective October 15th of this year. I am thus seeking a responsible position in R&D management requiring a Ph.D. with 18 years of experience and proven skills in polymer and specialty chemical research.

I have extensive experience and knowledge in the following chemical specialties:

- Organic & Polymer Specialty Chemicals
  - Water Treatment Chemicals
  - Oil Field and Mining Chemicals
  - Consumer Products Based on Water Soluble Polymers

- Polymers, Rubbers and Plastics
  - New Polymers and Plastics - Synthetic Approach
  - New Polymers and Plastics - Physio-Chemical Approach

- Adhesives, Coatings, Polymer Alloys and Composites

As you can see from the enclosed resume, my reputation as a creative, innovative scientist has led to 35 registered patents and 14 new product introductions. Perhaps I can make a similar contribution to your company?

I have no geographical restrictions and, in fact, would enjoy living on the West Coast. My current salary is $75K per year.

Should you have an appropriate opening in your Research Center, I would welcome the opportunity to meet with you personally. I can be reached at (312) 472-5535 during the day and at (312) 472-0088 during evenings and weekends.

Thank you for your consideration, and I look forward to hearing from you.

Sincerely,

Carolyn R. Steinman

Carolyn R. Steinman

Enclosure

274

Sample Broadcast Letter—To Employer

125 Deerborne Street
Heeley, VT 43506
March 18, 1997

Ms. Sarah D. Bowlings
Senior Vice President, Human Resources
Hawthorne Publishing Company
8000 Monroe Avenue
Chicago, IL 37787

Dear Ms. Bowlings:

I am an attorney with broad corporate experience in industrial relations and labor law.

My background includes substantial experience in collective bargaining, arbitration, equal employment opportunity, NLRB proceedings, contract administration and preventive employee relations programs.

I am seeking a corporate position with emphasis on employee relations law. I am open to relocation. Salary requirements are in the mid $70K range.

I will be happy to provide additional information. Thank you for your consideration.

Sincerely,

Rodney G. Smith

Enclosure

Sample Broadcast Letter—To Employer

822 Fern Avenue
Forest Glen, IN 23994
October 4, 1995

Mr. J. Walter Pringe
President & Chief Operating Officer
Walburn Manufacturing, Inc.
18 Collings Way
Trenton, NJ 19883

Dear Mr. Pringe:

As President & Chief Operating Officer of a leading firm in the small appliance manufacturing field, I am sure that you are aware of the importance and value of a top-flight Chief Financial Officer. If you are in the market for such an individual, you may want to give serious consideration to my credentials.

With 14 years of progressively senior financial management experience in manufacturing, I have logged a very satisfying record of achievement in such areas as cash flow improvement, profit enhancement and application of sophisticated IS techniques. In my current position as Controller and Chief Financial Officer for a $10 million autonomous division of a major company in the health care industry, I have established an excellent reputation for cost control. Under my leadership, cost reduction task forces have been successful in improving net earnings by 15% through application of creative cost reduction control techniques.

Since my current company is family owned, it has become quite apparent to me that meaningful future advancement is not a realistic probability. I have therefore decided to seek employment elsewhere.

My current compensation is $95,000 per year plus bonus. My requirements are in the $90K range plus comprehensive benefits package.

Should you be in the market for a top-flight Financial Officer who can add profits to your bottom line, I would appreciate hearing from you.

Sincerely,

Sandra A. Dawson

Sandra A. Dawson

Enclosure

Sample Broadcast Letter—To Employer

725 Peachtree Lane
Rochester, NY 27132
July 2, 1995

Mr. David Ramstead
Vice President Operations
Smith Burgstrom Company
2732 Birmingham Way Road
Fort Smith, AK 13950

Dear Mr. Ramstead:

Because of the outstanding reputation of your company as a leader in the field of small electrical devices, I am interested in exploring the possibility of employment with your firm in a senior operations management capacity.

An M.S. degreed Electrical Engineer with over 20 years experience in the electrical and electronics industries, I have held a variety of positions of increasing responsibility. Most recently, I have been Plant Manager of Davidson Electronics' plant in Rochester, New York, where I have enjoyed a reputation for efficiency and profitability. During the last three years, this plant has consistently set new production and profitability records with 1994 showing an increase in net profits of nearly 25%!

Unfortunately, although Davidson has been good to me, there appears to be little opportunity for advancement in the foreseeable future. As you may be aware Davidson has only three manufacturing facilities with the Rochester Plant being the largest. At this point in time, Davidson management is not aware of my decision to seek other employment.

I have no geographical preferences or restrictions. Salary requirements are in the high $80K range and are negotiable as appropriate with the specific opportunity.

Should you have a suitable opportunity and wish to discuss my qualifications in greater detail, I can be reached on a confidential basis at my office during normal business hours. My office number is (315) 472-5252.

I look forward to hearing from you.

Sincerely,

Donald A. Carlton

Donald P. Carlton

Enclosure

Sample Broadcast Letter—To Employer

2004 Jansen Street, NW
Atlanta, GA 11399
February 22, 1997

Ms. Carolyn A. Tarkin
Vice President Technology
Orlando Pharmaceutical Corporation
1825 Bisque Avenue, SW
Orlando, FL 88795

Dear Ms. Tarkin:

During my 20 year career in research and development, I have successfully managed numerous product development programs in the pharmaceutical and health care industries. As a leader in the pharmaceutical field, I felt that perhaps Orlando Pharmaceutical may have an interest in my background and accomplishments.

In addition to the qualifications set forth on the enclosed resume, I feel that it is important for you to know that I have a reputation for being extremely creative in the area of new product development. I also possess the ability to effectively translate market need into practical laboratory solutions. This has accounted for an excellent reputation with marketing management for developing products which consistently meet marketing objectives.

While the work at Sampson Chemical is both challenging and rewarding, recent downswings in the economy have forced severe reduction of the Company's R&D budget. This has seriously hampered my ability (and the ability of other R&D scientists) to respond to business requirements. For this reason, I am seeking a position in a growth-oriented organization where I may more fully utilize my talents and energy.

Salary requirements are in the $70-80K range with some flexibility dependent upon cost-of-living, future opportunity and other similar factors. Although I have no absolute geographical restrictions, I do have a preference for the Southeast.

Thank you for your consideration. I look forward to hearing from you.

Sincerely,

Linda R Barlett

Linda R. Barlett

Enclosure

Sample Broadcast Letter—To Executive Search Firm

825 Needham Road
Bellville, OH 13970
July 27, 1995

Mr. R. James Drillpenny
Burstrom & Bailings
Executive Search Division
795 Fifth Avenue, Suite 2075
New York, NY 19553

Dear Mr. Drillpenny:

Enclosed please find my resume for your review and consideration against either current or future search assignments in the field of human resources.

I am seeking a responsible and challenging corporate or division level position as a human resources generalist. Consideration would also be given to a senior level position in the field of organization effectiveness with either a manufacturing company or consultant. As you can see from my resume, I am well qualified for either of these areas.

My decision to leave Faulings Manufacturing, Inc. is a confidential one and is predicated by lack of company and personal growth. In five short years, Faulings has sold two divisions and four additional manufacturing plants. Shutdown of a fifth plant is scheduled for year-end. Future business strategy calls for further consolidation and the outlook for future personal growth, therefore, does not look particularly encouraging.

My current salary is in the mid $70K range with salary review scheduled for next month. Salary requirements will vary depending upon nature of position, defined advancement opportunity, location, cost-of-living, etc. Although I admittedly have a preference for the East Coast, I would be willing to discuss the possibility of other locations.

Since Faulings Manufacturing Inc. is unaware of my decision to seek other employment, I would appreciate your treating this inquiry with appropriate sensitivity. In this regard, I would prefer if at all possible to keep contact to my home during evenings or weekends. Should this prove inconvenient, however, my wife, Peggy, will be pleased to relay messages to me during working hours if necessary.

Thank you for your consideration, and I look forward to the prospect of discussing appropriate career opportunities with you or a member of your staff.

Sincerely,

Jonathan P. Peters

Jonathan P. Peters

Enclosure

Sample Broadcast Letter—To Executive Search Firm

45 Puritan Road
Plymouth Meeting, PA 19337
September 21, 1998

Mr. Craig Holston
President
Holston Executive Search, Inc.
22 Wollington Avenue
Wharton Circle, PA 85537

Dear Mr. Holston:

I am an experienced Controller and CPA seeking an opportunity for further career advancement in accounting/financial management. Some of my accomplishments are outlined in the enclosed resume.

My ability to creatively deal with rapid growth and to manage and develop people, in addition to my technical qualifications, should allow me to make a significant contribution to the right company.

My compensation, with performance bonuses, has averaged in the high $90K range for the past three years.

I will be happy to provide additional information if my experience and qualifications match the requirements of any of your current search assignments.

Sincerely,

Mary C. Walters

Mary C. Walters

Enclosure

Sample Broadcast Letter—To Executive Search Firm

33 Bakers Row
Cedar Hill, WA 45459
May 26, 1996

Ms. Michele Brown
Executive Search, Ltd.
1835 Washborn Avenue
Chicago, IL 89774

Dear Ms Brown:

In the course of your search activities you may have a requirement for an accomplished Manager of Operations.

My career has covered responsible positions with major companies in their industry: General Electric, U.S. Steel, I.B.M. and International Paper Company. I have substantial experience in the manufacture of electronics, steel, business machines and paper. Review of my resume will demonstrate a record of increasing responsibility and personal growth.

The enclosed resume briefly outlines my manufacturing accomplishments over the past 14 years. There are no geographical restrictions and salary requirements are in the $85-95K range.

If it appears that my qualifications meet your current needs in the manufacturing or related fields, I would be happy to further discuss my background with you in greater depth.

Thank you for your consideration.

Sincerely,

Samuel G. Kingstone

Samuel G. Kingstone

Enclosure

Sample Broadcast Letter—To Executive Search Firm

3807 Green Tree Terrace
Smithsonville, OH 83972
August 24, 1993

The Brenton Company
Executive Search Division
215 East Market Street
Detroit, MI 87705

Dear Search Consultant:

I am writing to you in hopes that you are currently providing service to client firms seeking uniquely talented sales and marketing management professionals. With a consistent track record of success within the plastics and special chemical industries, I believe that I could contribute immediately to a variety of business development situations.

I have enclosed my resume to provide you with the details of my background and skills. I would be most anxious to discuss my career goals with you -- even if on a purely exploratory basis.

If you have any immediate questions, do not hesitate to call. Should you have employment opportunities which you feel may be of interest to me, I would appreciate hearing from you.

Thank you for your consideration.

Sincerely,

Cynthia A. Ruthers

Cynthia A. Ruthers

Enclosure

Sample Broadcast Letter—To Executive Search Firm

35 Pierce Street
Grassom, TX 88339
April 5, 1997

Ms. Judith Beerson
Senior Account Executive
Baxter, Wilcox & Sloan Executive Search
325 Ollander Circle
Cleveland, OH 89776

Dear Ms. Beerson:

If any of your client searches require a seasoned International Sales Manager, I would appreciate your consideration of the enclosed data.

While my international experience with technical products has permitted me to sell successfully in a variety of markets, I feel that I have the most to offer a company that wants to build a solid, international distributor network. This would be true of either a company new to the export market or an established firm that would like to improve their overseas market position.

By nature, the enclosed resume is only a brief summary of my qualifications. I would be pleased to expand on it personally at your convenience should you have an appropriate opportunity with one of your clients. My current compensation at Pearson Plastics is $85,000 per year.

I hope to hear from you soon.

Sincerely,

Barbara A. Johnson

Barbara A. Johnson

Enclosure

Sample Cover Letter—Response to Advertisement

1832 Briarwood Circle
Radley, VA 43117
November 12, 1993

Mr. Joseph B. Cartigen
Technical Employment Manager
Hartwell Engineering, Inc.
325 Riverside Place, Suite 108
Norfolk, VA 19870

Dear Mr. Cartigen:

Your ad in the Sunday edition of *The Baltimore Sun* for a Senior Project Engineer caught my attention and interest! It appears that my professional qualifications and career interests are very much in line with your requirements. Consider the following:

> Your ad calls for a B.S. in Mechanical Engineering with five plus years project experience in the design, installation, start-up and debugging of modern high-speed tissue paper machines. Project responsibility, including supervision of three to five professionals, with focus on forming devices is highly desirable.

> I have had eight years experience with Brunson Paper Company as Project Engineer in the area of paper machine project engineering. I have handled projects of up to $25 million with supervision of five to eight contract engineers and designers. Project responsibility has included preliminary design, installation, start-up and debugging. I have just completed successful start-up of a Beloit twin-wire forming machine with speeds of over 5,000 feet per minute and full computer control. My specific responsibility was for the wet end of the machine including both headbox and formers.

Salary requirements are in the high $65K range plus moving cost reimbursement. I am free to travel extensively and open to the prospect of future relocation.

I can be reached at the project site on a confidential basis during the day at (315) 742-0978. Additionally, I can be reached at my motel room during evening hours at (315) 742-7749, Room 325.

I would welcome the opportunity to further discuss your requirements in greater detail and am hopeful that I will be hearing from you shortly. Thank you for your consideration.

Sincerely,

Scott M. Criswell

Scott M. Criswell, PE

Enclosure

Sample Cover Letter—Response to Advertisement

948 Elm Avenue
Stouffer, CA 09735
January 15, 1996

Box J-9587
The Philadelphia Inquirer
P.O. Box 8963
Philadelphia, PA 19101

Dear Sir/Madam:

Enclosed please find my resume in response to your recent advertisement in *The Philadelphia Inquirer* for a Director of Operations. This position sounds very interesting, and I think that you will find my background to closely parallel your requirements.

Your ad states that you are looking for a "seasoned manufacturing manager with over ten years experience in the manufacture of sheet metal fabricated assemblies". As my resume will attest, I have over 15 years experience in the fabrication of residential and commercial air conditioning and heating units, making extensive use of sheet metal assembly.

Additionally, your ad states that you require "a mature individual who has had P&L responsibilities for a multi-location operation employing at least 1,000 employees and accounting for at least $100 million in annual sales volume". As Operations Manager for Trefton Manufacturing, I currently have P&L responsibilities for four manufacturing facilities totaling 1,500 employees and sales volume of $128 million. I also have a B.S. degree in Mechanical Engineering as called for in your advertisement.

If you agree that my background is a close match for your requirements, I would welcome the opportunity to meet with you personally for the purpose of further exploring the prospects of employment with your company.

Salary requirements are in the mid $90K range with some flexibility for negotiation dependent upon details of the total compensation and benefits package.

I can be reached during the day on a confidential basis at my office. My office phone number is (209) 375-8945.

Thank you for your consideration, and I look forward to hearing from you.

Sincerely,

Robert S. Peterson

Robert S. Peterson

Enclosure

Sample Cover Letter—Response to Advertisement

85 Country Club Lane
Shaker Heights
Cleveland, OH 14457
February 18, 1995

Ms. Sandra B. Perkins
Employment Manager
Basker & Jardell, Inc.
801 Riley Square
Ridley Hills, MA 87013

Dear Ms. Perkins:

Enclosed please find my resume in response to Basker & Jardell's ad for a Senior Cost Accountant in this Sunday's *Boston Globe*. This position is very much in line with my current career objective, and I would appreciate the opportunity of discussing it further with you during a personal interview.

The following professional highlights from my background appear to be in keeping with your position requirements:

- B.A. Degree in Accounting from Cornell University
- Five years cost accounting experience in manufacturing
- Understanding and ability to apply modern cost theory
- Excellent oral and written communications ability (Editor of College Newspaper)
- Excellent rapport with manufacturing personnel
- High energy level and volume producer
- Not afraid to work long hours to get the job done

Since Boston is my home, I would welcome the opportunity to return to my native state. Future relocation, however, is not objectionable. Salary requirements are in the low $70K range.

I can be reached on a confidential basis at my office during the day -- (914) 376-4435. Evening calls to my home are preferable, however. My home phone is (914) 376-4475.

I appreciate your consideration and look forward to hearing from you shortly.

Sincerely,

Stephen H. Ralston

Stephen H. Ralston

Enclosure

Sample Cover Letter—Response to Advertisement

Apartment 10A
Ridgewood Arms Apts.
25 Rawley Avenue
Bakersville, ME 57332
June 14, 1994

Mr. Martin D. Smith
Vice President Human Resources
Delray Manufacturing Company
668 Parker Street
Springfield, MA 07727

Dear Mr. Smith:

Wednesday's edition of *The Springfield Newspaper* was a pleasant surprise. Your ad for a Human Resource Assistant brightened my day and gave me reason to hope that one can enter the field of Human Resources without prior experience. Hurrah for Delray Manufacturing Company!

Please consider my credentials carefully since they appear to be a close match for your job requirements. Consider the following highlights:

- M.S., Human Resources Management, Michigan State, 1994
- Honors Graduate, G.P.A. 3.3/4.0
- President of Student Government Association
- Editor-In-Chief, Student Newspaper
- Vice President, Delta Sorority
- Captain, Women's Swim and Tennis Teams

As you can see, I appear to have the academic and leadership credentials called for in you ad. Beyond these, however, I have a high energy level, am very results-oriented and have a strong desire for a career in Human Resources.

I would welcome the opportunity for a personal interview to further discuss my qualifications I am sure that I can convince you of my potential for a bright career in Human Resources if given the chance!

Please call me at my home -- (315) 744-5234. I look forward to hearing from you shortly.

Sincerely,

Mary Anne King

Mary Anne King

Enclosure

Sample Cover Letter—Response to Advertisement

35 Cranberry Road
Green Forest Subdivision
Montgomery, AL 57556
December 12, 1995

Box R-334
The Atlanta Journal
305 West Peachtree Street
Atlanta, GA 37224

Dear Sir/Madam:

I read with great interest your ad in this Sunday's edition of *The Atlanta Journal* calling for a Research Engineer, Injection Molding. I would like to be considered for this position and feel that I have sufficient qualifications to warrant your serious interest.

Consider the following as they relate to your requirements:

- M.S. Degree in Mechanical Design Engineering
- B.S. Degree in Plastics Technology
- Five years with Hilton Plastics as a Research Design Engineer
- Eight patents for injection molded packages

I have enclosed a resume which provides a fairly complete summary of my education and experience. I would be pleased to answer additional questions concerning my background and would welcome the opportunity of discussing this opportunity with you during a personal interview.

Salary requirements are in the $80-85K range subject to negotiation depending upon specifics of the opportunity in question. Although open to relocation, I must confess to a preference for the Southeast.

Since I am not actively on the job market, I request that my application be handled in strictest confidence. I prefer not being contacted at the office and would appreciate all calls being directed to my home during evening hours. My home phone is (917) 374-0956.

Thank you for your consideration, and I look forward to hearing from you shortly.

Sincerely,

John B. Duncan

John B. Duncan

Enclosure

Sample Cover Letter—To Personal Referral

818 Kimberly Lane
Shillington, PA 19432
June 22, 1993

Mr. B. David Carter
Vice President of Marketing
Jarzan International, Inc.
35 Europe Avenue
Philadelphia, PA 19830

Dear Mr. Carter:

John Bristol, a close friend of mine, suggested that I contact you. John and I worked together in sales and marketing for the Mittinger Company. This was our first job following college and we went through the Sales Training Program together. From there, we both went on to blaze new sales records for the Company!

I ran into John last week at the Electronics Convention in Atlanta. After explaining my current situation to him, he suggested that I contact you directly and feel free to use him as a reference as well.

Mr. Carter, my current contract with Tollerston Marketing Consultants expires next month. Since long-range growth opportunities appear rather limited, I don't plan to renew this relationship. I am thus on the market in search of a senior sales management position.

John advises me that you are searching for a National Sales Manager and, from what he describes, it appears that I could well be the person you are looking for. Additionally, your position sounds like a close match for my immediate career objectives. Perhaps there is sufficient reason for us to explore this possibility during a personal meeting.

I am enclosing my resume for your review and consideration. Of course, this is only a thumbnail sketch of my background and experience. I would appreciate the opportunity to more fully discuss my qualifications with you personally.

I will be in the Philadelphia area next week and plan to give you a call. Perhaps we can get together for a brief meeting over lunch.

Thank you for your consideration, Mr. Carter, and I look forward to talking with you.

Sincerely,

Rodney B. Smith

Rodney B. Smith

Enclosure

Sample Cover Letter—To Personal Referral

814 Butternut Lane
Burnt Hills, OK 43225
January 25, 1995

Ms. Katherine Marcus
Director of Human Resources
Holstetter Manufacturing Company
497 Dry Gulch Road
Tulsa, OK 47789

Dear Katherine:

It appears that we have a close mutual friend. John Carlson and I go back a few years. We have done quite a bit of sailing together including one three-week charter out of Norfolk to Bermuda. I understand that you have done your share of sailing as well. John tells me that the two of you are planning a charter trip out of St. Thomas in October. Sounds like a challenging and interesting trip. Wish I could join you.

While sailing with John last weekend, he mentioned that he knew you quite well and suggested that I contact you for some assistance on a personal matter to see if you could be of some help. I would very sincerely welcome any thoughts, ideas or suggestions you might have.

After 13 years as Human Resources Manager for Houston Minerals, the company has decided to close its doors on June 1st of this year. This unfortunate circumstance places me in the position of needing to locate a new position.

Although I know that it is highly unlikely that your company has an appropriate opening at this time, I would very much welcome your assistance and guidance in my job search. As a respected leader in the human resources community, perhaps some of your professional acquaintances may have a suitable opening or may know of one who does. Katherine, if it wouldn't be too much of an imposition, I would appreciate if you could provide me with the names of other professionals who you feel might be of possible assistance in helping me to identify an appropriate opportunity.

I am enclosing a copy of my resume for your use. Please feel free to use it as you may see fit.

I will plan to call you within the next couple of days to see if we can arrange a meeting. Thank you, Katherine, for your help.

Sincerely,

Lee Briton

Lee Briton

Enclosure

Sample Cover Letter—To Personal Referral

8 Pickering Way
Hawthorne, PA 19372
May 15, 1993

Mr. Jeffrey R. Davis
Director of Operations
The Boston Carvinger Company
18 Bay Bridge Road
Boston, MA 55793

Dear Mr. Davis:

I understand that you are a close personal friend of David Thatcher. Dave and I grew up together in Wyomissing Hills and were co-captains of the high school football team. During our twentieth class reunion last week, I mentioned a personal matter to Dave and he suggested that I might contact you for some guidance and assistance.

After a challenging and rewarding career in manufacturing with the Davidson Company, it appears that I will be seeking a new career opportunity closer to the Boston area. My wife's parents live near Frammingham and Sally has been wanting to move back to the area. Although I have thoroughly enjoyed my career with Davidson, I must admit to a desire to return as well. In any event, we have made the decision and are in the process of seeking a new career opportunity in the Boston area. In this regard, I would appreciate your assistance.

I know that it is highly unlikely that The Boston Carvinger Company has an appropriate opportunity at this time, and I am not contacting you for that purpose. Instead, as a member of the greater Boston manufacturing community, I felt that you might be in a position to provide me with the names of a few good contacts who might be of assistance in my job search. Even if they do not have immediate openings within their own companies, perhaps they could refer me to others who do.

Mr. Davis, I will be in Boston next week and would appreciate the opportunity to meet with you. Perhaps we could get together over lunch or dinner. I will call you to see if we can arrange a convenient time.

In the meantime, I am enclosing a copy of my resume to give you a better understanding of my background. As a manufacturing executive, I would value your thoughts on the effectiveness of this resume. Perhaps you could give me some pointers during our meeting.

Thank you very much for your assistance, and I look forward to meeting with you personally. Dave speaks very highly of you.

Sincerely,

David B. Johnson

David B. Johnson

Enclosure

Sample Cover Letter—To Personal Referral

82 Fulton Street
Jamesville, NY 13779
March 22, 1996

Ms. Katherine B. Harrison
Director of Engineering
Berrington Engineering Associates
857 North Arlington Drive
Syracuse, NY 57786

Dear Ms. Harrison:

A close personal friend and past sorority sister from Syracuse University, Joan Mattersby, suggested that I contact you. Joan and I were in many of the same engineering classes together at Syracuse and managed to keep one another afloat. Joan tells me that the two of you have been doing some interesting project work together for the Women in Business Association in the greater Syracuse area. I understand that your membership drive has gone tremendously well and that Association membership has more than tripled in the past year alone. Quite an accomplishment! Joan is quite excited with the potential for future impact of this organization on the business community.

Joan felt that as a fellow woman engineer and successful engineering executive, you might be willing to help me with a personal situation. I would certainly welcome your advice and support.

Following completion of my M.S. degree in Mechanical Engineering in 1986, I accepted a position as Research Engineer with Hunter Laboratories here in Jamesville. Although the position was described as heavily research-oriented initially, it has not turned out that way. I find that I am spending 80% or better of my time in reduction-to-practice work, with less than 20% on true research and development projects. I have thus decided to seek other employment where there is greater opportunity to do conceptual, creative work.

Although I know that it is unlikely that Berrington has an appropriate position available, I would still appreciate if you could review my credentials. I have enclosed a copy of my resume for this purpose. More importantly, however, perhaps you could provide me with a list of personal contacts who might know of someone currently in search of a creative, young research engineer. If you could, I would be most appreciative.

If your busy schedule permits, it would be nice if we could have lunch together sometime during the next few weeks. I will give you a call sometime early next week to see if we can work out an appropriate time to get together.

Thank you, Ms. Harrison, for your help.

Sincerely,

Regina A. Schweiz

Regina A. Schweiz

Enclosure

Sample Cover Letter—To Personal Referral

935 Jefferson Avenue
Washington, DC 37052
April 22, 1994

Mr. J. Perrington Russel
Senior Vice President & Partner
Smith, Brennen & Russel Associates
Financial Consultants
300 Franklyn Place, Suite 100
Washington, DC 37775

Dear Mr. Russel:

At Friday's meeting of the Darlington Investors Club, I was speaking to a friend of mine, Donald G. Crystal, President of the District of Columbia National Bank. He mentioned that you are currently searching for a Director of Taxes and suggested that I contact you.

I have an MBA in Finance from the University of Pennsylvania's Wharton School and over 20 years experience in taxes. I understand, by the way, that you are also a Wharton School graduate.

Mr. Russell, as my enclosed resume will attest, I have held a wide variety of positions of increasing responsibility in the field of taxes, starting as a Tax Accountant and ending with my current position as Manager of Corporate Taxes with Scherling Corporation. In my current position, I manage a staff of eight tax accountants in the preparation of all federal, state and local returns. Annual returns are valued at $85 million.

In the last three years, through creative and innovative approaches, I have saved Scherling $1.8 million in tax reductions. Through a new, creative approach in the area of foreign leasing, I expect to realize another $1 million in tax savings by year end.

From what Donald describes as your requirements, it would appear that my background is a fairly good match. If you agree, perhaps we could meet to explore this matter in greater detail on a more personal basis.

I will plan to call you next week to see if you are interested in arranging a meeting. I would very much appreciate this opportunity to talk with you.

Thank you for your consideration, and I look forward to the possibility of meeting with you personally.

Sincerely,

R. Samuel Gothing

R. Samuel Gothing

Enclosure

16

THE
TOP 50
EXECUTIVE
SEARCH FIRMS

For those uninitiated in the ways of the employment market, there has long been a lot of confusion about the difference between the employment agency and the executive search firm. It is important for those in search of a new position to be knowledgeable of employment sources so that they have a good understanding of the roles of each and know what to expect. Further, without a clear understanding of these employment sources and how they function, you will end up frustrated and disillusioned and will not know how to capitalize on the individual expertise of each.

It is important that you understand the difference between the executive search firm and the employment agency. After conveying this understanding, we will take a detailed look at each of these services in an effort to distinguish the overall role of each in the employment process as well as how each functions. Let's start first with the employment agency.

There are thousands of employment agencies across the United States. Many are independent agencies working solely on their own except for an informal, loosely defined affiliation with a few other independent agencies. Others are part of a large franchise organization in which, although the agency is owned by an individual or autonomous group, the manner in which the agency functions is governed by a contract with the franchisor. This contract may stipulate certain constraints on the franchise, such as limiting the geographical territory in which the franchise may operate, restricting the franchisee's business to certain career disciplines (marketing, sales, engineering, and so on), or limiting the franchisee to certain industries.

The main distinction between the executive search firm and the employment agency lies in three principal areas.

1. Who is represented by the firm?
2. Who pays the firm's fee?
3. How does the firm operate?

EMPLOYMENT AGENCIES

The employment agency represents the individual who is in search of a job. With the employment agency, therefore, you are frequently required to sign a contract authorizing the agency to act in your behalf in search of a position for you. As with any contract, in order to be binding the contract must provide for "valuable consideration." In the case of the employment agency contract, the valuable consideration is the agent's fee that you must pay to the agency upon acceptance of a position with a company with whom the agency has placed you in contact. These employment agency fees can be substantial and are charged on the basis of a percentage of first year's anticipated income (salary plus all incentive payments).

Although there is some variation in employment agency fees, the industry standard appears to be based on a formula of 1 percent per $1,000 of annual income. Thus, under the terms of the normal agency contract, an anticipated first year's income of $20,000 would yield an employment agency fee of $4,000. Likewise, an income of $25,000 would result in an employment agency fee of $6,250. Most employment agencies with this type of standard contract have a cutoff or maximum fee of 30 percent on incomes of $30,000 and above. Thus an annual income of $50,000 would yield, under the terms of such a contract, an employment agency fee of $15,000.

The fee schedule below is representative of those employment agencies now charging an agency fee of 1 percent per $1,000 of first year's income with a maximum cap on fees of 30 percent. This should enable you to get a fairly close estimate of what your obligation would be under such an agency contract.

There are some variations between these firms. One common variation to the standard schedule is one that calls for 1 percent plus 1 percent for every $1,000 of the first year's

Normal Agency Fee Schedule*

First Year's Income ($)	Agency Fee (%)	Range of Fees ($)
14,999 and under	15	2,250 and under
15,000–15,999	15	2,250–2,400
16,000–16,999	16	2,560–2,720
17,000–17,999	17	2,890–3,060
18,000–18,999	18	3,240–3,420
19,000–19,999	19	3,610–3,800
20,000–20,999	20	4,000–4,200
21,000–21,999	21	4,410–4,620
22,000–22,999	22	4,840–5,060
23,000–23,999	23	5,290–5,520
24,000–24,999	24	5,760–6,000
25,000–25,999	25	6,250–6,500
26,000–26,999	26	6,760–7,020
27,000–27,999	27	7,290–7,560
28,000–28,999	28	7,840–8,120
29,000–29,999	29	8,410–8,700
30,000 & Over	30	9,000 & Up

*Based upon 1% per $1,000 for the first year's income, with a maximum of 30%.

estimated income. The fee schedule below is representative of firms falling into this category.

I am sure that after reviewing these fee schedules you will come to have a lot of respect for the size of the typical employment agency fee. Many people would shudder at the thought of having to pay an agency fee in the range of $9,000 or more. Yet such fees are not uncommon for those whose annual salaries fall into the over $30,000 range. You should therefore approach the signing of an employment agency contract with a great deal of respect and caution.

This does not mean that you should shy away from working with employment agencies. You should simply be well aware of the obligation that you create when you sign the agency contract. Don't despair, however, since most of the better employers will agree to pay the employment agency fee on behalf of the professionals they hire. To be sure that this is the case, though, ask the employment agency, prior to agreeing to an interview, whether the prospective employer

Agency Fee Schedule*

First Year's Income ($)	Agency Fee (%)	Range of Fees ($)
14,999 and under	15	2,250 and under
15,000–15,999	16	2,400–2,560
16,000–16,999	17	2,720–2,890
17,000–17,999	18	3,060–3,240
18,000–18,999	19	3,420–3,610
19,000–19,999	20	3,800–4,000
20,000–20,999	21	4,200–4,410
21,000–21,999	22	4,620–4,840
22,000–22,999	23	5,060–5,290
23,000–23,999	24	5,520–5,760
24,000–24,999	25	6,000–6,250
25,000–25,999	26	6,500–6,760
26,000–26,999	27	7,020–7,290
27,000–27,999	28	7,560–7,840
28,000–28,999	29	8,120–8,410
29,000 & Over	30	8,700 & Up

*Based upon 1% + 1% per $1,000 of the first year's income, with a maximum of 30%.

with whom you will be interviewing is willing to pay the agent's fee. Should the prospective employer be unwilling to do so, you may want to think twice before agreeing to an employment interview.

One way of safeguarding yourself against the payment of an employment agency fee is to write across the face of the employment agency contract—"Will interview for fee paid positions only." This places the responsibility for assuring that you are directed to "fee paid only" interviews on the agency. Although I'm not an attorney, it would appear to me that you have shifted the bulk of the responsibility to the agency. In any event, however, you have certainly alerted the employment agency that you are unwilling to pay an agency fee. Even though you may have taken this action, I would still advise you to ask in advance of any interview whether the prospective employer has agreed to pay the agency fee if you are hired. In this way, you are absolutely certain that you will never find yourself in the position of having to pay a sizable fee.

For the inexperienced job seeker, one of the most confusing and bewildering aspects of any job-hunting campaign is the selection of a good employment agency. This task is complicated by the fact that there are literally thousands of employment agencies in the United States. Some have poor reputations from the professional standpoint and have conducted themselves in less than commendable fashion. There are many agencies that are good and handle themselves professionally. Unfortunately, however, the few that do not have accounted for some employment "horror stories," several of which I am sure you have heard.

It is important that you have some good advice regarding the selection of an agency that will truly represent your best interests and do a thoroughly professional job in helping you to find the position and employer that you seek. Let's first, however, examine the dangers of making a poor selection—some of the unnecessary experiences that you may encounter in utilizing a source that does not have your best personal and professional interests in mind.

Agencies who conduct themselves in an unprofessional manner are known among employment professionals as "body shops." These agencies operate on the premise that they are in business simply to make money. The more people that they are able to place, the more agency fees, or placement fees, will come rolling into their coffers. They care little about the individual employment candidate they represent; they are concerned only with making a placement and earning an agency commission. These are the agencies described by the professional employment community as the ones who attempt to "place a square peg in a round hole." Having received the employment candidate's resume, their typical mode of operation is to pick up the telephone and call numerous employers in an effort to "pitch" their candidate. They care little whether the company with whom they are speaking has an appropriate opening or whether such openings are in line with the qualifications and interest of the employment candidates they represent.

Such agencies are looked upon by the professional employment community with disdain. The experienced employment professional has usually trained his or her administrative assistant to screen out phone calls from such firms and will refuse to even talk to them. The reason for such action is simple. Too many times in the past the employment professional has experienced a situation where the agency has grossly misrepresented the qualifications and/or the experience of the candidate they are representing. The result has been that the employer agrees to an interview with the candidate only to discover, during the course of the interview, that the candidate does not possess the skills and qualifications as presented by the agency. This proves to be both embarrassing and expensive to the employment manager. First, the employment manager is embarrassed to discover that the candidate is not qualified for the employment opening. Second, he or she is embarrassed by having to tell the candidate that he or she does not have the qualifications sought. If told at the beginning of the interview, the employment manager may terminate the interview early and the job candidate is frequently both hurt and angered. Much of this anger and hostility is directed toward the employer rather than the agency who has made the referral. Unfortunately, the candidate has not been present when his or her qualifications have been discussed with the employer and thus may be left with the impression that the employment manager is careless or incompetent. Should the employment manager elect to proceed with the interview schedule and use the valuable time of busy managers to interview an individual who is clearly unqualified for the position, he or she will likely incur the wrath of these managers and risk earning a reputation for carelessness or incompetence.

In addition to the embarrassment and hard feelings caused by this situation, there may be considerable expense involved. There can be travel expenses reimbursed by the company up to several hundred dollars (plane fare, meals, lodging, and so on). In addition, there is the time lost by the employment manager as well as the managers who interviewed the candidate. In salaries alone (not considering the lost production), this could easily result in costs of $100 or $200 (depending on the levels of the managers involved).

These "body shop" agencies earn an extremely unsatisfactory reputation in the employment community. The effect is that knowledgeable candidates with good qualifications, who have taken the time to research agencies, avoid these firms. These agencies thus frequently end up representing those employment candidates who have poor qualifications and are hard to place. This further renders such agencies useless as far as the employment professional is concerned.

From the employment candidate's standpoint, there is much at risk when selecting such an agency to represent you. One great danger, if you are currently employed, is that such firms may not use proper discretion in handling your resume. Many mass mail your resume to numerous employers. In such cases it is not entirely uncommon for the resume of an unknowing candidate to be sent to the candidate's current employer. In the case of better employers this may simply result in some embarrassment; in other cases, however, it may result in termination of the employee's employment.

On the other side of the employment equation, these agencies may grossly misrepresent a job to the employment applicant, indicating that the position pays considerably more than it in fact does, that the position has considerably more scope and authority than it really does, or that promotional opportunities are substantially greater than they really are. Such employment agencies appear to be substantially more motivated by receiving commissions than they are in deriving professional satisfaction from helping people locate a position that will satisfy their career objectives.

By contrast, there are also some excellent agencies out there. It is simply a matter of finding out who they are and how to make contact with them. There are techniques I would like to suggest to you in accomplishing this. First, if you know someone who is a human resources manager or employment manager in a major corporation, you might inquire of them which agencies they utilize and which they feel conduct themselves in a professional manner. This alone may not be a significant help since companies tend to gravitate toward those better employment agencies who specialize in their industries. Thus they may refer to you agencies that are proficient in finding people in the steel and automotive industries, but if you are in the chemical industry, this would be of little or no help to you. Where possible, therefore, it would be a good practice to attempt to make contact with human resource managers or professional employment individuals within your own industry. This is particularly true if your background is only marketable to the industry in which you currently work. Thus, if you are an engineer with considerable experience in the steel industry, the likelihood is that your background is far less marketable in other industries. Conversely, if your background is in a more generic function (for example: accounting, finance, or human resources), there is a high likelihood that you will be able to cross industry lines with little or no effort.

Another good technique to use in identifying the better employment agencies is to check for advertisement in professional publications related to your career or field. After identifying a number of these agencies, call some of these firms on the phone without disclosing your name. Generally describe your background to them and tell them that you do not wish to disclose your name until you have had an opportunity to find out more about their firm. Request the names and telephone numbers of some employment candidates with whom they have recently worked. Having done this, call these individuals and introduce yourself. The following are some questions you might use:

1. Did the agency appear to have a good understanding of your background and qualifications such that they did a good job of representing you to prospective employers?

2. Did the agency appear to have contact with the better employers within your industry?

3. Did the agency do a reasonably thorough job of explaining to you the job opportunities of prospective employers? Was the agency able to be factual in describing the reporting relationships of the position, job scope and accountability, promotional prospects, compensation levels, company benefits, and relocation expense reimbursement policy?

4. Did the agency do a good job in representing your interests during the negotiation phase with the prospective employer? Were the terms of the employment offer totally satisfactory?

5. If you were to be back in the labor market at some future point in time, would you consider using this agency again?

6. In your opinion, during the course of your relationship with the agency, did anything happen that caused you to feel that the agency was less than professional or ethical?

7. Who were you dealing with at the agency?

Having received answers to these questions from four or five employment candidates with whom the agency has worked, you are in a good position to judge whether the agency is the type of firm with whom you would like to deal.

EXECUTIVE SEARCH FIRMS

Unlike the employment agency, the executive search firm does not represent the individual. Instead, these firms are retained by the employer to search out qualified individuals to fill key positions within their client company. All fees are charged directly to the employer, with no fee charged to the successful candidate found by the search firm to fill the position.

The better executive search firms are highly respected within the employment community. They frequently belong to an association that requires them to operate in accordance with an extremely rigid code of ethics and conduct. Inappropriate behavior would cause a member firm to be immediately dismissed from the association. Member firms are very protective of their professional reputation and will not tolerate devious or unethical behavior on the part of other association members.

Perhaps the best known of these associations is the Association of Executive Search Consultants, Inc., headquartered in Stamford, Connecticut. This association is comprised of some 50 member firms and subscribes to a very tightly enforced code of ethics. The membership of this organization is believed to represent the top 50 executive search firms in the United States. A select listing of the association's membership is contained at the end of this chapter, along with a few other select firms who are also well known in the executive search field.

Generally speaking, these search firms handle management and executive searches only (with salaries in the over $75,000 per year range). On occasion, however, they may agree to handle client searches for some technical or professional positions in the under $75,000 range that are particularly difficult to fill.

When writing to an executive search firm, it is important to remember that they may not be working on a compatible search at the time that your resume arrives. Additionally, they will make no attempt to help you find employment unless they coincidentally have a compatible opening with one of their client firms. It is important, therefore, that you acknowledge this fact in your cover letter. See Chapter 14 for guidance in the preparation of effective cover letters when writing to executive search firms.

If you are in search of a management or executive position, it is recommended that you write to some of the more reputable executive search firms as part of your overall job-hunting strategy. Should they not have an immediate search assignment that is compatible with your qualifications and interests, provided you have reasonable credentials, they will likely file your resume for future reference. There is always the possibility that an appropriate search assignment may be just around the corner and that you will be hearing from them.

The following listing of the top 50 executive search firms is provided for your convenience. They are listed by geographical region for ease in focusing on those geographical areas that are in line with your preference.

Top Executive Search Firms

Northeast

BARGER & SARGEANT, INC.
22 Windermere Rd., Ste. B
P.O. Box 1420
Center Harbor, NH 03226-1420
(603) 253-4700

BATTALIA WINSTON
300 Park Ave.
New York, NY 10022
(212) 308-8080

BOYDEN WORLD CORPORATION
625 Stanwix St., Ste. 2405
Allegheny Tower
Pittsburgh, PA 15222-1423
(412) 391-3020

375 Park Avenue, Ste. 1008
New York, NY 10152
(212) 980-6480

55 Madison Ave., Ste. 400
Morristown, NJ 07960-7354
(201) 267-0980

364 Elwood Ave.
Hawthorne, NY 10532-1239
(914) 747-0093

CANNY, BOWEN INC.
200 Park Ave. 49th Fl.
New York, NY 10166-4998

101 Federal St.
Boston, MA 02110-1800

CHRISTENSON & HUTCHISON
466 Southern Blvd.
Chatham, NJ 07928
(201) 966-1600

GOULD & MCCOY, INC.
300 Park Ave.
New York, NY 10022
(212) 688-8671

HEIDRICK & STRUGGLES, INC.
125 S. Wacker Drive, Ste. 2800
Chicago, IL 60606-4590
(312) 372-8811

245 Park Ave., Ste. 3230
New York, NY 10167-0152
(212) 867-9876

One Post Office Sq., Ste. 3570
Boston, MA 02109
(617) 423-1140

104 Field Point Rd.
Greenwich, CT 06830
(203) 629-3200

**INTERNATIONAL MGMT.
ADVISORS, INC.**
516 Fifth Ave.
New York, NY 10036-7501
(212) 768-4121

**THE JOHN LUCHT
CONSULTANCY INC.**
The Olympic Tower
641 Fifth Ave.
New York, NY 10022
(212) 935-4660

**A.T. KEARNEY EXECUTIVE
SEARCH**
153 E. 53rd St.
New York, NY 10022
(212) 751-7040

Four Landmark Sq., Ste. 302
Stamford, CT 06901
(203) 969-2222

**KENSINGTON MGMT.
CONSULTANTS, INC.**
2 Research Drive
Shelton, CT 06484
(203) 925-9555

KORN/FERRY INT'L.
237 Park Ave.
New York, NY 10017
(212) 687-1834

1 Palmer Sq.
Princeton, NJ 08542
(908) 647-4131

101 Federal St., 24th Floor
Boston, MA 02110
(617) 345-0200

81 Wethersfield Ave.
Hartford, CT 06114
(203) 727-0721

One Landmark Sq.
Stamford, CT 06901
(203) 359-3350

LAMALIE AMROP INT'L.
489 Fifth Ave.
New York, NY 10017-6105
(212) 953-7900

LAWRENCE L. LAPHAM, INC.
80 Park Ave., Ste. 3K
New York, NY 10016
(212) 599-0644

OLIVER & ROZNER ASSOC., INC.
598 Madison Ave.
New York, NY 10022
(212) 688-1850

PAUL RAY BERNDSTON
101 Park Ave.
New York, NY 10178
(212) 370-1316

**RUSSELL REYNOLDS
ASSOC., INC.**
200 Park Ave.
New York, NY 10166
(212) 351-2000

45 School St., Old City Hall
Boston, MA 02108
(617) 523-1111

SPENCERSTUART
55 E. 52nd St.
New York, NY 10055-1021
(212) 407-0200

2005 Market St., Ste. 2350
Philadelphia, PA 19103
(215) 851-6200

695 E. Main St.
Financial Centre
Stamford, CT 06901
(203) 324-6333

TASA INTERNATIONAL
750 Lexington Ave., Ste. 1800
New York, NY 10022
(212) 486-1490

THORNDIKE DELAND ASSOC.
275 Madison Ave., 13th Floor
New York, NY 10016
(212) 661-6200

WARD HOWELL
  INTERNATIONAL, INC.
99 Park Ave., Ste. 2000
New York, NY 10016-1699
(212) 697-3730

One Landmark Sq., Ste. 1810
Stamford, CT 06901
(203) 964-1481

WILLIAM WILLIS WORLDWIDE
  INC.
164 Mason St.
Greenwich, CT 06830-6611
(203) 661-4500

Southeast

THE BRAND CO., INC.
8402 Red Bay Ct.
Vero Beach, FL 32963
(407) 231-1807

HEIDRICK & STRUGGLES, INC.
303 Peachtree St., Ste. 3100
One Peachtree Ctr.
Atlanta, GA 30308
(404) 577-2410

76 S. Laura St., Ste. 2110
Jacksonville, FL 32202
(904) 355-6674

2000 K St. NW, Ste. 610
Washington, DC 20006
(202) 466-5410

A.T. KEARNEY EXECUTIVE
  SEARCH
225 Reinekers Lane
Alexandria, VA 22314
(703) 739-4624

1100 Abernathy Rd., Ste. 900
Atlanta, GA 30328-5603
(404) 393-9900

Miami Center, Suite 3180
201 South Biscayne Blvd.
Miami, FL 33131
(305) 577-0046

KORN/FERRY INT'L.
303 Peachtree St. NE, Ste. 1600
Atlanta, GA 30308
(404) 577-7542

900 19th St. NW
Presidential Plaza
Washington, DC 20006
(202) 822-9444

LAMALIE AMROP INT'L.
13920 N. Dale Mabry
Tampa, FL 33618-2489
(813) 961-7494

191 Peachtree St., NE
Atlanta, GA 30303-1747
(404) 688-0800

LOCKE & ASSOC.
2410 Nations Bank Plaza
Charlotte, NC 28280
(704) 372-6600

4144 Carmichael Rd., Ste. 20
Montgomery, AL 36106
(205) 272-7400

ROBISON & MCAULAY
1350 First Citizens Plaza
128 S. Tryon St.
Charlotte, NC 28202
(704) 376-0059

ROPES ASSOC., INC.
333 N. New River Drive E., Ste.
4000
Ft. Lauderdale, FL 33301-2240
(305) 525-6600

RUSSELL REYNOLDS ASSOC., INC.
The Hurt Bldg., 50 Hurt Plaza,
Ste. 600
Atlanta, GA 30303
(404) 577-3000

1700 Pennsylvania Ave. NW, Ste. 850
Washington, DC 20006
(202) 628-2150

SPENCERSTUART
1201 W. Peachtree St.
One Atlantic Ctr., Ste. 3230
Atlanta, GA 30309
(404) 892-2800

TASA/FLEMING
9300 Shelbyville Rd., Ste. 1010
Hurstbourne Place
Louisville, KY 40222
(502) 426-3500

240 N. Washington Blvd., Ste. 322
Sarasota, FL 34236
(813) 366-7979

**WITT/KIEFFER, FORD,
    HADELMAN & LLOYD**
4800 Hampden Lane, Ste. 1050
Bethesda, MD 20814
(301) 654-5070

Midwest

**AIM EXECUTIVE CONSULTING
    SERVICES**
35000 Chardon Rd., Ste. 425
Willoughby Hills, OH 44094
(216) 975-1144

6605 W. Central Ave., Ste. 250
Toledo, OH 43617
(419) 841-8998

4060 Executive Drive
Beavercreek, OH 45430
(513) 427-3388

BOWDEN & CO., INC.
5000 Rockside Rd., Ste. 550
Cleveland, OH 44131
(216) 447-1800

BOYDEN WORLD CORPORATION
2 Prudential Plaza
180 N. Stetson Ave., Ste. 5050
Chicago, IL 60601
(312) 565-1300

HEIDRICK & STRUGGLES, INC.
125 S. Wacker Drive, Ste. 2800
Chicago, IL 60606-4590
(312) 372-8811

600 Superior Ave. E., Ste. 2500
Cleveland, OH 44114
(216) 241-7410

THE HEIDRICK PARTNERS, INC.
20 N. Wacker Drive, Ste. 2850
Chicago, IL 60606
(312) 845-9700

HODGE-CRONIN & ASSOC., INC.
9575 W. Higgins Rd., Ste. 904
Rosemont, IL 60018
(708) 692-2041

**A.T. KEARNEY EXECUTIVE
SEARCH**
222 W. Adams St.
Chicago, IL 60606
(312) 648-0111

1200 Bank One Ctr.
600 Superior Ave. E.
Cleveland, OH 44114-2650
(216) 241-6880

8500 Normandale Lake Blvd.,
   Ste. 1730
Minneapolis, MN 55437
(612) 921-8436

KORN/FERRY INT'L.
2508 IDS Center, 80 S. 8th St.
Minneapolis, MN 55402
(612) 333-1834

120 S. Riverside Plaza, Ste. 918
Chicago, IL 60606
(312) 726-1841

KUNZER ASSOC., LTD.
2001 Spring Rd.
Oak Brook, IL 60521
(708) 574-0010

LAMALIE AMROP INT'L.
1375 E. Ninth St., Ste. 1320
One Cleveland Ctr.
Cleveland, OH 44114-1724
(216) 694-3000

123 N. Wacker Drive, Ste. 950
Chicago, IL 60606-1700
(312) 782-3113

LAUER, SBARBARO ASSOC., INC.
30 N. LaSalle St., Ste. 4030
Chicago, IL 60602
(312) 372-7050

MCFEELY WACKERLE SHULMAN
20 N. Wacker Drive, Ste. 3110
Chicago, IL 60606
(312) 641-2977

PAUL RAY BERNDTSON
10 S. Riverside Plaza, Ste. 720
Chicago, IL 60606
(312) 876-0730

**RUSSELL REYNOLDS ASSOC.,
   INC.**
3050 Norwest Ctr., 90 S. Seventh St.
Minneapolis, MN 55402
(612) 332-6966

200 S. Wacker Drive, Ste. 3600
Chicago, IL 60606
(312) 993-9696

S. K. STEWART & ASSOC.
Box 40110
Cincinnati, OH 45240
(513) 851-7060

SPENCERSTUART
401 N. Michigan Ave.
Chicago, IL 60611-4244
(312) 822-0080

TASA/FLEMING
1428 Franklin St.
P.O. Box 604
Columbus, IN 47202
(812) 376-9061

WARD HOWELL INT'L., INC.
300 S. Wacker Drive, Ste. 2940
Chicago, IL 60606
(312) 236-2211

1250 S. Grove Ave., Ste. 201
Barrington, IL 60010
(708) 382-2206

**WITT/KIEFFER, FORD,
   HADELMAN & LLOYD**
2015 Spring Rd., Ste. 510
Oak Brook, IL 60521
(708) 990-1370

Southwest

EASTMAN & BEAUDINE, INC.
1370 One Galleria Twr.
13355 Noel Rd., LB-31
Dallas, TX 75240
(214) 661-5520

HEIDRICK & STRUGGLES, INC.
1999 Bryan St., Ste. 1919
Dallas, TX 75201
(214) 220-2130

**A.T. KEARNEY EXECUTIVE
  SEARCH**
3050 Post Oak Blvd., Ste. 500
Houston, TX 77056
(713) 621-9927

Lincoln Plz.
500 N. Akard St., Ste. 4170
Dallas, TX 75201
(214) 969-0010

6930 E. First St.
Scottsdale, AZ 85251
(602) 994-3032

KORN/FERRY INT'L.
1100 Louisiana, Ste. 2850
Houston, TX 77002
(713) 651-1834

500 N. Akard St.,
3950 Lincoln Plaza
Dallas, TX 75201
(214) 954-1834

LAMALIE AMROP INT'L.
1301 McKinney St., Ste. 3520
Chevron Tower
Houston, TX 77010-3034
(713) 739-8602

1601 Elm St., Thanksgiving Twr.
Ste. 4246
Dallas, TX 75201-4768
(214) 754-0019

PAUL RAY BERNDTSON
301 Commerce St., Ste. 2300
Ft. Worth, TX 76102
(817) 334-0500

Texas Commerce Tower
2200 Ross Ave., Ste. 4500W
Dallas, TX 75201
(214) 969-7620

**RUSSELL REYNOLDS ASSOC.,
  INC.**
First Interstate Bank Plaza
1000 Louisiana, Ste. 4800
Houston, TX 77002
(713) 658-1776

1900 Trammell Crow Ctr.
2001 Ross Ave.
Dallas, TX 75201
(214) 220-2033

SPENCERSTUART
1111 Bagby, Ste. 1616
Houston, TX 77002-2594
(713) 225-1621

1717 Main St., Ste. 5300
Dallas, TX 75201-4605
(214) 658-1777

**WARD HOWELL
  INTERNATIONAL, INC.**
1000 Louisiana St., Ste. 3150
First Interstate Bank Plaza
Houston, TX 77002
(713) 655-7155

1601 Elm St., Thanksgiving Twr.,
  Ste. 900
Dallas, TX 75201
(214) 749-0099

2525 E. Arizona Biltmore Cir.,
  Ste. 124
Phoenix, AZ 85016
(602) 955-3800

**WITT/KIEFFER, FORD,
   HADELMAN & LLOYD**
8117 Preston Road, Ste. 690
Dallas, TX 75225
(214) 739-1370

432 N. 44th St., Ste. 360
Phoenix, AZ 85008
(602) 267-1370

Rocky Mountain States

**AIM EXECUTIVE CONSULTING
   SERVICES**
1600 Stout St., Ste. 1800
Denver, CO 80202
(303) 893-0146

**A.T. KEARNEY EXECUTIVE
   SEARCH**
One Tabor Ctr.
1200 17th St., Ste. 950
Denver, CO 80202
(303) 572-6175

West Coast

BOYDEN WORLD CORPORATION
275 Battery St., Ste. 420
Embarcadero Center West Tower
San Francisco, CA 94111
(415) 981-7900

ROBERT W. DINGMAN CO., INC.
32129 W. Lindero Canyon Rd.,
Ste. 206
Westlake Village, CA 91361
(818) 991-5950

LEON A. FARLEY ASSOC.
468 Jackson St.
San Francisco, CA 94111
(415) 989-0989

HEIDRICK & STRUGGLES, INC.
Four Embarcadero Ctr., Ste. 3570
San Francisco, CA 94111
(415) 981-2854

2740 Sand Hill Rd.
Menlo Park, CA 94025
(415) 854-9300

300 S. Grand Ave., Ste. 2400
Los Angeles, CA 90071
(213) 625-8811

**HOUZE, SHOURDS &
   MONTGOMERY, INC.**
Greater LA World Trade Ctr.
One World Trade
Long Beach, CA 90831-1840
(310) 495-6495

**A.T. KEARNEY EXECUTIVE
   SEARCH**
One Lagoon Drive, Ste. 220
Redwood City, CA 94065
(415) 595-4300

Biltmore Twr.
500 S. Grand Ave.
Los Angeles, CA 90071
(213) 624-8328

KORN/FERRY INT'L.
1800 Century Park E., Ste. 900
Los Angeles, CA 90067
(310) 552-1834

Embarcadero Corp. Ctr.
2483 E. Bayshore Rd., Ste. 101
Palo Alto, CA 94303
(415) 856-2611

600 Montgomery St., 31st Floor
The Transamerica Pyramid
San Francisco, CA 94111
(415) 956-1834

1300 Dove St., Ste. 300
Newport Beach, CA 92660
(714) 851-1834

100 E. Wardlow
Long Beach, CA 90807
(213) 595-1101

601 S. Figueroa, Ste. 1900
Los Angeles, CA 90017
(213) 624-6600

1940 116th Ave. NE
Bellevue, WA 98004
(206) 462-1100

KREMPLE & MEADE, INC.
P.O. Box 426
Pacific Palisades, CA 90272
(310) 459-4221

PAUL RAY BERNDTSON
2029 Century Park E., Ste. 1000
Los Angeles, CA 90067
(310) 557-2828

**RUSSELL REYNOLDS ASSOC.,
   INC.**
101 California St., Ste. 3140
San Francisco, CA 94111
(415) 392-3130

333 S. Grand Ave., Ste. 4200
Los Angeles, CA 90071
(213) 489-1520

SPENCERSTUART
333 Bush St., Ste. 2500
San Francisco, CA 94104-2161
(415) 495-4141

555 S. Flower St., Ste. 4455
Los Angeles, CA 90071-2420
(213) 620-0814

3000 Sand Hill Rd.
Building 2, Ste. 175
Menlo Park, CA 94025
(415) 688-1285

WARD HOWELL INT'L., INC.
16255 Ventura Blvd., Ste. 400
Encino, CA 91436-2394
(818) 905-6010

**WITT/KIEFFER, FORD,
   HADELMAN & LLOYD**
2000 Powell St., Ste. 1645
Emeryville, CA 94608
(510) 420-1370

2030 Main St., Ste. 620
Irvine, CA 92714
(714) 851-5070

Canada

**THE CALDWELL PARTNERS
   INT'L.**
1840 Sherbrooke St. W.
Montreal, PQ H3H 1E4
Canada
(514) 935-6969

999 W. Hastings St., Ste. 750
Vancouver, BC V6C 2W2
Canada
(604) 669-3550

400-3rd. Ave. SW, Ste. 3450
Calgary, AB T2P 4H2
Canada
(403) 265-8780

64 Prince Arthur Ave.
Toronto, ON M5R 1B4
Canada
(416) 920-7702

HEIDRICK & STRUGGLES, INC.
BCE Pl., 161 Bay St., Ste. 2310
Toronto, ON M5J 2S1
Canada
(416) 361-4700

**A.T. KEARNEY EXECUTIVE
  SEARCH**
Box 10, Ste. 2300, 20 Queen
Street W.
Toronto, ON M5H 3R3
Canada
(416) 977-6886

KORN/FERRY INT'L.
40 King St. W., Ste. 1814
Scotia Plaza, P.O. Box 118
Toronto, ON M5H 3YZ
Canada
(416) 366-1300

SPENCERSTUART
1981 Ave. McGill College .
Montreal, PQ H3A 2Y1
Canada
(514) 288-3377

One University Ave., Ste. 801
Toronto, ON M5J 2P1
Canada
(416) 361-0311

**TANTON MITCHELL/PAUL RAY
  BERNDTSON**
710-1050 W. Pender St.
Vancouver, BC V6E 3S7
Canada
(604) 685-0261

WARD HOWELL INT'L., INC.
141 Adelaide St. W., Ste. 1800
Toronto, ON M5H 3L5
Canada
(416) 862-1273

International

BOYDEN WORLD CORPORATION
364 Elwood Ave.
Hawthorne, NY 10532-1239
(914) 747-0093
(Australia, Belgium, Brazil, Columbia, Denmark, Finland, France,
Germany, Greece, Hong Kong, Hungary, India, Indonesia, Italy, Japan,
Malaysia, Mexico, The Netherlands, Norway, Poland, Portugal,
Republic of China, Singapore, South Africa, South Korea, Spain,
Sweden, Switzerland, Thailand, United Kingdom)

HEIDRICK & STRUGGLES, INC.
303 Peachtree St., Ste. 3100
One Peachtree Ctr.
Atlanta, GA 30308
(404) 577-2410
(Australia, Belgium, Finland, France, Germany, Japan, Spain,
Sweden, United Kingdom)

A.T. KEARNEY EXECUTIVE SEARCH
222 W. Adams St.
Chicago, IL 60606
(312) 648-0111
(Belgium, France, Germany, The Netherlands, Norway, Spain, United Kingdom)

KORN/FERRY INT'L.
1800 Century Park E., Ste. 900
Los Angeles, CA 90067
(310) 552-1834
(Argentina, Australia, Belgium, Brazil, Columbia, France, Germany, Hong Kong, Hungary, Italy, Japan, Luxembourg, Malaysia, Mexico, The Netherlands, Norway, Singapore, Spain, Sweden, Switzerland, Thailand, United Kingdom, Venezuela)

RUSSELL REYNOLDS ASSOC., INC.
200 Park Ave.
New York, NY 10166
(212) 351-2000
(Australia, Belgium, France, Germany, Hong Kong, Italy, Japan, Singapore, Scotland, Spain, United Kingdom)

SPENCERSTUART
55 E. 52nd St.
New York, NY 10055-1021
(212) 407-0200
(Australia, Belgium, Brazil, France, Germany, Hong Kong, Italy, Japan, The Netherlands, Spain, Switzerland, United Kingdom)

TASA INTERNATIONAL
750 Lexington Ave., Ste. 1800
New York, NY 10022
(212) 486-1490
(Argentina, Australia, Austria, Belgium, Brazil, Chile, Columbia, France, Germany, Hong Kong, Ireland, Italy, Mexico, Singapore, South Africa, South Korea, Spain, Switzerland, United Kingdom, Venezuela)

WARD HOWELL INTERNATIONAL, INC.
99 Park Ave., Ste. 2000
New York, NY 10016-1699
(212) 697-3730
(Australia, Austria, Belgium, Brazil, Moscow, Czech Republic, France, Germany, Greece, Hong Kong, Hungary, Italy, Japan, The Netherlands, New Zealand, Poland, Portugal, South Africa, South Korea, Spain, Switzerland, Taiwan, United Kingdom, Venezuela)

INDEX